Jamaica Kincaid
and Caribbean
Double Crossings

Jamaica Kincaid and Caribbean Double Crossings

Edited by
Linda Lang-Peralta

Newark: University of Delaware Press

Associated University Presses
2010 Eastpark Boulevard
Cranbury, NJ 08512

The paper used in this publication meets the requirements of the American National Standard for Permanence of Paper for Printed Library Materials Z39.48-1984.

Library of Congress Cataloging-in-Publication Data

Jamaica Kincaid and Caribbean double crossings / edited by Linda Lang-Peralta.
   p.   cm.
   Original versions of these contributions were presented at the 2002 American Comparative Literature Association in San Juan, Puerto Rico.
   Includes bibliographical references and index.
   ISBN-10: 0-87413-928-7 (alk. paper)
   ISBN-13: 978-0-87413-928-0 (alk. paper)
   1. Kincaid, Jamaica—Criticism and interpretation—Congresses.   2. Caribbean Area—In literature—Congresses.   3. Postcolonialism in literature—Congresses.   4. Imperialism in literature—Congresses.   I. Lang-Peralta, Linda.   II. American Comparative Literature Association.

   PR9275.A583K5653   2006
   813'.54—dc22   2006002596

PRINTED IN THE UNITED STATES OF AMERICA

Contents

Acknowledgments

MANY FRIENDS AND COLLEAGUES HAVE SUPPORTED THIS PROJECT from its inception. The contributors have been a pleasure to work with because of their inspiration, enthusiasm, and patience. Paget Henry contributed insightful suggestions for the conceptual framework of the book. Many thanks go to Kim White and Rene Freshour for timely research, Irene Gorak for assistance with the manuscript, and Catherine O'Neil for excellent editing suggestions. The Metropolitan State College of Denver provided helpful financial support, including a sabbatical leave. For constant support of innumerable kinds, I thank my husband, Tim Peralta.

Grateful acknowledgment is made to the following publishers for use of quoted material

For "'Another line was born . . . ': Genesis, Genealogy, and Genre in Jamaica Kincaid's Mr. Potter" by Jana Evans Braziel:

Excerpts from MR. POTTER by Jamaica Kincaid. Copyright © 2001 by Jamaica Kincaid. Reprinted by permission of Farrar, Straus and Giroux, LLC.

From Mr. Potter by Jamaica Kincaid, published by Chatto & Windus. Reprinted by permission of The Random House Group Ltd.

For "Carribbean Impossibility: The Lack of Jamaica Kincaid" by Thomas W. Sheehan:

Reprinted by permission of Farrar, Straus and Giroux, LLC: Excerpts from THE AUTOBIOGRAPHY OF MY MOTHER by Jamaica Kincaid. Copyright © 1996 by Jamaica Kincaid. Excerpts from MY GARDEN (BOOK): by Jamaica Kincaid. Copyright © 1999 by Jamaica Kincaid. Excerpt from A SMALL PLACE by Jamaica Kincaid. Copyright © 1988 by Jamaica Kincaid.

For "A Little Miss in the Land of Little Women: Louisa May Alcott and Jamaica Kincaid" by Maria Soledad Rodriguez:

This is an expanded and revised version of an essay that originally appeared in *La Torre* VII, no. 25 (July–September 2002): 333–42.

Jamaica Kincaid
and Caribbean
Double Crossings

Introduction

LINDA LANG-PERALTA

JAMAICA KINCAID RELATES A REMARKABLE STORY ABOUT HER LITER-
ary past. Once while she was charged with watching her little brother,
she became engrossed in reading a book instead. When her mother returned home and found a soggy diaper, she was furious at the fifteen-
year-old Kincaid. Her mother gathered all of Kincaid's books together,
poured kerosene over them, and set them ablaze. In *My Brother* (1997),
Kincaid reflects on this event: "It would not be so strange if I spent the
rest of my life trying to bring those books back to my life by writing
them again and again until they were perfect, unscathed by fire of any
kind. . . . The source of the books has not died, it only comes alive again
and again in different forms and other segments."[1] Kincaid's writing
draws on that "source" and explores the complexity of identity in various genres.

After a British colonial upbringing on the Caribbean island of Antigua, Kincaid, née Elaine Potter Richardson, left her home in 1966, well
before her country gained independence in 1981. Although she now
lives in Vermont, she writes frequently and frankly about Caribbean
postcolonial issues, most notably in *A Small Place* (1988). Her work has
given her a wide international influence but a troubled reception in the
Caribbean, which she often depicts in a negative light.[2] In "A Small
Place Writes Back," Jane King expresses a Caribbean perspective on
Kincaid's work: "Fine, so Kincaid does not like the Caribbean much,
finds it dull and boring and would rather live in Vermont. There can
really be no difficulty with that, but I do not see why Caribbean people
should admire her for denigrating our small place in this destructively
angry fashion."[3] As Moira Ferguson notes, "As an African-Caribbean
writer Kincaid speaks to and from the position of the other."[4] Her characters are often maligned by history and subjected to a foreign culture,
while Kincaid herself has become an increasingly mainstream American
writer. She has become a prominent voice who conceptualizes Caribbean culture for North Americans not only as a writer for the *New*

Yorker and other periodicals but also as an author whose fiction is widely read in educational institutions across America—typically *Annie John* in high school and the short story "Girl" in college literature courses.

At the Bottom of the River (1985), the collection of stories in which "Girl" is included, and which first established Kincaid's literary career, was more heavily influenced by Obeah imagery than by history, Paget Henry observes. For example, "Kincaid's mother images go way beyond everyday or biological constructions and are distinguished by a mythic coding that is very reminiscent of African mother goddesses."[5] The author's mother and grandmother were steeped in the Obeah belief system that is based on the power of transformation and followed its practices. In Henry's view, Kincaid's "shift in emphasis" toward a more historical perspective "demonstrates clearly the tension between poeticism and historicism that has divided the Caribbean philosophical imagination in the postcolonial period" (46). Indeed, this tension is evident in much Caribbean literature.

In one of her many published interviews, Kincaid has admitted a shift in her work: "In my first two books, I used to think I was writing about my mother and myself. Later I began to see that I was writing about the relationship between the powerful and the powerless. That's become an obsessive theme, and I think that it will be a theme for as long as I write. And then it came clear to me when I was writing an essay that became "On Seeing England for the First Time" that I was writing about the mother—that mother I was writing about was really Mother Country. It's like an egg; it's a perfect whole. It's all fused some way or other."[6]

In addition to the mother and the motherland, several recurrent themes run through Kincaid's recent fiction and nonfiction, whether she writes about visiting her brother, creating her garden, or traveling to China or the Himalayas. She repeatedly expresses ambivalence and self-consciously comments on her increasing identification with the consumer culture that revels in the same type of conquest she attacks in Caribbean history. Several times she notes the necessity of recognizing the cost of the American lifestyle to others in the world. She writes various versions, fiction and nonfiction, of key events in her life: reciting Wordsworth's poem on daffodils and coming to loath it, experiencing displacement in her family when her brothers were born, visiting her mother and confronting their relationship. Kincaid's depiction of familial relationships often becomes a critique of Caribbean history and an analysis of the complexity of constructing a postcolonial identity. Her tone ranges from fiery rage, as in *A Small Place*, to calm assessment, as in *My Garden (Book):*.

In Kincaid's later texts, ambivalence remains evident in the complex feelings she expresses for her family and her home. She comes to some conclusions about herself in *My Brother*: "I love the people I am from and I do not love the people I am from, and I do not really know what it means to say so, only that such a thing as no love now and much love now, these feelings are not permanent" (148–49). Even without her conflicted feelings about her family, she could not have lived among them as a writer in Antigua. Her brother mimics her British accent on the telephone, and Kincaid quotes her brother's speech, emphasizing the difference in their use of the colonizers' language. Comparing her brother's life to hers, she writes, "In his life there had been no flowering, his life was the opposite of that, a flowering, his life was like the bud that sets but, instead of opening into a flower, turns brown and falls off at your feet" (162–63). It is through writing, even though it is in what she calls the criminal's language, that she survives by creating her identity: "I became a writer out of desperation" (195–96).

Where Sarah Brophy characterizes *My Brother* as "an act of examining her conquering self as a split and devastated being,"[7] I would argue that Kincaid, with intense self-awareness, presents herself as being far from devastated. She is the person she has created, as well as split, and for all her repetition of "What to do?" she valorizes her literary productivity, her Vermont family, and her extravagant garden.

Much has been written about Kincaid's early writings, including a 1998 collection of essays edited by Harold Bloom, who concludes the introduction by saying, "So far, [Kincaid's] best work has emerged from recollections of childhood and of her complex relationship to her mother. Her current meditations upon gardening have implicit in them a new development in her work, which her admirers, common readers and critics together are likely to welcome."[8] However, relatively little has been published on her exciting work since the 1990s, work that includes rich analyses of issues central to literary criticism in recent years: the identity of the postcolonial subject, the effects of imperialism, and the double consciousness of the diasporic writer. In this groundbreaking collection of essays, scholars have given Kincaid's "new development" the serious critical attention it deserves.

In the contributions that follow, scholars from the Caribbean and scholars who focus on Caribbean literature explore Kincaid's recent fiction and nonfiction: *A Small Place* (1988), *Lucy* (1990), *The Autobiogra-*

phy of My Mother (1996), *My Brother* (1997), *My Garden (Book):* (1999), *Mr. Potter* (2002), and *Among Flowers: A Walk in the Himalayas* (2005). Early versions of these essays were originally presented in San Juan, Puerto Rico at the 2002 American Comparative Literature Association annual meeting in association with the University of Puerto Rico, Rio Piedras. The essays offer a fresh look at Kincaid's work, drawing upon the theories of Homi Bhabha, Jacques Lacan, Jacques Derrida, and Édouard Glissant, with a special focus on the construction of identity in the literary traditions and the historical context of the Caribbean.

The comparative studies included in this collection suggest that Kincaid has written "again and again" the books that her mother set on fire, locating herself among writers such as Charlotte Brontë, Louisa May Alcott, and Jean Rhys. Kincaid often describes herself as a writer in relation to other writers, as she told interviewer Kathleen Balutansky in 1998: "I would happily sacrifice any amount of reading of any of my books for people to read *Jane Eyre*. You can't begin to understand me until you read certain things. I didn't begin to understand myself until I read certain things. The things that were most important to me were written by people who didn't look like me."[9] Comments such as these encourage critics to offer intertextual readings of Kincaid's work, as Maria Soledad Rodriguez, Evie Shockley, Joanne Gass, and I do in the essays included here.

By ignoring traditional generic distinctions, critics can make further illuminating connections in Kincaid's work. The theme of identity constructed within a historical context transcends genre boundaries, as demonstrated in the essays by Thomas Sheehan, Derik Smith and Cliff Beumel, Jeanne Ewert, and Jana Evans Braziel.

These contributions attest to the intriguing nature of the "different forms and other segments" that have emerged from the ashes of Kincaid's books to forge her art. We look forward to that source continuing to "come . . . alive again and again" for future readers.

NOTES

1. Jamaica Kincaid, *My Brother* (New York: Farrar Straus Giroux, 1997), 197–98.
2. Lizabeth Paravisini-Gebert, *Jamaica Kincaid: A Critical Companion* (Westport, CT: Greenwood Press, 1999), 33.
3. Jane King, "A Small Place Writes Back," *Callaloo* 25 (2002): 899.
4. Moira Ferguson, *Colonialism and Gender Relations from Mary Wollstonecraft to Ja-*

maica Kincaid: East Caribbean Connections (New York: Columbia University Press, 1993), 136.

5. Paget Henry, *Caliban's Reason: Introducing Afro-Caribbean Philosophy* (New York: Routledge, 2000), 46.

6. Moira Ferguson, "A Lot of Memory: An Interview with Jamaica Kincaid." *Kenyon Review* 16 (1994): 176.

7. Sarah, Brophy, "Angels in Antigua: The Diasporic Melancholy in Jamaica Kincaid's *My Brother*," *PMLA* 117 (2) (March 2002): 269.

8. Bloom, Harold, ed., *Jamaica Kincaid: Modern Critical Views* (Philadelphia: Chelsea House, 1998), 2.

9. Kathleen M. Balutansky, "On Gardening: An Interview with Jamaica Kincaid, *Callaloo* 25 (2002): 799–800.

A Little Miss in the Land of Little Women: Louisa May Alcott and Jamaica Kincaid

MARIA SOLEDAD RODRIGUEZ

"AT THE COST OF BEING DEEMED EFFEMINATE, I WILL ADD THAT I . . . worshipped . . . *Little Women.*"¹ When I read the author's name under those words, I couldn't believe it: Theodore Roosevelt, the United States President as famous for hunting as for making war, was Louisa May Alcott's admirer! Then I read: "I identified passionately with Jo." This admission by one of the twentieth century's most notable feminists, Simone de Beauvoir, also surprised me. Wasn't Louisa May Alcott's book supposed to be sentimental, and therefore second-class, fiction? Hadn't the author herself characterized this type of writing as "moral pap for the young"?² I continued reading: "Where else . . . could we have read about an all-female group who discussed work, art, and all the Great Questions — or found girls who wanted to be women and not vice versa?" This, from a leader of the women's revolution in the United States, Gloria Steinem. I kept searching for Alcott admirers and found African-American poet Sonia Sanchez: "I understood what it was like being an outsider. . . . I didn't identify with Beth and all the others. . . . They were too formal, and they were the women you expected them to be, but Jo broke the mold." In 1994, another African-American author, Ann Petry, had this to say: "I felt as though I was part of Jo and she was part of me." A seeming tribute to the fictional character that has become the symbol of young women's desire for independence and the ever-present danger that they might have to compromise it, as Jo March does, under the onslaught of the attractive masks of domesticity.

With that background, then, it should have come as no surprise to me that there's another very strong narrative voice in literature today that pays tribute to the author of *Little Women*. Like Louisa May Alcott, Jamaica Kincaid is a true daughter of Charlotte Brontë, and as such, to borrow a phrase from Christine Doyle, Kincaid too "translates Bron-tëan values within sites of meaning important to herself."³ In this, she resembles other novelists of the West Indies who turned to nineteenth-century England for models. But I don't want to dwell on those transatlantic connections. Instead, I want to explore two areas of the intertextual relationship of Alcott and Kincaid: first, the relation of text to text and author to author, and second, what it clarifies about the contentions made by some, like Carol Boyce Davies, that Jamaica Kincaid seems to have given up her Caribbean identity and implicitly become Americanized,[4] and others, like Belinda Edmondson, who refute Boyce Davies by saying that there is no hegemonic intertextual presence of United States texts in Kincaid's works.[5]

In her 1990 novel, *Lucy*, Jamaica Kincaid places her main character "at the crossroads of cultures and identities: Antiguan and American."[6] Lucy is nineteen, has just arrived in the United States, and works for a middle-class family: "I was only an unhappy young woman living in a maid's room, and I was not even the maid. I was the young girl who watches over the children and goes to school at night."[7] Later on, when she identifies with the painter Gauguin for leaving his own country, she will describe herself in clearer terms: "I was a young woman from the fringes of the world, and when I left home I had wrapped around my shoulders the mantle of a servant" (*L*, 95). This is the first similarity to Jo March, whose dubious status when she undertakes a similar job is also an issue. When Jo says she feels restless and anxious for something more and therefore wants to go to New York, where she is going to be hired by Mrs. Kirk to teach her children while she tries her luck as a writer, Jo's mother replies: "My dear, go out to service in that great boardinghouse?"[8]

In Kincaid's novel, Lucy does two things: she interprets her culture for others and the culture of the United States for herself, especially as it threatens to entrap her in its scripts of female domesticity and neocolonization. Although exile is supposed to help one explore privilege and freedom in the North, the construction of a new hybrid identity, which might seem open to many possibilities,[9] could be as limiting as the identity one is seeking to leave behind. In order to create a new self, then, Lucy dwells on concepts like family and gendered identity that still resonate in the United States with echoes of Alcott's texts, and she examines those possibilities.

Little Women tells us the story of Jo March: how she goes from being a disgruntled rebel with a sharp tongue to the "little woman" her father had desired. Through her rebellions, she expresses "a woman's legitimate longing for a larger sphere of activity,"[10] and, according to Catharine R. Stimpson, her appeal is to "readers who resist the cult of womanhood."[11] When one hears the temperamental Jo March speaking, there is no doubt that she's Lucy's precursor: "You don't know; you can't guess how bad it is! It seems as if I could do anything when I'm in a passion; I get so savage, I could hurt anyone and enjoy it. I'm afraid I shall do something dreadful some day, and spoil my life, and make everybody hate me" (*LW*, 79–80).

According to Judith Fetterley, much of the popularity of *Little Women* "derives from its embodiment of a cultural fantasy of the happy family. At the heart of this family is, of course, the kind of Mom we all at some time or other are made to wish we could have had."[12] The daughters have a conflict between their individual rights and those of the family, which gives them an important but restricted sense of identity.[13] In the March household, Marmee takes over the father's role when he leaves for Washington during the Civil War. She becomes the spokesperson for the patriarchy, for the father who is present through her when she enforces his domestic ideal of little womanhood, taking special pains to help Jo to suppress her personality as she has done with her own.[14] In this, she resembles the mother in *Lucy* who, though far from her daughter, is nevertheless in her memory a dominating presence that transmits limiting Victorian notions about respectability. Just as "through her mother Jo explores her feelings about herself and her psychological dependence on women,"[15] Lucy can be said to do the same. Even the two phrases, "little woman" and "little miss" are likewise associated with the two mothers. Marmee is the model her daughters want to become, the pilgrim struggling, just as they are, to reach perfection as little women. Jo is very much like her, the mother's confidante. Mother and daughter both get strength from this. On the other hand, Lucy is addressed as "Little Miss" by Mr. Thomas in a context in which she says he is thinking about how much like her mother she is becoming. When she speaks, he hears her imitation of her mother's voice, and responds by naming her "Little Miss" (*L*, 107). Ironically, in her attempt to get away from the world of the "little miss" in which she mimics her mother's speech, she winds up in the land of little women where Alcott's text provides the background against which Kincaid will question the cultural authority of the United States in terms of gender. Just as *Little Women* was given publicity as a work that "would civilize as well as entertain the young,"[16] one of the issues Kincaid will debate is the domestication of the "savage" girl-child. Other issues the two novels have in common are the desire for self-authorization and the primary role each mother plays in the protagonists' lives. Moreover, Kincaid even grapples with the concept of "family" which underlies the much broader one of the melting pot in the United States: "How nice everyone was to me, though, saying that I should regard them as my family and make myself at home. I believed them to be sincere, for I knew that such a thing would not be said to a member of their real family. After all, aren't family the people who become the millstone around your life's neck?" (*L*, 7–8).

The "family" Kincaid creates as a counterpoint to Lucy's is the one Ann Douglas finds in *Little Women*, one in which the five closely knit figures "are the only mythic American characters from the Victorian era unashamedly, believably, actively capable of love, friendship, loyalty, and sheer fun."[17] It is precisely that myth that Kincaid puts to the test in her novel, which also has a mother whose name shares the first three letters and syllable of the mother in *Little Women*. Marmee becomes Mariah, who says: "I have always wanted four children, four girl children" (*L*, 26) and has exactly four daughters whose names are Louisa, May, Jane, and Miriam, and a father and husband relegated, like the one in *Little Women*, to the periphery of the action. At one point in *Lucy*, Mariah is represented as having as great an influence over her daughters as Marmee has over hers: "the children were happy to see things her way" (*L*, 36). Whether Mariah will have a strong influence on Lucy, though, is not decided in as straightforward a manner: "The times I loved Mariah it was because she reminded me of my mother. The times I did not love Mariah it was because she reminded me of my mother" (*L*, 58). These contradictory feelings about her mother and Mariah (and implicitly about Marmee) will mark Lucy's relationships. At times she will catch herself acting like a replica of her mother or doing things in ways Mariah had taught her; at others, she will assume her own stand in opposition to what either one thinks; and sometimes she will privilege one of them, mostly her mother, over the other.

This can often be seen in scenes involving Mariah's children. For example, the youngest, five-year-old Miriam, is the one Lucy loves most: "She must have reminded me of myself when I was that age, for I treated her the way I remembered my mother treating me then" (*L*, 53). Edyta Oczkowicz thinks Lucy's love for Miriam "reflects and activates her need and capacity for self-love, the first condition of becoming one's own person,"[18] but in the context of this discussion, it assumes greater significance, since it will put the two mothers, Lucy's and Mariah, at odds with each other. Once when she's trying to feed Miriam stewed plums and yogurt "specially prepared for her by her mother" (*L*, 44), Lucy says the same things her mother used to tell her to convince her to eat, but she "always did it in a low voice, so that Mariah would not overhear. Mariah did not believe in this way of doing things" (*L*, 45).

At other times, Lucy sides with one of Mariah's children against her: "She moaned against the vanishing idyll so loudly that Louisa, who was just at the age where if you are a girl you turn against your mother, said, "Well, what used to be here before this house we are living in was built?" It was a question I had wanted to ask, but I couldn't bear to see the hurt such a question would bring to Mariah's face" (*L*, 73).

In those words, Lucy identifies closely with Louisa (note the similar-sounding names — Lucy and Louisa) and both diverge from Jo March, whose bouts with a bad temper were much tamer and never included such relentless criticism of the mother. At the same time, Lucy shows signs of being more mature than when she hadn't been able to stop herself from saying things that hurt others.

Furthermore, in *Little Women* there are two alternatives to the domestic ideal: Jo's unconventional character and the fellowship of women itself.[19] When she moves in with the family in New York, Lucy is given a chance to observe this female community closely as she herself is fighting for her own independence. In her new home, she is the "different" one, the "dark" one like Jo March, and they share some qualities: doing daring things, being blunt, and repeating that they don't want to get married. Jo dreams of assuming the masculine role of supporting her family, and Lucy sends money to her mother after her father dies, leaving her penniless. Besides this, they both literally carry similar secrets close to their hearts. In a letter to Jo, Marmee says: "I write a little word to tell you with how much satisfaction I watch over your efforts to control your temper," and Jo pins it inside her frock, "a shield and reminder, lest she be taken unaware" (*LW*, 119). Lucy, for her part, carries her mother's letters inside her bra. That unopened bundle becomes a double shield: from the mother's influence because she doesn't read her letters, and from the new culture because they won't allow her to succumb to its influences. The bundle "suggests a continuing, though muted, discourse with home."[20] In both instances, it's the mother, more than the letters themselves, that is present in the daughter's life.

There are some significant differences between them, however. Jo's disappointment over not being born a boy is much stronger than that of Lucy, who limits herself to resenting her parents' privileging her brothers. In addition, the "ultimately tamed Jo"[21] is neutralized by her marriage to the somewhat older Bhaer,[22] whereas at the end of the novel Lucy, who has criticized her mother for marrying an older man and asked her why she had betrayed herself that way (*L*, 127), is sad, but in her own apartment, in her own room, and in her own bed.

Kincaid takes this a step further. In *Little Women*, there are two emotional triads. The first one is when the oldest sister, Meg, becomes engaged, and Jo, who tells Marmee she's in love with Meg sometimes (*LW*, 166), says she wishes she could marry her herself so as to keep her safe in the family. The second is when Laurie, who proposes to and is rejected by Jo, courts and eventually marries her younger sister, Amy. Jamaica Kincaid dovetails these two triads: Lucy has a relationship of lesbian overtones with Peggy, whose name is another version of Meg's, and we're given to understand that Peggy and Paul have started an affair of their own, which Lucy doesn't mind: "I only hoped they would not get angry and disrupt my life when they realized I did not care" (*L*, 163).

Although Jo seems to have found fitting resolutions to both of her conflicts by preserving the family at close quarters and conforming to notions of domesticity, Lucy certainly doesn't. Antonia McDonald-Smythe comments about the possibilities of her relationships in New York: "While Mariah, Paul and Peggy can assume the role of a substitute community, Lucy forecloses that possibility by holding them at emotional arms' length. . . . Because Lucy is less like them than she is willing to admit and because Mariah is still too untouched by the hardness and rawness of life to earn Lucy's respect and therefore love, the mother remains the un-challengeable source of that community."[23]

And yet there is a lot more to be said about the Lucy that goes into the home of Lewis, Mariah, and the four daughters. Whereas Alcott's Civil War background conjures the image of "a house conflicted but not divided, a family that offered an analogy and possibly a corrective to America,"[24] the war itself is a metaphor for the internal conflicts of the March sisters as they make their pilgrimage to little womanhood:[25] "I'll try and be what he loves to call me, a 'little woman,' and not be rough and wild, and do my duty here instead of wanting to be somewhere else," said Jo, thinking that keeping her temper at home was a much harder task than facing a rebel or two down South" (*LW*, 14).

Jo's war took place at home, then, and by all accounts little womanhood won. Lucy steps into the supposedly reunited American house, the legacy of the Alcott one, where the myth of the ideal family, that safe haven that will guarantee the growing-up process, reigns. At its center "Mariah, with her pale yellow skin and yellow hair, stood still in this almost celestial light, and she looked blessed, no blemish or mark of any kind or her cheek or anywhere else" (*L*, 27). But instead of a house standing tall around Mariah, what Lucy sees is ruins. There is a mark after all. The marriage is in trouble. Lucy perceives this with the vision her Antiguan upbringing has given her: "The whole thing had an air of untruth about it" (*L*, 47) and "I knew that the end was here, the ruin was in front of me" (*L*, 118). Her use of the word "ruin" is significant. In another part, she says of Paul, "He loved ruins; he loved the past, but only if it had ended on a sad note" (*L*, 156). He had driven her around the countryside, to a plantation in ruins, a landmark of the spirit of adventure he admires. It had belonged to someone who had made his money in the area she comes from, the Caribbean. In this way, Jamaica Kincaid combines the ruins of Victorian America's values as transmitted through *Little Women* and the ruins of the plantation, thus tying in Victorian-American domesticity and colonialism.

The (surrogate) mother-(immigrant) daughter relationship between Mariah and Lucy can also be viewed more closely on those terms. Two situations make this quite clear. The first is related to the confessed admirer of Louisa May Alcott, Simone de Beauvoir, the first two lines of whose book, *The Second Sex*, Mariah gives Lucy to read, making her angry: "Mariah had completely misinterpreted my situation. My life could not really be explained by this thick book that made my hands hurt as I tried to keep it open" (*L*, 132). Lucy then goes on to mention that what has been on her mind for half of her life has been the end of her relationship with her mother, "perhaps the only true love in [her] whole life [she] would ever know" (*L*, 132), a topic to which Simone de Beauvoir doesn't give much attention in the book. The last quotation so strangely reminiscent of Jo March's saying that mothers are the best lovers in the whole world also manages to distance Lucy from de Beauvoir's and Mariah's feminism, and approximate her to Louisa May Alcott. In fact, what Ann Douglas says about the Victorian-American author can easily be applied to the contemporary Kincaid: "Alcott is perhaps the only American author of her generation to invest the girl's need for her mother with the psychological, emotional and political depth recent post-Freudians have granted it, and to realize the confidence and sense of self its satisfaction can bring."[26] Even more, in her rejection of de Beauvoir's book, Lucy is again emphasizing the complicity of colonialism and domesticity. Moira Ferguson concurs: "Another representation of cultural imperialism that signs Mariah unmistakably as part of the colonizing project. . . . Having unburdened her problems with motherhood and colonial intervention on to Mariah, Mariah then exchanges for this knowledge a famous bourgeois feminist text embedded in eurocentric beliefs and principles."[27]

Furthermore, Lucy says that Mariah "spoke of women in society, women in history, women in culture, women everywhere. But I couldn't speak, so I couldn't tell her that my mother was my mother and that society and history and culture and other women in general were something else altogether" (L, 131–32). She repeats this as, "I had to suppress the annoyance I felt at her for once again telling me about everybody when I told her something about myself" (L, 139). By having Lucy express such thoughts, Jamaica Kincaid is avoiding the repetition of "the Western-based paradigms that had reduced the colonized to an undifferentiated, un-individuated, homogeneous group,"[28] but even more, she is emphasizing the silencing and suppression of true feelings that can result from Mariah's growing influence, something Lucy will have to negotiate.

This is doubly determined in another scene, the one in which Mariah is against Lucy's moving into her own apartment and starts to resemble the "stoney-faced" Queen of the British Empire: "It was a last resort for her—insisting that I be the servant and she the master. She used to insist that we be friends, but that had apparently not worked out very well; now I was leaving. The master business did not become her at all, and it made me sad to see her that way" (L, 143). In one fell swoop, Mariah, whom Lucy has begun to esteem, falls right back into a role that goes against the liberal ideas she had been expressing throughout the novel. At the same time, Kincaid implies, that's because it was always there. The ruins all around her call attention to the fact that the little womanhood of domesticity and colonialism had built such strong edifices at one time that their trace is still very much in evidence.

There is an additional association in the Jo-Lucy relationship, which is Kincaid's main character's three names: Lucy Josephine Potter. Moira Ferguson points out that "her names are associated with plantocratic lineage, slave traders, (the English Potter family), and a Western symbol of evil, Lucifer."[29] Jo March, too, has a name associated with a wealthy Boston family, and she even says "I'm as proud as Lucifer" (LW, 327). Beyond this double association of Lucy and Jo with Lucifer, however, is another issue, one related to Milton's Lucifer in "Paradise Lost." In her discussion of Kincaid's earlier novel, Annie John, Antonia MacDonald Smythe comments: "Evelyn O'Callahan in Woman Version

offers a reading of the mother as Eve because of her collusion in the
imperial and patriarchal subjugation of women. I am suggesting that
the mother is closer to Milton's God, unwilling to accommodate transgression or individuality even while she recognizes herself in Annie.
The fact that the mother can be herself colonized is a sign of her humanity in much the same way that Milton's God is given to emotions of
anger and jealousy not befitting his status."[30]

The mother as God, in this sense, is confirmed by the protagonist
herself: "That my mother would have found me devil-like did not surprise me, for I often thought of her as god-like, and are not the children
of gods devils?" (*L*, 153). This, in turn, contributes to another intertextual relationship that Kincaid is establishing: she sets up the opposition
between the books from which Lucy had been taught to read and knew
well, among them the Bible, Shakespeare's works, and *Paradise Lost* (*L*,
152), and John Bunyan's allegory, *Pilgrim's Progress*. Published in 1678,
this work provides the metaphor of pilgrimage underpinning *Little
Women*: "Jo felt that it was a true guidebook for any pilgrim going the
long journey" (*LW*, 17). As Marmee says: "Our burdens are here, our
road is before us, and the longing for goodness and happiness is the
guide that leads us through many troubles and mistakes to the peace
which is a true Celestial City" (*LW*, 15).

Much has been written about the role Bunyan's work plays in Alcott's novel. After discussing interpretations proposing that it undermines the empowerment of young women, Anne K. Phillips analyzes
the pilgrim and his or her pilgrimage as applying not only to little
women, but also to men and women, and as representing the empowerment that results from "a lifelong spiritual commitment."[31] As for the
March sisters themselves, Phillips thinks they "find power and satisfaction through self-control,"[32] something which Elaine Showalter prefers
to describe as "female self-restraint."[33] Moreover, given the community
of Transcendentalists that surrounded Louisa May Alcott in Concord—
Emerson, Hawthorne, Thoreau, Fuller, and even her own father,
Bronson—it's easy to see why Phillips considers selfreliance as an application of principles of *Pilgrim's Progress* that helps the Marches go
beyond their material limitations.[34] One would have to concur, but only
up to a point. The mother's family keeps helping them out financially,
and Jo's inheritance definitely contributes to the Bhaers' prosperity at
the end. Amy herself can finally enjoy all the material comforts about
which she dreamed when she was growing up, even if she does over-
come her material desires during her pilgrimage from childhood to

adulthood. For example, although she doesn't give in to the temptation to accept Fred Vaughn's marriage proposal because he is rich, she does marry the very wealthy neighbor and family friend, Laurie. Whereas Bunyan opposes material wealth (Lucre) to morality, Alcott, one can conclude, tempers that opposition by allowing her characters to achieve certain material benefits. Her Celestial City includes the Palace Beautiful, the Laurence residence, which is fittingly situated in close proximity to the March house. As for Plumfield, which Jo inherits from Aunt March, Anne K. Phillips sees it as "another version of Plimouth Plantation" and a reminder of the values of the early settlers of New England,[35] the pilgrims who historically and allegorically founded their version of Eden in the United States. Their journey toward the New World is a movement toward the Celestial City, with its aura of promise and possibility and presupposes certain choices: not to continue living where they felt they were being oppressed, and setting up a value system more attuned to their beliefs.[36]

These two types of pilgrims, the ones coming to a new land, and the ones, like the March sisters, who make interior pilgrimages (whether for the freedom acquired by self-control, as Phillips argues, or because of the limiting ideology of domesticity the parents communicate, as others argue) are fused in *Lucy* through Kincaid's use of the figure of Lucifer. On the one hand, there's a reverse movement in this novel: instead of the new pilgrim going toward the Celestial City, Lucy, already one of the fallen by virtue of having been named for Satan himself (*L*, 152), arrives in the United States after she has been expelled from Paradise. That the city to which she travels is not a second Paradise is continually reaffirmed throughout the novel, in which everything is subject to her questioning at the same time that it falls short of all the descriptions she had been given before. Plus, there's the ever-present motif of ruins, of what has been destroyed to make way for what is. Kincaid even adds an analysis that could just as well apply to the great wealth of Mrs. March's family, Aunt March herself, or Mr. Laurence: "they made no connection between their comforts and the decline of the world that lay before them. I could have told them a thing or two about it" (*L*, 72).

From the beginning Lucy positions herself as a pilgrim so unlike the early ones that it's easy to miss the fact that her pilgrimage presupposes similar desires to get away from a place where one feels oppressed and to search for or create a value system more in tune with her own beliefs, even if they're still not fully formed. It is also easy to forget that her pilgrimage is as life consuming as Jo March's: "journey affords a construction of woman as open to infinite possibilities of signification," as MacDonald-Smythe points out.[37] According to Phillips, Jo's major battle is with her fiery temper,[38] and for Lennox Keyser, she fights for her independence but has so internalized the values that dictate a family should stay together that she feels guilty.[39] Judith Fetterley sees that guilt as coming more from being thought useless in a society that assigns roles she rejects like that of being an agreeable woman.[40] Lucy likewise feels the conflict between what she would like to say and, like Jo with Marmee, doesn't, so as not to hurt Mariah: "I couldn't bring myself to point out to her that. . . . I couldn't bring myself to ask her to. . . . Ordinarily that was just the sort of thing I enjoyed doing, but I had grown to love Mariah so much" (*L*, 73). However, instead of generally feeling guilty like Jo, especially when she gets manipulated by Beth into forgetting about living in New York and pursuing a writing career, Lucy represents what Antonia MacDonald-Smythe says about the author herself: "What seems to constitute power for Kincaid is the ability to take what you want unapologetically."[41]

By naming her protagonist Lucy, instead of some version of Caliban or even Sycorax, from Shakespeare's *The Tempest* (1611), Kincaid grants her the status afforded by an association with anyone whose quest to replace that lost Paradise with a new Eden is doomed, no matter how strong the representation of the new land as Adamic. Her voluntary exile from Antigua and her mother, then her move away from Mariah's home, are very different choices from those of Jo's, who is given a specific parcel of land with a house already on it. Lucy's is a much more individualistic choice, which is her saving grace, at the same time that by virtue of her name, in her quest for self-articulation, she makes the battles of postcolonial subjects ones that affect the human spirit as profoundly as any pilgrimage. From that perspective, she confronts in multiple ways the plan for self-improvement that Fetterley[42] perceives as the result of the application by the Marches of the ideas of *Pilgrim's Progress*: How can a descendant of slaves who comes from a former colony be "content" with everything? How can she renounce the "self" when that "self" has been formulated by colonialism, especially as transmitted to her through her mother? Even though "conquer yourself" sounds like such a grand suggestion, it belies the trauma of conquest in the Caribbean, again assuming that there is a "self" left to conquer. In the scene in the garden, when she tells Mariah that she wants to kill her special flowers, Lucy says: "I felt sorry I had cast her beloved daffodils in a scene she had never considered, a scene of conquered and conquests; a scene of brutes masquerading as angels and angels portrayed as brutes. It wasn't her fault. It wasn't my fault. But nothing could change the fact that where she saw beautiful flowers I saw sorrow and bitterness. The same thing could cause us to shed tears, but those tears would not taste the same." (*L*, 30). And, how "cheery" can she feel about her condition? "Mariah came up to me. . . . 'You are a very angry person, aren't you?' and her voice was filled with alarm and pity. Perhaps I should have said something reassuring; perhaps I should have denied it. But I did not. I said, 'Of course I am. What do you expect?'" (*L*, 96).

Even the issue of self-control, which for Jo March means putting the brake on her sharp tongue, is quite different for Lucy, for whom it becomes the opposite of being controlled, politically or whatever, by someone else. For example, when Paul gives her a photograph of herself naked from the waist up, she says "that was the moment he got the idea he possessed me in a certain way, and that was the moment I grew tired of him" (*L*, 155).

As for self-reliance, there's no doubt Lucy undertakes her pilgrimage by herself. She maintains a distance, though tenuous at times, from the family that is splitting up anyway, and, true to her name, she says: "I am alone in the world, and I shall always be this way—all alone in the world" (*L*, 93). Whereas the Marches represent a togetherness treasured all the more because they fought hard against anything interior or nonspiritual that threatened it, something else can be said of Kincaid's protagonist: "Although the figure of Lucifer comes from the culture of her colonizer, Lucy, now liberated, can freely choose to identify with him. . . . Her state of loneliness and alienation is the price she has to pay for her search for self-knowledge."[43]

That search is just beginning. Chapter 33 of *Little Women*, "Jo's Journal," is written in the first person. In it Jo March records her first impressions of New York. Significantly, toward the end of her novel, Kincaid will have Mariah give Lucy a red leather notebook with smooth white pages as a reminder of what Lucy herself had said when she was moving out of Mariah's apartment, that her life stretched out ahead of her "like a book of blank pages" (*L*, 163). There in New York, then, both Jo and Lucy have in their hands journals in which to begin their long road to self-authorization. However, it is in New York City, too, that Jo March meets the man she will marry, the one who convinces her about the existence of God and to stop writing the sensational stories that were starting to bring her some financial success. She comes under his moral influence more than anything, feels ashamed of having written the stories, and increasingly yields to his criteria. Lucy, too, feels some shame at the end of the novel, when she's just beginning to write. She expresses a desire to be able to love someone so much she could die from it. Moira Ferguson interprets this as a sign that Lucy is "on the way to self-articulation" after resisting the "grand narratives of marriage, religion, and cultural conformity."[44] Since self-articulation requires that she break away from the sense of doom imbedded in her first name, the strong desire she expresses to be able to love marks the giant step Jo was kept from taking, that of loving without having to give up her individuality.

Regarding Lucy's middle name, Josephine, Ferguson and others are silent about it. Lucy herself says: "I was named Josephine after my mother's uncle Mr. Joseph, because he was rich, from money he had made in sugar in Cuba, and it was thought that he would remember the honor and leave something for me in his will. But when he died it was discovered that he had lost his fortune a while before and did not even have a roof over his head; he had been living in an old tomb in the Anglican churchyard" (L, 149).

In this statement, she's indicating the empty inheritance she could expect at home where fortunes were in ruin: the uncle had already been dwelling among the dead. However, the name in the middle, the Josephine of Lucy Josephine Potter, has greater significance than that because it also alludes to Josephine (Jo) March, in Little Women. First, there are echoes of Jo's family's own plans for her to inherit something from Aunt March, which she eventually does. Plumfield becomes a school where the married Jo can be the daughter who "comes closest to realizing the ideal of imitating mother."[45] The opposite is true of Lucy's most earnest desire, which is to get as far away from her mother and from being a "Little Miss" as possible, without falling into a colonial relationship that comes with the acceptance of American dominance.[46] This would have been effected through an identification with Mariah's, and implicitly, Little Women's, worlds.

Jo is therefore a fitting precursor for Lucy without erasing her Caribbeanness. Quite the contrary, she throws new light on it. Kincaid's novel is founded on the opposition to the meanings of womanhood and cultural authority passed on from the discourse of Little Women. If, as Belinda Edmondson thinks, the metaphor of the relationship between a West Indian girl and her mother conveys "what it means to be a West Indian woman,"[47] this meaning is expanded in Lucy by the metaphor of the relationship between the immigrant West Indian girl and the surrogate mother whose life is modeled on the "perfect" female community in *Little Women*. Kincaid assumes an anticolonial stand as strong as that of other novelists, male or female, replying to the discourse of British texts. The colonizing project is thus rejected in both its narratives, that from England as well as that from the United States, at the same time that there is an undercutting of the female experience represented as universal when it is distinctly middle class.[48]

So, has Jamaica Kincaid forfeited her identity as part of the Caribbean literary tradition? In *Lucy* she has added meanings of womanhood that are founded on the Victorian-American gendered counterdiscourse of Louisa May Alcott. This doesn't mean, however, that the United States has replaced Britain as the hegemonic presence in her text. In fact, Lucy's Caribbeanness remains intact, safeguarded by her constant questioning of whatever she observes to avoid being subsumed into it. Kincaid expresses this well through the images of bars on windows that are mentioned twice in the novel. The first time, the bars are on the windows of Lewis and Mariah's tenth-floor apartment, put there to keep the children from falling out. Lucy's reaction is quite revealing: "I was confounded: Couldn't human beings in their position—wealthy, comfortable, beautiful, with the best the world had to offer at their fingertips—be safe and secure and never suffer so much as a broken nail?" (*L*, 85). With all their material and supposed emotional wealth, this couple still has to take measures to prevent the children from hurting themselves. It is also a way of controlling those children. This motif of imprisonment, something Lucy tried to evade by leaving Antigua (*L*, 95), is also reflected in her dream the first night she arrives. In it, she's holding a nightgown with a label that says "Made in Australia," and when she is awakened by the maid who dislikes her because of the way she talks, she remembers that Australia was partially settled by prisoners "so bad that they couldn't be put in a prison in their own country" (*L*, 9). For different reasons, then, they're all behind bars, the "perfect" family, the maid, and the stranger who has come to live with them.

The second time bars on windows are mentioned, Lucy is in the apartment she shares with Peggy: "Here the windows in the back had bars—not the decorative kind to keep children from falling out, but the crisscross kind to keep people who meant us no good from coming in; the windows in the front allowed the sun, when it shone, to come in plenty" (*L*, 147). Those bars keep out, like she herself does, those who will not do good to her. Although her new life is full of uncertainty, she is only partially behind bars because it includes some freedoms she didn't have before. However, she's far from implying that she's totally at home in the United States at that point. She's not even a part of the community that supposedly arises because of similar skin color. She distinguishes her people from the African-American waiters on a train, by saying: "On closer observation, they were not at all like my relatives; they only looked like them. My relatives always gave backchat" (*L*, 32), erasing that way any preconceived notions that West Indians and African-Americans, who seem subservient to her, are a homogeneous group. It is the characteristic of giving backchat that eventually distinguishes Lucy from Jo March. Whereas Jo says "the sharp words fly out before I know what I'm about" (*LW*, 80) and learns to suppress her anger before saying something she'll regret, Lucy ultimately doesn't position herself that way. She has not completely internalized voicelessness nor is she willing to keep silent about any injustice she may have suffered. This way, the talking back that might be interpreted as a reflection of an adolescent self is inscribed instead as a general cultural trait. It is no longer being rude, but an expression of one's perceptions and an inscription of oneself as a perceiving being. In her alignment with those who give backchat, she reaffirms her decision to continue speaking up. It is this quality of her Antiguan personality that usually alerts readers to her being the perpetual "Visitor" in the United States. As such, she provides a focus through which to view the new land in which she lives. In this context, one of the pictures Lucy has in her room is very revealing. It's one she took of a vase she had bought at a museum, a reproduction from the site of a lost civilization (*L*, 121). Kincaid's text itself is the picture she takes of a reproduction of *Little Women*, another lost civilization.

NOTES

This is an expanded version of an essay that originally appeared with the same title in *La Torre* VII, no. 25 (July–September 2002): 333–42.

1. This quotation and the ones in the paragraph that follows are taken from the Introduction to *"Little Women" and the Feminist Imagination: Criticism, Controversy, Personal Essays*, ed. Janice M. Alberghene and Beverly Lyon Clark (New York: Garland, 1999), xv and xvi.

2. 1877 journal entry cited by Elizabeth Lennox Keyser in "The Most Beautiful Things in All the World?: Families in *Little Women*," in *"Little Women" and the Feminist Imagination* (see note 1), 95n7.

3. Christine Doyle, "Transatlantic Translations: Communities of Education in Alcott and Brontë," in *"Little Women" and the Feminist Imagination* (see note 1), 263.

4. Carol Boyce Davies, "Writing Home: Gender and Heritage in the Works of Afro-Caribbean/American Women Writers," in *Out of the Kumbla: Caribbean Women and Literature*, ed. Carol Boyce Davies and Elaine Savory Fido (Trenton, NJ: Africa World Press, 1990), 60.

5. Belinda Edmondson, *Making Men: Gender, Literary Authority, and Women's Writing in Caribbean Narrative* (Durham, NC: Duke University Press, 1999), 4.

6. Edyta Oczkowicz, "Jamaica Kincaid's *Lucy*: Cultural 'Translation' as a Case of Creative Exploration of the Past," in *Jamaica Kincaid*, ed. Harold Bloom (Philadelphia: Chelsea House, 1998), 118.

7. Jamaica Kincaid, *Lucy* (New York: Plume/Penguin, 1991), 7. All subsequent references will be to this edition and will appear parenthetically in the text, designated by *L*.

8. Louisa May Alcott, *Little Women*, Introduction by Susan Cheever (1868; New York: The Modern Library, 2000), 319. All subsequent references will be to this edition and will appear parenthetically in the text, designated by *LW*.

9. Antonia MacDonald-Smythe, *Making Homes in the West Indies: Constructions of Subjectivity in the Writings of Michelle Cliff and Jamaica Kincaid* (New York: Garland, 2001), 23.

10. Lennox Keyser, "The Most Beautiful Things," 90.

11. Catharine R. Stimpson, "Reading for Love: Canons, Paracanons, and Whistling Jo March," in *"Little Women" and the Feminist Imagination* (see note 1), 73.

12. Judith Fetterley, *"Little Women*: Alcott's Civil War," in *"Little Women" and the Feminist Imagination* (see note 1), 32.

13. Ann Douglas, "Introduction to *Little Women*," in *"Little Women" and the Feminist Imagination* (see note 1), 49.

14. Kathryn Manson Tomasek, "A Greater Happiness: Searching for Feminist Utopia in *Little Women*," in *"Little Women" and the Feminist Imagination* (see note 1), 245.

15. Roberta Seelinger Trites, "Queer Performances: Lesbian Politics in *Little Women*," in *"Little Women" and the Feminist Imagination* (see note 1), 145.

16. Susan R. Gannon, "Getting Cozy with a Classic: Visualizing *Little Women*," in *"Little Women" and the Feminist Imagination* (see note 1), 116.

17. Douglas, "Introduction," 62.

18. Oczkowicz, "Jamaica Kincaid's *Lucy*," 124.

19. Tomasek, "A Greater Happiness," 238.

20. MacDonald-Smythe, *Making Homes*, 97.

21. Angela M. Estes and Kathleen M. Lant, "Dismembering the Text: The Horror of Louisa May Alcott's *Little Women*," *Children's Literature* 17 (1989): 99.

22. Fetterley, *"Little Women*: Alcott's Civil War," 39.

23. MacDonald-Smythe, *Making Homes*, 97.

24. Douglas, "Introduction," 48.

25. Fetterley, *"Little Women*: Alcott's Civil War," 28.

26. Douglas, "Introduction," 58.

27. Moira Ferguson, *"Lucy* and the Mark of the Colonizer," in *Jamaica Kincaid*, ed. Harold Bloom (see note 6), 64.

28. MacDonald-Smythe, *Making Homes*, 6.

29. Ferguson, *"Lucy* and the Mark," 67.

30. MacDonald-Smythe, *Making Homes*, 69 n 13.

31. Anne K. Phillips, "The Prophets and the Martyrs: Pilgrims and Missionaries in *Little Women* and *Jack and Jill*," in *"Little Women" and the Feminist Imagination* (see note 1), 214.

32. Ibid., 215.

33. Elaine Showalter, *Sister's Choice: Tradition and Change in American Women's Writing* (Oxford: Clarendon, 1991), 53.

34. Phillips, "The Prophets and the Martyrs," 215.

35. Ibid., 225.

36. Ibid.

37. MacDonald-Smythe, *Making Homes*, 23.

38. Phillips, "The Prophets and the Martyrs," 223.

39. Lennox Keyser, "The Most Beautiful Things," 88.

40. Fetterley, *"Little Women*: Alcott's Civil War," 34.

41. MacDonnald-Smythe, *Making Homes*, 20.

42. Fetterley, *"Little Women*: Alcott's Civil War," 30.

43. Oczkowicz, "Jamaica Kincaid's *Lucy*," 129.

44. Ferguson, *"Lucy* and the Mark," 67.

45. Fetterley, *"Little Women*: Alcott's Civil War," 37.

46. Boyce Davies, "Writing Home," 61–62.

47. Edmondson, *Making Men*, 3.

48. Jan Susina, "Men and *Little Women*: Notes of a (Resisting) Male Reader," in *"Little Women" and the Feminist Imagination* (see note 1), 162.

"Smiling with my Mouth Turned Down": Ambivalence in Jamaica Kincaid's *Lucy* and *My Garden (Book):*

LINDA LANG-PERALTA

"ISN'T IT SO THAT LOVE AND HATE EXIST SIDE BY SIDE?" ASKS THE protagonist in Jamaica Kincaid's novel *Lucy* (20). Lucy feels deeply ambivalent toward just about everything in her life: her mother, her Antiguan home, her new North American home, her employer, herself. As reviewer Elaine Kendall notes, "You can almost believe Kincaid invented ambivalence."[1] Some critics see Kincaid's work in universal terms, explaining the confused emotions as a part of the maturation process.[2] Indeed, Kincaid depicts the confused adolescent jumble of emotions with which one can identify, in whatever location one was raised. However, a closer analysis suggests that the ambivalence about personal relationships that emerges in Kincaid's writing, especially since *Annie John*, is steeped in history and politics unique to her West Indian home, Antigua.

In Kincaid's writing, binaries develop within characters as well as among characters and locations, emphasizing the complexity of identity. According to Ashcroft, Griffiths, and Tiffin, in the colonial situation, "the state between the binarism . . . will evidence the signs of extreme ambivalence manifested in mimicry, cultural schizophrenia, or various kinds of obsession with identity, or will put energy into confirming one or other side of the binarism."[3]

Originally a psychological term meaning to have conflicting emotions, ambivalence in Homi Bhabha's criticism refers to "the complex mix of attraction and repulsion that characterizes the relationship between colonizer and colonized."[4] The colonizer expects mimicry, but that mimicry can also pose a threat. On the other hand, the ambivalence in the colonized undermines the authority of the colonizer because the desired mimicry in the colonized can easily veer toward mockery. According to Bhabha, "The *menace* of mimicry is its *double* vision which in disclosing the ambivalence of colonial discourse also disrupts its authority" (88). Further emphasizing the duality in the colonial experience, Bhabha asserts, "The ambivalence of mimicry—almost but not quite— suggests that the fetishized colonial culture is potentially and strategically an insurgent counter-appeal. . . . its 'identity-effects' are always crucially *split*" (91).

Victoria Burrows takes this concept a step further in her analysis of Kincaid by suggesting that "Acknowledging the reality of the possibilities of holding contradictory views without constantly striving for their eradication offers the potential for a shift in terms and a relational politics that holds within it explicit—rather than implicit—tensions that can then become productive."[5] The "obsession with identity" that Ashcroft, Griffiths, and Tiffin emphasize and the ambivalence-as-resistance described by Bhabha are both evident in Kincaid's writing, most notably in *Lucy*, and, in fact, seem to be the source of inspiration for that writing.

In *Lucy*, the protagonist explicitly resists attempts to make her mimic the behavior of those around her. Rather than "mimic," Kincaid uses another term to describe what Lucy's mother wants her to do: "echo" her. Lucy's struggle against being an echo causes a breakdown in communication between characters, but allows Kincaid to make her use of the language of the colonizer a site of resistance. *Lucy* reveals the futility of attempting to create an identity separate from one's history, culture, and family.

Whereas Kincaid's earlier text *Annie John* (1985) depicts a young girl growing up in Antigua and developing ambivalent feelings toward her mother and her home, *Lucy* traces a protagonist's first venture away from her colonized island home as she takes a position as *au pair* for the four children of a North American family. Although the setting is America rather than Britain, the characters' European ancestry and associations with "the victors" are emphasized. The newness of everything that Lucy encounters in this different situation provides many opportunities for Kincaid to chart the contrasts between life in Antigua and the United States. The employer/employee relationship also allows the author to comment on power relations in this live-in situation and compare them with those in a colonial context.

From the beginning of the text, as Lucy contrasts her new and old homes, her reactions are clearly ambivalent: "It was all so new that I had to smile with my mouth turned down at the corners (4)." This is the type of sentence in Kincaid's work that "heads toward its own contradiction," in Derek Walcott's words.[6] In addition to the figure of the mother, snow and daffodils are two cathected figures for the nineteen-year-old Lucy. When she sees snow, something she never saw in the Caribbean, she refuses to love it even though she finds it beautiful because she doesn't want to be hurt again by loving: she "didn't want one more thing that could make [her] heart break into a million little pieces at [her] feet" (23). She both loves and fears the beauty surrounding her because of her vulnerable emotional state caused by her relationship with her mother.

Her reaction to the snow's beauty is made more complex and intense because she remembers her mother telling her that she and Lucy's father used to watch a Bing Crosby film set in a snowy clime every Christmas eve. Lucy describes her reaction to hearing the story: "I felt strongly how much I no longer liked even the way she spoke; and so I said, barely concealing my scorn, 'What a religious experience that must have been.'" Lucy's ambivalence toward her own behavior is clear: "I walked away quickly, for my thirteen-year-old heart couldn't bear to see her face when I had caused her pain, but I couldn't stop myself" (22). One wonders, taking Kincaid's cue that the mother and the oppressor are linked, if "the way she spoke" referred to the British accent and if the sarcastic reaction has to do with the admiration of a film that represents the culture of the oppressor. The film (probably Michael Curtiz's *White Christmas*, 1954), the British accent, and even the West Indians have all been transported to the island. Ironically, the setting of *White Christmas* is Vermont, Kincaid's current home.

Lucy clearly sees her mother along with the British and Americans as the powerful, while she identifies with the powerless. Her relationship with her mother has hurt her so deeply that she feels she can never love again. Later in the novel, Lucy observes that "for . . . half of my life, I had been mourning the end of a love affair, perhaps the only true love in my whole life I would ever know" (132). The change in their relationship occurred when Lucy's three brothers were born. While her parents turned all their attention to the boys' futures, imagining them attending an English university and becoming important professionals, they completely ignored her future. Lucy, at that point, began to call her mother "Mrs. Judas" (130). The love affair with her mother that ended in betrayal affected all future emotional ties.

It is this sense of "loss" and "betrayal," a fall from "a state of wholeness, in which . . . division is unknown" that Diane Simmons sees as the fundamental aspect of Kincaid's work.[7] However, this view does not fully take into account the rebellious urge to create a new identity, separate from mother, home, and oppressor. It is significant as well that there never was a pure, whole culture or relationship in the Caribbean to which she could return. After struggling to achieve some measure of independence, Lucy writes in her journal, "I wish I could love someone so much that I would die from it" (164). This expression of a simultaneous desire for an intense emotion and death, the cessation of all emotion, is indicative of the type of "split" identity that Bhabha describes. The only love that she has known has been that for her mother, and it has broken her heart, so she cannot desire love without desiring death, the end of pain. Likewise, she has known love for her motherland, Antigua, as it existed as a colonial dominion of the Queen Mother, who has caused her pain and made her a "minion." Thus, the pervasive ambivalence is directed toward not only the mother figure, but also the mother country and the Queen Mother who has dominated the homeland, as well as other oppressors. The mother and the motherland in *Lucy* are inextricably intertwined, as Kincaid herself has noted.

In addition to the snow, the mention of daffodils also elicits a well of complex emotions on the part of Lucy, who remembers her British education. Mariah, Lucy's employer, wants to share her excitement over this spring bounty. However, Lucy remembers that when she was a ten-year-old student at Queen Victoria Girl's School, she was asked to recite the poem about daffodils to an auditorium full of people. She does so, being at "the height of [her] two-facedness," and is praised for "how nicely [she] had pronounced every word. "While she is praised for mimicking English idioms so accurately, she is acting falsely: making "pleasant little noises that showed both modesty and appreciation," even though her deep resentment led her to "erase from [her] mind, line by line, every word of that poem" (18). In a dream after the event, daffodils chased her down a cobblestone street and buried her, indicating the event's serious effect on her. This image of being buried in daffodils seems to represent the profoundly oppressive effect of the colonial education, which blanketed her with a false identity, language, and culture.

The mimicry involved in the recitation sets the stage for the resistance that wells up inside of her when Mariah takes her to see actual daffodils. Lucy recognizes their beauty and simplicity, but before even knowing what type of flowers they are, she feels the urge to destroy them. After learning that they are daffodils, when trying to explain her violent reaction to Mariah, she asks, "Do you realize that at ten years of age I had to learn by heart a long poem about some flowers I would not see in real life until I was nineteen?" (30). As in the scene above with her mother, she regrets hurting Mariah: "I had cast her beloved daffodils in a scene she had never considered, a scene of conquered and conquests" (30). The daffodils had become for her a symbol of barbaric colonization.

In reciting Wordsworth's poem, she is being forced to express the emotion this English man felt for a flower she had never seen. She resists by vowing to forget the poem that is so alien to her but that she can recite so much like her colonizers who had valorized them. Likewise, Mariah wants Lucy to mimic/share/echo her feelings about the daffodils, but Lucy resists. Mariah's desire is exactly what Lucy hates in her mother, who wants Lucy to "echo" her. Thus, the mother and Mariah both play the role of colonizer, while Lucy resists the role of the colonized, one who mimics. Lucy veers away from mimicry and toward mockery when she asks herself how Mariah got to be the type of person she is. Later in her relationship with Mariah, her refusal to mimic her friend's emotions and views becomes more pronounced: "I would not bend. It was hollow, my triumph, I could feel that, but I held on to it just the same" (41). Thus, she mimics to the extent that she is in a position to resist.

"Obsession with identity" (Ashcroft) and "double vision" (Bhabha) lead to a breakdown in communications. Initially, Lucy tries to communicate, but in many instances fails, even though English is the language in common. This lack of communication isolates her: when Lucy first arrives at Mariah and Lewis's, the maid dislikes her because she speaks like a nun, and when the maid sings a popular song, Lucy sings a calypso. Lucy relates a dream to Mariah and her husband, Lewis, to show them she has embraced them as part of her life, but they raise their eyebrows, interpreting the dream in Freudian terms. Even though she has received a British education, she is perceived as a foreigner in this new place, and that image is reinforced when she sees everything a bit differently from those around her.

In this different location, Lucy learns to interpret things in new ways. In Antigua, the sun would always mean heat, but in North America, the winter sun means cold. There are also new signifiers, such as snow and lakes, causing her to learn a new language. She must also react to these new entities: she finds the snow beautiful but fears to love it, and she dislikes the lake in comparison with the sea of her home. Ultimately, she makes her own decisions about how to respond to new aspects of her existence, rather than imitating others. She misses certain aspects of her home—the color of the sky at sunset, the mullet and figs her grandmother used to prepare for her, but she refuses to read her mother's letters because they would cause her pain. She appreciates aspects of her new home, such as the four seasons and snow, but her reactions to them are always ambivalent because of her history.

Kincaid emphasizes the slippery nature of language in this novel. The relation between the signifier and the signified often becomes as complex as the emotions themselves. Various interpretations of utterances and gestures are offered; they can mean one thing or they can mean the opposite. As Lucy remembers a scar on the face of her mother's friend, she relates that it resulted from an embrace not of love but of anger. At a sensitive moment in a discussion with Mariah, she hears the children's screams, not knowing if they result from pain or pleasure. Language has more than one meaning for Lucy, as does ambivalent emotion.

As Lucy distances herself from home both geographically and emotionally, she hopes to be "free to take everything just as it came and not see hundreds of years in every gesture, every word spoken, every face" (31). She is unable to free herself, however, as she observes imperialism and oppression proliferating all around her. She comes to the conclusion that rulers live in places with four seasons, northern countries. When the wealthy Mariah becomes an environmental activist, Lucy remarks, "Like her, all of the members of this organization were well off but they made no connection between their comforts and the decline of the world that lay before them" (72). Lucy's history allows her to see issues from multiple perspectives, whereas Mariah, with her privileged background, has a more limited perspective.

On the train to the Great Lakes, Lucy observed that everyone sitting down to dinner looked like Mariah (fair), and all those waiting on them looked like her (with skin color the "brown of a nut rubbed repeatedly with a soft cloth" [5]). When Mariah shows Lucy the cultivated fields of which she is so fond, Lucy identifies with the laborers whose efforts resulted in the beautiful scene: "Well, thank God I didn't have to do that," she muses, noting that her remark had many meanings (33). At a cocktail party, Lucy "had just begun to notice that people who knew the correct way to do things such as hold a teacup, put food on a fork and bring it to their mouth without making a mess on the front of their dress—they were the people responsible for the most misery, the people least likely to end up insane or paupers" (98–99). Mariah's friend

Dinah, who has an affair with Mariah's husband, looks at Lucy as "the girl" (58). Lucy bristles at Mariah's malapropism, "minion," that makes her remember her "dominion" home. Lucy, who has Carib Indian blood from her grandmother, also resents Mariah's assertion that she has Indian blood, asking "How do you get to be the sort of victor who can claim to be the vanquished also?" (41). In her essay "The Flowers of Empire," Kincaid admits, "I only mind the absence of this acknowledgment: that perhaps every good thing that stands before us comes at a great cost to someone else."[8] It is partly the absence of this acknowledgment in those around her that causes miscommunication, ambivalence, and resistance.

Her acute perception of power relationships causes Lucy to become fiercely independent, resolving that she will never accept harsh judgments again (51). She moves into an apartment with a friend, takes a job as a photographer's assistant, and consciously attempts to decolonize her mind, having cut off all communication with her mother. Of course, she can never escape her mother because, as she recognizes, Lucy IS her mother (90). The reason she has not read her mother's letters, she finally admits, is that she "would die from longing for her" (91). Lucy traces her own transformation. She compares herself to a man, a hero, after leaving home with the mantle of a servant. In order to become a hero, she has had to turn her back on the mother who limited her horizons and made her a second-class citizen to her brothers. Also, she has had to separate herself from Mariah, the surrogate mother who had to become an equal friend for Lucy's maturation process to become complete. And she had to leave her home, the dominion, and strike out for the place in which she might become a doctor if she wished, or a photographer. Mariah calls Lucy an angry person, and it is probably ambivalence that fuels this anger and creates the resistance that propels Lucy to become a hero in her own eyes instead of a servant.

The link between the colonized home and the home of the colonizer is the similarity between Lucy's mother and Mariah: "The times that I loved Mariah it was because she reminded me of my mother. The times that I did not love Mariah it was because she reminded me of my mother" (58). But there is one important difference: "This was a way in which Mariah was superior to my mother, for my mother would never come to see that perhaps my needs were more important than her wishes" (63–64). It is significant that Mariah and Lucy manage to salvage their friendship after Lucy moves out, leaving the newly single Mariah and her children. Mariah recognizes Lucy's desperate need for

independence. Her time with Lewis and Mariah taught her an important lesson, however. She muses, "I had thought the untruths in family
life belonged exclusively to me and my family" (77). Being able to compare her family with another allows her to place her own family's problems in perspective.

Once Lucy can recognize the "good mother" in her friend Mariah
and acknowledge that there is such a thing as a good mother, once she
can analyze her feelings and place them in the context of refusing to
sing "Rule Britannia!" she can move on and realize she can count on
intuition to guide her. Her mother's guidance has not allowed for her
potential; Britain's rule was foreign to her. Her "double vision" enables
her to recognize these truths. Her ambivalence prevents her from being
subject to anyone: Mariah, her lovers, her friend Peggy. She struggles
for freedom and independence, realizing that she had "memory,"
"anger," and "despair" (134) as her supports. The tone in this passage
is realistic but hopeful as she recognizes not only her limitations, but
also her creativity and strengths.

In *Lucy*, as in many of Kincaid's texts, personal relationships are conceptualized in terms of the political and historical past of the Caribbean.
Relationships involve an oppressor and one who is oppressed. The oppressor demands mimicry, while the oppressed resists, at times turning
mimicry into mockery. The mother is viewed as the colonizer who
smothers identity, an identity that is already complex because it contains aspects of African, Caribbean, and European cultures. The language of the colonizer not only mimics the oppressors but also becomes
a site of resistance as Kincaid explores the impossibility of constructing
new identities without "see[ing] hundreds of years in every gesture,
every word spoken, every face" (31). When her lover Paul gives her a
photograph he took of her cooking, covered only from the waist down,
she realizes, "That was the moment he got the idea he possessed me in
a certain way, and that was the moment I grew tired of him" (155).
Their relationship loses its uniqueness when she understands that "he
loved things that came from far away and had a mysterious history"
(156). He cannot see her apart from her history, just as she cannot see
their relationship in terms other than colonizer and colonized. For this
reason, she is not upset when he begins a relationship with her room-
mate.

The "obsession with identity" emphasized by Ashcroft, Griffiths, and
Tiffin and the ambivalence that involves resistance described by
Bhabha are both evident in the novel *Lucy*, but they also appear in her

later texts, *A Small Place* (1988), *My Brother* (1997), and *My Garden (Book):* (1999). I will focus on the last in order to demonstrate Kincaid's shift to the other side of the binary. The intense focus on identity is readily apparent, even in a book on gardening, and Kincaid still clearly valorizes one side or the other of the binarism; however, her more recent texts suggest an increasing identification with the side of the binary that she previously attacked and a more positive view of the ambivalence and irritation that lead to her artistic productivity.

In *My Garden (Book):*, Kincaid reminds the reader that "the two things I like most, [are] history and gardening/botany."[9] This nonfiction book confesses an obsession with her garden in Vermont, while analyzing the acquisitive desire and tendency toward conquest that this type of gardener experiences. Her tone is milder here than in previous texts, partly because she is analyzing the ways in which her passion for acquiring foreign seeds and plants elicits feelings and behavior that she had previously criticized. She associates the beginning of her gardening with reading a book about the conquest of Mexico by William Prescott (6). While visiting a flower show in England, she has an attack of acquisitiveness when she sees a striking flower. She admits, "I wanted immediately to put the thing I was seeing in my handbag and take it home" (102). Her consumerism is not limited to gardening, however. Her family wants to buy a neighbor's lovely house, and finds a way to do so. She writes, "That house was at least twenty times as big as the house I grew up in, a house in a poor country with a tropical climate, but I had lived in America for a long time and had adjusted to the American habit of taking up at least twenty times as much of the available resources as each person needs" (37). She reveals here a double vision much like that of Lucy's. She is acutely aware of her consumerism but revels in it.

As she admires complementary colors in her garden, she admits, "I had crossed a line; but at whose expense? I cannot begin to look, because what if it is someone I know? I have joined the conquering class: who else could afford this garden . . . ? My feet are (so to speak) in two worlds" (123). In this Rousseauistic confessional mode, she examines her own complicity with a system that led her to create her divided identity, her double vision. Now that she has become part of the system, driven partly by her obsession to create the perfect garden, she cannot forget those who actually make her consumerism possible. Describing the history of botany and its relation to conquest, she mildly laments, "I only mind the absence of this admission, this contradiction: perhaps every good thing that stands before us comes at a great cost to someone else" (152). In *My Garden (Book):* she admits that her passions are bought from others in transactions that impoverish both parties. As she traces the intersections of the histories of conquest and botany, she reminds the reader that the desire to conquer, control, name, import, and export affects the rest of the world, such as her tiny island of Antigua.

In *My Garden (Book):* she describes a trip to China with a group of people who shares her passion to study botany and acquire seeds. The irony is that she emphasizes her capitalistic consumerism in a communist country without much political comment. Here she becomes the tourist, against whom she railed in *A Small Place*, which attacks tourists who visit Antigua, the British who made a conquest of the island, and the independent Antigua of the late 1980s. According to Moira Ferguson, "In *A Small Place* tourists are a collective Columbus, new colonists, brash cultural invaders."[10] This small book does not let its readers forget the ways in which the past colors the present in the Caribbean. Curiously enough, in *My Garden (Book):*, Kincaid is not only a tourist, but she is not even a very nice tourist, bitching (in her words) about the restrooms, offering quite frank observations about the habits of the Chinese, as well as her tour companions, and blaming it all on what she calls a small nervous breakdown. The book ends with a series of revealing associations: China/Garden of Eden/comfort/discomfort. She writes, "Eden is like that, so rich in comfort, it tempts me to cause discomfort; I am in a state of constant discomfort and I like this state so much I would like to share it" (229). This concluding observation sheds light on the whole text, since it explains why the English would leave the England they loved so much to go live among those they disliked (Antiguans).

She comes to understand this desire, it seems, through her passion for gardening. In the Museum of Garden History, she comes across a book of songs that Walter Jekyll wrote for the people of Jamaica, observing that "he did not like black people, so naturally, he had to go and live among them. For some people, a fixed state of irritation is oxygen. I understand this all too well" (113). She again writes of irritation in a positive light when reminiscing about her trip to China in *Among Flowers: A Walk in the Himalayas* (2005): "I suppose I felt that thing called alienated, but it was so pleasant, so interesting, so dreamily irritating to be so far away from everything I had known."[11] Her multilayered perceptions and ambivalent emotions coalesce in irritation, which inspires her to create, whether it be a garden or a book.

In her garden book, Kincaid seems to answer many of the questions raised in previous texts. In *A Small Place*, she couldn't understand why the English would have chosen to live among the Antiguans, but here she seems to find an answer in her own identity. In *Lucy* and again in the garden book, she angrily describes having to recite Wordsworth's poem about daffodils, but she reveals that blooming in her garden is an exquisite yellow daffodil that ultimately turns a creamy color she finds irresistible. In Antigua she had not understood why the English had brought plants from their conquered lands to create a botanical garden, and she had not learned the names of those plants. Now she travels as far as China and the Himalayas to bring back foreign plants to her garden, carefully listing their scientific names.

She has not forgotten history, but she seems to have gained an understanding of the human weaknesses that create it. Memory is the key to understanding present identity. However, most frustratingly for her, the language she uses to list the history of crimes is that of the criminals. She writes in *A Small Place*, "But what I see is the millions of people, of whom I am just one, made orphans: no motherland, no fatherland, no gods, no mounds of earth for holy ground, no excess of love which might lead to the things that an excess of love sometimes brings, and worst and most painful of all, no tongue."[12] Writing, even if it is in the colonizers' language, is her only means of expressing her anger. There is no way to right the wrongs, but she can write about the wrongs. The multiple perspectives that she has gained from this history, along with the irritation that it generates in her, inspires her productivity, leading her repeatedly to construct selves in writing, expressing the ambivalence located at the source of her art.

NOTES

The quotation in the title is from Jamaica Kincaid's novel *Lucy* (New York: Plume/Penguin, 1991), 4. All further references to this edition will be noted in the text.

1. Elaine Kendall, review of *Lucy* by Jamaica Kincaid, *Los Angeles Times Book Review*, October 21, 1990.

2. Susan Kenney, review of *Lucy* by Jamaica Kincaid, *New York Times Book Review*, April 7, 1985, 6.

3. Bill Ashcroft, Gareth Griffiths, and Helen Tiffin, "Ambivalence," in *Key Concepts in Post-Colonial Studies* (New York: Routledge, 1998), 24.

4. Homi Bhabha, *Location of Culture* (London: Routledge, 1994): 12.

5. Victoria Burrows, *Whiteness and Trauma* (New York: Palgrave, 2004), 13

6. Quoted in Diane Simmons, *Jamaica Kincaid* (New York: Twayne, 1994), 4.

7. Ibid., 1.

8. Jamaica Kincaid, "The Flowers of Empire," *Harper's Magazine*, April 1996, 24.

9. *My Garden (Book):* (New York: Farrar Straus Giroux, 1999), 110.

10. Moira Ferguson, *Colonialism and Gender Relations from Mary Wollstonecraft to Jamaica Kincaid* (New York: Columbia University Press, 1993), 133.

11. Jamaica Kincaid, *Among Flowers: A Walk in the Himalayas* (Washington, DC: National Geographic, 2005), 3.

12. Jamaica Kincaid, *A Small Place* (New York: Farrar Straus Giroux, 1988), 31.

The Horrors of Homelessness: Gothic Doubling in Kincaid's *Lucy* and Brontë's *Villette*

EVIE SHOCKLEY

JAMAICA KINCAID'S 1990 NOVEL, *LUCY*, IS A WORK WHOSE DECEPTIVELY simple language and short length belie the complexity of both its engagement with literary tradition and its critique of the ideological framework sustaining power imbalances in and among Western(ized) societies. In this essay, I attempt to unpack some of the concerns of this highly compressed text by looking at *Lucy* in a comparative context. As I will discuss in more detail below, Kincaid, via *Lucy*, quite pointedly addresses Charlotte Brontë and the heroine and readers of Brontë's 1853 novel, *Villette*, so that the earlier work acts as a lens through which *Lucy*'s readers can focus more clearly on some of the later novel's most important analyses of the function of identity in maintaining the status quo between relatively powerful and relatively disempowered people(s). By the same token, the text of *Villette* reveals a greater ambivalence in its understanding of identity when read in conjunction with Kincaid's novel. The precariousness of Brontë's heroine's social position becomes more clearly visible, even as its stability, in comparison to the position of Kincaid's heroine, becomes a critical aspect of my reading of the text.

Both *Lucy* and *Villette* are texts whose authors use gothic conventions (the tropes, settings, and plot devices that recurred formulaically in the classic gothic romances of the late eighteenth century[1]) to represent and interrogate their heroines' societal marginality. In particular, the gothic figure of the double (or the doppelgänger) becomes an important part of the lexicon of gothic conventions used by Brontë and Kincaid, binding these narratives from beginning to end, endowing them with a reciprocal resonance greater than either could individually generate. Lucy Potter, the au pair-heroine of Jamaica Kincaid's novel, is the double of the very Victorian Lucy Snowe, governess-heroine of Charlotte Brontë's novel. The two Lucys haunt one another, across the boundaries of narrative, as well as those of geography, time, and race. I argue that by examining the significant similarities and differences between Kincaid's *Lucy* and Brontë's *Villette*, we can obtain a more nuanced understanding of the ways in which mutually constructing identity categories—race, class, gender, sexuality, and nationality—operate in modern England and America, as well as what identity means in these works. In both works, gothic conventions—the double, as noted, but also such tropes as the ghost, the haunted ruins, and the "unspeakable horror"— manifest the social terrors involved in negotiating the shifting boundaries of identity. By tracing this parallel across an ocean and a century, we can begin to see the way these texts are further linked by the oppressive force that domestic ideology imposes on their authors, a force that generates the terror revealed in the novels through gothic conventions. We can also delineate differences in the efficacy of women's agency in the twentieth-century African American and British Victorian contexts.

Texts from these two cultures are rarely juxtaposed in literary criticism. As a consequence of artificial and arbitrary epistemological boundary drawing, general connections between the cultures, not to mention specific linkages between texts like *Lucy* and *Villette*, get lost in a disciplinary blind spot. My comparative reading of these novels helps to illustrate, as I argue elsewhere, that both British Victorian culture and twentieth-century African American culture are subject to a nearly all-encompassing "tyranny of domesticity," which is to say that domestic ideology's behavioral norms radically overdetermine the identities— and, hence, the living conditions and opportunities—of members of these cultures. I would like to provide a brief outline of the reasons for seeing domestic ideology as a tyrannical influence in the British and African American contexts, as background for a closer examination of the novels.

Anne McClintock explains in *Imperial Leather: Race, Gender and Sexuality in the Colonial Contest* that domestic ideology posits the "home" and the "family," literally and metaphorically, as the fundamental units of societal organization at all levels.[2] Utilizing cultural meanings that are attached to biological relationships, social roles based upon one's race, class, gender, sexuality, and nationality are both prescribed and naturalized. I see such roles as performative, in the sense in which Judith Butler has described gender as performative: "that is, constituting the identity it is purported to be."[3] In other words, I extend her analysis of gender to include racial, class, sexual, and national identities, as well, understanding these social roles not as fixed, but as perpetually unstable, their performativity a necessarily ongoing process that depends from moment to moment on our *doing* what a given identity "is." Domesticity, then, can be described as a command performance of various (and often competing) social roles, which are assigned both arbitrarily and deliberately at once. Thus, men are said to be "naturally" the heads of households and the fathers of nations, despite the fact that they must individually be taught and reminded to "be a man"; the construction of stereotypes that feminize black males in relation to white males serves to exclude black men from privileges reserved for "real (white) men." Likewise, blacks are said to be "naturally" part of a unified racial family, despite the fact that black leaders in the United States must frequently urge their "brothers and sisters" to act out of a common "black national" interest. Debates over the so-called "authenticity" of African Americans accused of "acting white" (read: performing "whiteness") ironically serve to police the boundaries of "blackness" using the same ideology that is employed to strengthen the exclusionary boundaries of "whiteness" against blacks.[4] In this way, the ideology works to render our performance of various social roles "logical" and "natural" through analogies to the "logical" and "natural" relationships between husbands and wives, parents and children, sisters and brothers.

These "familial" relationships form a "household" hierarchy—typically with "fathers" at the top and "daughters" at the bottom—in which the differing natures and degrees of the contributions of its members are supposed to explain and justify the varying degrees of power each member holds. In other words, domestic ideology's norms underwrite a system of dramatically uneven allocation of societal resources that privileges some identities over others (e.g., men over women, Americans over Antiguans) and typically punishes those whose behavior takes them outside of their prescribed boundaries. Thus, one's life conditions and options depend to a significant degree upon which social roles one has been assigned and how consistently one performs those roles according to societal expectations. I argue that, in the British Victorian and twentieth-century African American cultures, the degree to which these norms and performances hold sway is peculiarly tyrannical, so much so that members of these cultures understand there to be *terrifying* consequences for the failure to properly perform prescribed identities. Indeed, these terrors often outweigh the *horrors* of successful performances, for persons whose relatively disempowered identities (e.g., "woman," "laborer," "nonwhite") are assigned behaviors that are distinctly and stereotypically negative, such that to perform "properly" is to court humiliation (or worse) in exchange for the small rewards that attend conformity with expectations.[5] This "tyranny of domesticity" emerges in these two cultures in the frighteningly wide gap between the supposed caste-like fixity of class and racial identities (in the Victorian and African American contexts, respectively), and the demonstrable mutability of those identities and the other identities against which they are constructed.

To put it another way, in both cultures, people—faced with frighteningly rapid change and uncertainty—found themselves both relying upon and imprisoned within this paradoxically superrigid, yet hyperelastic network of rules-for-being. The developing Victorian middle classes, whose wealth alone was insufficient to justify their new claims to power, evolved and perpetuated, as markers of worthiness, various idealized performances of identity that even their most vocal proponents could not consistently sustain. They set in motion the ideology of domesticity that we know today and think of as virtually synonymous with Victorianism. According to this ideology, the privilege of ruling England—of voting in parliamentary elections, to take the case of the 1832 Reform Bill—rightfully belonged to the moral, stable, thrifty, devoted (i.e., domesticated) middle classes. The ideology distinguished these worthies from the "savage" poor and working classes, as well as from the "decadent" aristocracy that had formerly held uncontested sway over the nation.[6] A wide selection of "conduct" books (such as *Hints for Practical Economy in the Management of Household Affairs* and *The Compleat Housewife or, Accomplished Gentlewoman's Companion*) were available to instruct members of this new class-based community how to recognize one another, operating as scripts, we might say, for the performance of domesticity.[7] The rules for proper performance of domesticity were so detailed and dogmatic that, often, only a performance of performance was possible, as when the Victorian "gentlewoman" of lesser means, working side-by-side with her maid all day to clean her house up to standards, throws off her gloves and apron and takes up her needlework just moments before the arrival of visitors or the return of the "man of the house."[8]

By contrast, America's class system is far less rigid. Without taking American democratic rhetoric at its word, we can nonetheless recognize the relative freedom many in the United States have felt to believe in the possibility of upward mobility and the cherished, collective national fantasy of the rags-to-riches tale. But such potential mobility has been basically unavailable to African Americans, among others. Indeed, "blackness"—color and culture—has been treated as a marker for poverty or working-class status, as opposed to "whiteness," which has been constructed as a sign of middle- or upper-class status, actual or potential.[9] While post-Reconstruction African Americans—the first nationwide generation of free (not *freed*) blacks in the United States— embraced many of the ideological standards of domesticity, even those among them who met those standards were rarely recognized as worthy of the societal resources and privileges they had certainly, in one fashion or another, earned. African Americans, having thus learned that even their successful performances of domesticity would go unrecognized, entered the twentieth century with this ideology both on their backs—in their economically enforced capacity as domestic workers in white homes, a legacy of slavery—and tangling their feet—insofar as they were required (but not thought able) to "prove" their humanity and their right to political power by mimicking white, middle-class domestic values without having individually or collectively the financial resources to support their efforts.[10]

Against this background, I introduce a concept called "gothic homelessness," which I developed as a way of thinking about the meaningful similarities between Kincaid's and Brontë's narratives. *Lucy*, written by a twentieth-century African American who has immigrated to the United States from the small Caribbean nation of Antigua,[11] and *Villette*, authored by a British Victorian of shabbily genteel middle-class standing, both feature heroines who are domestic workers. As such, their occupations place them at odds with the privileged gender norms, which state that "true women" (read: "ladies") do not work to earn a living, but rather dedicate themselves to creating a domestic haven for their own families. Our heroines repeatedly articulate their dis-ease with the liminal social positions they occupy, as women who work for money in other women's homes, in cultures that punish them for being "improperly" and "abnormally" independent of fathers or husbands or sons. Their resulting social marginality leaves them in the state of "gothic homelessness," a dis-eased condition that is at once psychological—in terms of the uneasiness that troubles the mind of the affected person— and social—in terms of the sense that person has of being treated by others like the "carrier" of some societal abnormality.[12]

Gothic homelessness, then, is the state of the individual who is unwilling and/or unable to achieve or maintain performances of ideologically privileged norms and, as a result, comes to be located socially outside or on the margins of domestic space and the communities privileged by domestic ideology. Gothic terror and horror saturate the environment of such individuals, whose double nightmare is that of seeing through the supposed fixity of domestic ideology's identity boundaries, while at the same time being unable to control those boundaries—to shift or transgress them purposefully—so as to obtain and sustain a desired social outcome. By comparing the strategies of Kincaid's and Brontë's heroines for coping with and mitigating their gothic homelessness, we can obtain a more complete understanding of the operation of domestic ideology to maintain the status quo in both their cultures and the relative significance of power differentials created by varying combinations of identities.

Lucy and *Villette* beg to be read together. Indeed, Kincaid's work is a conscious rewriting of Brontë's. She points to the earlier novel by repeating the names of the heroine, Lucy, and her romantic interest, Paul, and by carefully informing us that Lucy Potter's favorite authors are named "Emily, Charlotte, [and] Jane."[13] We can begin tracing the double here, with Potter's remark that "In my mind, I called myself [by these] names" (Kincaid, 149)—whereby she seeks to identify herself with these writers whose works she feels so passionately about. If Kincaid is creating a double of Brontë's heroine in *Lucy*, she also, as author and as woman, imagines *Brontë* as a double for *herself*. The similarities in the premises of the novels—young woman crosses the ocean, takes employment as a nanny, falls in love, and misses home—reflect not only Kincaid's literary choices, but additionally the actual correspondences between her life, the life of Brontë's Lucy, and Brontë's own life, parallels that must have led Kincaid to see *Villette* as fertile ground for her literary reworking in the first instance. In other words, because both novels are significantly autobiographical,[14] it is ultimately the analogy between the two writers' lives that underwrites Kincaid's revision of Brontë's text.

But Kincaid does not simply revisit Brontë's story, she doubles it, creating an uncanny relationship between the two novels that draws our attention to the horrors that plague each heroine. An early passage from *Lucy* does the work of linking Potter with her Victorian double, and at the same time, shows her to be doubled within herself—double-consciousness being a familiar motif in the African American literary tradition.[15] She maps her inner division upon the vast differences between her homeplace, Antigua, and her new place of employment, New York City: "[T]his realization now entered my life like a flow of water dividing formerly dry and solid ground, creating two banks, one of

which was my past—so familiar and predictable that even my unhappi-
ness then made me happy now just to think of it—the other my future,
a gray blank, an overcast seascape on which rain was falling and no
boats were in sight" (Kincaid, 5–6). Lucy Potter is gothically doubled
internally as a result of the contingency of the path she has chosen: a
rejection of the horrifying known in favor of the terrifying unknown.
She has for years wanted nothing so much as to escape from her island
"home" and the gendered, ideologically mandated difference between
the way her parents treat her and the way they treat her younger brothers. But having placed an ocean between herself and her family, she is
forced to acknowledge that the source of her longing for escape is a
longing for *belonging*, a desire that will always flow away from the place
where she is, the satisfaction of which is continually deferred.

This seascape metaphor also serves to invoke her double, Lucy
Snowe, who similarly resorted to a seascape metaphor in speaking of a
turning point her life. In *Villette*, we learn indirectly that Snowe begins
her life and grows up as a member of a middle-class household. She
never explains her change in circumstances, except in an elliptical passage, in which she invites the reader to imagine her spending her adolescence as a passenger on a craft at sea:

> [I]t cannot be concealed that . . . I must somehow have fallen over-board,
> or that there must have been wreck at last. . . . To this hour, when I have
> the nightmare, it repeats the rush and saltness of briny waves in my throat,
> and their icy pressure on my lungs. I even know there was a storm, and that
> not of one hour nor one day. For many days and nights neither sun nor stars
> appeared; we cast with our own hands the tackling out of the ship; a heavy
> tempest lay on us; all hope that we should be saved was taken away. In fine,
> the ship was lost, the crew perished.[16]

On one side of this storm, Snowe is a little girl of the middle classes,
enjoying a visit to her godmother; on the other side, she appears as a
bereaved and penniless young woman, "faded" and "hollow-eyed" from
her ordeals (Brontë, 96). This shadowy catastrophe leads ultimately to
her decision to leave her "little island," like Lucy Potter, and seek employment on the nearby continental mainland.

Potter's description of her future as a desolate seascape recalls
Snowe's metaphorical tempest. However, where Lucy Snowe begins on
a ship, facing the water's danger only when it capsizes, Lucy Potter,
from the start, must negotiate the stormy sea with "no boats . . . in sight"
(Kincaid, 6). Kincaid thus signifies on the racial and national differences

that distinguish these two otherwise similarly situated young women. The gap between their parallels and their disparities is a gothic space, which continually haunts Lucy Potter's narrative in the form of what we might call, after Deborah McDowell, the "changing same."[17] Even after a century of "progress," a woman named Lucy might find that her most attractive option is to leave her "homeland" for low-paying domestic employment in another country. The significance and consequences of exercising this option, however, are dramatically different for the two women, even as they remain linked through the (il)logic of the ideology of domesticity.

Lucy Snowe finds that leaving England offers her the possibility of recapturing her lost economic identity (and thus her lost gender identity). Having formed her identity as a middle-class gentlewoman, she finds herself, in the aftermath of her unspecified familial disaster, in a state of gothic homelessness, where her performances of the class and gender identities she desires are either disabled or dismissed. She tries to shore up her self-identity with the small signs and tokens that mark members of the class community in which she imagines herself. When she travels to London to seek employment, for example, she manages to correct the rudeness of the inn staff by name-dropping, asserting her familial connection to businessmen she believes the older members of the staff will remember with respect. She enjoys her minor triumph, noting, "my position in [their] eyes was henceforth clear, and *on a right footing*. . . . A ready and obliging courtesy now replaced [their] former uncomfortably doubtful manner" (Brontë, 108; emphasis mine). Her dis-ease with her initial reception by the staff derives from her growing recognition of the conflict between domestic ideology's dogma that her class status is inherent—"in her blood," we might say—and her lived experience of needing a middle-class bank account and a middle-class kinship network in order to properly perform a middle-class identity.

Domestic ideology mandates that Snowe's performance of being middle class conform to certain gendered expectations, one of which is that she limit her labor to the unpaid homemaking services of daughter to father, or preferably wife to husband, and otherwise live a life of leisure. Thus, when the inn staff treat her like a working-class woman, she suffers from an unbearable cognitive dissonance, marked by the gothic convention of the specter. "All at once my position rose on me like a ghost," she says (Brontë, 107), realizing that ladylike conduct is a luxury she can no longer wholly afford. This gothic crisis of identity is particularly significant in that it provokes her not to resign herself to performing a working-class womanhood, but rather to rededicate herself to the performance of middle-class gentility. Immediately upon experiencing this ghostly displacement of her class identity, Lucy Snowe discards her plan of finding employment in London and determines to leave England. She follows this decision with a morning's performance of the role of woman of leisure: sightseeing, shopping, dining, napping, even indulging unwarrantedly in the thrill of consumerism: "I bought a little book—a piece of extravagance I could ill afford; but I thought I would one day give or send it to Mrs Barrett [formerly a servant in her family's household]. Mr Jones [the bookseller] . . . seemed one of the greatest, and I one of the happiest, of beings" (Brontë, 109). This purchase enables her to feel herself in the "proper" relation to the businessman, and, prospectively, to reassert her position as benefactor vis-à-vis her former servant, from whom she has recently been forced to seek advice on obtaining employment.

Why does Brontë's narrative take this odd turn? I suggest that we are to understand Lucy as making a strategic attempt to end her feeling of gothic homelessness. She cannot bear the prospect of having her performance of middle-class domesticity fail or go unrecognized, as her first evening in London has shown her it will, when she can drop neither names nor coins enough in support of her role. Shrewdly, she decides to take her show on the road, if you will—to renew her performance on the mainland of Europe where it will be valued more highly. That is, Lucy decides to capitalize upon the fact that performance of domesticity involves a performance of nationality. To live in accordance with domestic ideology is to be "civilized," and to be civilized is to be English. And while her attempt to use relocation to resituate herself from the margins to the center of the domestic space is never wholly successful—indeed, she faces quite a stunning defeat in the novel's concluding section—her experiences do tend to bear out her expectation that, on the Continent, she will be more likely perceived as quite the proper gentlewoman, because she is English—regardless, to some extent, of her actual economic status.

Kincaid's Lucy has a very different set of goals than Brontë's. Whereas Lucy Snowe's gothic homelessness derives from her desire to move from the margins of domestic space *in*, Lucy Potter's gothic homelessness is associated with her determination to move from the margins *out*. Snowe—whose name, chosen for its "coldness,"[18] also comes to signify "whiteness" in light of Kincaid's novel—wishes desperately to find a way to perform domesticity successfully in accordance with ideological standards, a desire all the more heartbreaking for her efforts to conceal and disguise it in her narrative. Potter, on the other hand, wants to break free of the constraints of domestic ideology altogether, seeing it as little more than an oppressive trap—and the poignancy of her desire lies in her inability to prevent herself from longing for the comforts that come with the cage. She struggles futilely to avoid accepting a normative "familial" role in each new context she encounters, in a society in which interpersonal relationships, particularly intimate ones, are routinely translated into domestic ideology's terms. Racial and national differences play an important role in creating the distinctions between the desires and expectations of the two women in this regard.

Unlike Snowe, Lucy Potter does not hold a privileged class relationship to domestic ideology. Potter occupies a set of identities—black, female, colonized, and poor—that are marginal within the framework of this ideology. Crucially, it is her mother's betrayal that teaches her that domestic ideology did not, *could not*, have a place for her that she was willing to accept. This betrayal is narratively depicted through recourse to the gothic double. Lucy is her mother's double—or vice versa—a fact that goes from making her proud to making her furious. She and her mother have a fairly seamless relationship until she turns nine, when the first of her brothers is born. The way her parents plan for her brothers' futures—education abroad, great careers—was not how they had planned for hers. She can forgive her father for this, she tells us, but not her mother, who: "knew me . . . as well as she knew herself: I, at the time, even thought of us as identical; and whenever I saw her eyes fill up with tears at the thought of how proud she would be at some deed her sons had accomplished, I felt a sword go through my heart, for there was no accompanying scenario in which she saw me, her only identical offspring, in a remotely similar situation. To myself I then began to call her Mrs. Judas, and I began to plan a separation from her that even then I suspected would never be complete" (Kincaid, 130–31). It is at this moment that Lucy begins to comprehend fully the extent to which domestic ideology privileges the male within the normative "family."

Potter rejects this "family," which for her is not just her mother, father, and brothers, or even more distant relatives, but the whole racial/national community of Antigua. The "homeland," she decides, is the "home" she must escape, in order to create a home for herself that would not hold within its very existence the seeds of her oppression. But her mother, as her double, symbolizes for Lucy the inescapability

of this "home" she wants so badly to leave behind. Here, we might note
Moira Ferguson's argument that Kincaid's "doubled articulation of
motherhood as both colonial [e.g., the 'motherland'] and biological explains why the mother-daughter relations in her fiction often seem so
harshly rendered."[19] Lucy's mother's words haunt her: "'You can run
away, but you cannot escape the fact that I am your mother'" (Kincaid,
90). Thus her bitter response: "How else was I to take such a statement
but as a sentence for life in a prison whose bars were stronger than any
iron imaginable?" (Kincaid, 90–91). Like Lucy Snowe, she hopes that
moving outside her national "home" will provide her with the means of
reconstructing her identity, and she obtains employment as the au pair
of a wealthy New York family.

But just as Snowe's move to Labassecour does not enable her to shed
her disempowered status fundamentally, Potter arrives in the United
States only to find a narrative repetition of the mother-daughter double
that she fled Antigua to elude. That is, her white employer, Mariah,
becomes a mother-like double for Lucy:

> Mariah wanted all of us, the children and me, to see things the way she
> did. . . . But I already had a mother who loved me, and I had come to see
> her love as a burden and had come to view with *horror* the sense of self-
> satisfaction it gave my mother to hear other people comment on her great
> love for me. I had come to feel that my mother's love for me was designed
> solely to make me into an echo of her; and I didn't know why, but I felt that
> *I would rather be dead* than become just an echo of someone. (Kincaid, 35–36;
> emphasis added)

The "horror" here is doubled and redoubled. First, Kincaid's language
subtly implicates the ghastly history of white American exploitation of
black women as domestic workers. African American women were employed more often as domestics than in any other type of job during the
first half of the twentieth century and have been essential, yet invisible,
components of white families' performances of domesticity.[20] Thus,
Lucy's horror derives in part from the way that the rhetoric of "family"
was historically used both to violently reconstruct the exploitative economic relationship as one of mutual caring and to write out of existence
the workers' biological families.[21] Moreover, Lucy begins to see, here,
the terrifying limitlessness of domestic ideology's scope suggested by
Mariah's role in her life. She feels a growing affection for Mariah,
which frightens her, and her fear expresses itself in gothic terms. For
example, she contrasts the way Mariah's daughter sees her—as a

"beautiful golden mother pouring love over growing things"—to Potter's own view of Mariah as "a hollow old woman, all the blood drained out of her face, her bony nose bonier than ever, her mouth collapsed as if all the muscles had been removed" (Kincaid, 46), as if by constructing Mariah as a corpse, Lucy can distance herself from the position of "daughter." For if this blonde, blue-eyed, wealthy, white American can double her impoverished, Afro-Caribbean mother (and attempt to make a double of Lucy as well), Lucy can only conclude that "there is no escape" (Kincaid, 36).

Potter's intertextual double, Lucy Snowe, is also delineated as a daughterly double of her first employer. Before Snowe is driven to seek employment outside of England's borders, she works for a few months as the "maid, or rather companion" of an aging invalid, Miss Marchmont (Brontë, 95). Unlike Potter, however, Snowe chooses to minimize the distance between herself and her mistress. Though Lucy's tasks will be to fetch and carry and wait upon Miss Marchmont hand and foot, she prefers to name herself "companion," rather than "maid," an indication that she welcomes the opportunity to see herself in as close a light to a mother/daughter relationship with her employer as possible. Because Victorian social practices blurred the lines between wage labor and kinship services—such that cleaning, child care, and nursing duties might be performed by persons hired on the basis of a "character" (i.e., a reference) or, just as easily, on waged or unwaged terms, by members of the family or family-like circles of close friends and neighbors[22]— Lucy can use terminology that disguises the extent to which her class status has altered. She takes pains to describe Miss Marchmont's scoldings as "rather like an irascible mother rating her daughter, than a harsh mistress lecturing a dependent" (Brontë, 96). By constructing her relationship with her employer as a *familial* one, Lucy is able to avoid facing, for a while longer, the frightening fact that she is "dependent" upon paid employment for her survival.

But Miss Marchmont proves to be more than like a mother to Lucy; by the novel's conclusion, the reader realizes that the older woman is like Lucy herself. Brontë constructs Miss Marchmont as Lucy's own double through the parallels in the termination of the two women's marital prospects. The night of Miss Marchmont's death is described in gothic tones, dark and stormy, characterized by a "wind . . . wailing at the windows" like a "Banshee" (Brontë, 97–98). The sound of the "Banshee" at the windows of a house augurs the death of someone therein, according to legend (Brontë, 98, 597). To this mournful accompaniment, Miss Marchmont reminisces over the death of her beloved fiancé thirty years earlier, a tragedy from which she has never emotionally recovered. Hours later, before morning, Lucy finds that the elderly woman has expired, proving the Banshee legend to be true, within the context of the novel. Thus, in the closing chapter of *Villette*, when Lucy addresses the storm that attacks the ship carrying her fiancé, M. Paul Emanuel, by saying "Peace, peace, Banshee—'keening' at every window!" (Brontë, 595), we can be under no illusions about the conclusion of her story. Miss Marchmont's fate—to continue alone, unmarried, and self-supporting, until her hair is "like snow upon snow" (Brontë, 105)—is ultimately Lucy Snowe's fate. Through the course of the narrative, Lucy's hopes and fears concerning her relationship to M. Paul must be understood in light of the specter of Miss Marchmont's lonely, cramped existence. Lucy's double here is a haunting reminder of the fragility of the boundaries that domestic ideology represents as solid. To close and lock the windows of the home is no defense against death—if the Banshee serenades, death can penetrate the domestic space. And the death of the "man of the house" can necessitate the transgression of normative identity boundaries for the surviving "gentlewoman," who may have to compromise her performances of class and gender by taking paid employment to keep herself in food and shelter.

Arguably, it is M. Paul's dark, pronounced "foreignness" that makes him a potentially attainable marriage partner for Lucy Snowe, whose demoted class status and voluntary exile leave her little likelihood of marrying an English "gentleman." At the same time, through his death, the novel seems to punish Lucy for the "crime" of attempting to transgress domestic ideology's national and sexual boundaries so far as to marry a man of a different nationality. Lucy Potter, too, finds that she is haunted by the imposition of ideological definitions upon her sexual relationships. But, as we have come to expect, the impact of domestic ideology in this area of her life manifests itself differently than it does for Lucy Snowe. Snowe's longing for marriage is entirely absent from Potter's emotional landscape. Potter transgresses national and sexual boundaries not to achieve marriage, but indeed to avoid it. Because domestic ideology's constraints upon women's sexual lives are imposed upon her most directly by her mother's conventional teachings and rules, Lucy makes it her business to challenge them consistently, beginning early in her adolescence to welcome or invite sexual pleasure whenever and wherever she may find it. For example, she recalls with satisfaction the list of people whose "tongues I had held in my mouth," which includes Tanner, her first sexual partner; her grade-school best friend; a boy she met in the library near her house; her friend Peggy, with whom she shares her first apartment upon moving out of Mariah's home; and Hugh, the brother of a would-be friend of Mariah's (Kincaid, 82).

The relationship she begins with Paul (a gothic doubling of Lucy Snowe's fateful relationship with M. Paul) is grounded, for her, on the immediacy and strength of her desire: "When he held my hand and kissed me on the cheek, I felt instantly deliciously strange; I wanted to be naked in a bed with him" (Kincaid, 97). It is not long before Lucy has her wish, and thus commences her "life with Paul," a life which was primarily sexual (Kincaid, 113). She describes it to Mariah as "an adventure," with such surprises as the fact that she is "thrilled by the violence of it" and simply that "such pleasure could exist and . . . be available to me" (Kincaid, 113). She separates this relationship from traditional romantic values, noting matter-of-factly that Paul first tells her he loves her the night she has arrived at his door directly from another man's bed. Lucy Potter seeks nothing from Paul that domestic ideology would dictate that a "man" should provide for the "woman" he loves: not fidelity, not marriage, not financial support. The relationship between this Lucy and Paul, as Potter establishes it, is a far cry from the one between Brontë's pair, in which M. Paul was to provide Lucy Snowe with a name, a home, and, above all, a gender role that she could not perform convincingly without him.

But Potter can only keep domestic ideology out of her unconventional affair for so long. The moment in which she recognizes its insertion is captured in a photograph Paul takes of her cooking food: "In the picture I was naked from the waist up; a piece of cloth, wrapped around me, covered me from the waist down. That was the moment he got the idea he possessed me in a certain way" (Kincaid, 155). This "certain way" bothers her because it evokes an imperialist approach to ownership, in Lucy's mind. She notes: "He loved *ruins*; he loved the past but only if it had ended on a sad note, from a lofty beginning to a gradual, rotten decline; he loved things that came from far away and had a mysterious history" (Kincaid, 156; emphasis mine). Paul has exoticized Lucy and she recognizes this as another construction of her identity (dark, mysterious, somewhat pitiable, immigrant woman, therefore desirable) that she can credit to domestic ideology. This understanding presents Lucy with another frightening example of the fluidity of the

ideology's boundaries. She has rebelled against the ideologically mandated performance of sexuality that her mother advocates—"clean, vir-
ginal, beyond reproach" (Kincaid, 97)—but finds that, as a black
Antiguan woman, the liberated sexuality she has invented for herself
can and will be read against the ideological backdrop that constructs
black women as licentious. In other words, black women fall into an
ideological double-bind, with regard to sexuality: to exercise the "right"
to be more sexual is to fall into the stereotypical role assigned to blacks,
but to exercise the "right" to be less sexual (or even asexual) is to be
co-opted into the ideological requirement of asexuality imposed on
women.[23] Lucy's fear is gothically manifested in the language of haunt-
ing/haunted "ruins," but also in the reappearance of the double: insofar
as Paul's imperialist emotional investment in the "sad," "mysterious,"
"far away" Caribbean islands marks the death knell for his relationship
with her, it recalls the way M. Paul's death by shipwreck separates him
from Lucy Snowe during his return from overseeing his family's "interests" in colonial Guadeloupe.

Ultimately, neither Lucy Potter nor Lucy Snowe is able to manipulate or avoid domestic ideology to her own satisfaction. Lucy Snowe's
expatriate construction of England as the "home" from which she goes
forth to "civilize" the world, which affords her a somewhat more comfortable performance of class and gender, is repeatedly interrupted by
the appearance in Labassecour of old English friends and acquain-
tances. Their common nationality return her gender and class performances to the context in which they fail to meet domestic ideology's
standards; she can only be at "home" in England when her environment
is wholly un-English. Likewise, Lucy Potter is forced to recognize, finally, that to define "home" and "family" in the way she wants to—to
invent herself without regard to the prescriptions of domestic ideology—she must continually weaken and ultimately sever her ties to people and places she cares about. "Familial" affection, she learns, is the
reward for ideological conformance—and that which she must sacrifice
in her attempt to construct a different existence. She is alone by choice
at the novel's conclusion, but the tears she sheds over the pages of her
journal signal the instability of her achievement.

Both heroines end their narratives in mournful resignation, homeless
and horrified, each in her own gothic way. Reading their stories com-
paratively enables us to see more clearly not only the extent to which
their cultures place them in similarly terrifying positions of vulnerability
and marginality, but also the significance of the degree and manner in

which their goals and strategies diverge. We recognize, among other things, that nationality, in an international context, acts as a lens through which one's gender, class, and other identity performances are refracted. Snowe's Englishness, among the Labassecouriens, becomes a credential of the status of "gentlewoman" that she desires, whereas Potter's Antiguan background inevitably marks her in New York as a domestic and a laborer, rather than someone with a "proud" future, like her brothers. The nexus of nationality and race becomes, in this reading, a focal point for examining the interplay between the exploitative and the exploitable in the nature of identity construction within domestic ideology. The lexicon of gothic conventions—the ghost, the ruins, and, of course, the double—supplies both Kincaid and Brontë with a means of expressing their dis-ease with the options available to them as women in societies tyrannized by domestic ideology. This shared literary device arises from the shared cultural phenomenon of ideologically inspired social terror: similarities that are fundamentally important to the narratives insofar as they productively heighten our understanding of what the differences in the identities of Kincaid and Brontë (and Potter and Snowe) mean for their ability to manipulate and increase their gender- and class-constrained opportunities. The importance of the comparative context for a fuller, more complicated understanding of Kincaid's fundamental concerns and engagements in writing *Lucy* cannot be overstated. The manifestation of the gothic lexicon connecting *Lucy* to its nineteenth-century doppelgänger rewards the transgression of the epistemological boundaries between British Victorian and twentieth-century African American literary studies. Undoubtedly, it is clear to all her readers that Kincaid's *Lucy* is horribly haunted—but some of her ghosts materialize only when we identify whom Kincaid herself is haunting.

NOTES

1. I have borrowed here (without capitalization) the phrase "Classic Gothic," Judith Wilt's useful shorthand for gothic romances produced during the genre's formative period in England (approximately 1764–1830). Wilt, *Ghosts of the Gothic: Austen, Eliot, & Lawrence* (Princeton, NJ: Princeton University Press, 1980), 12, 23.

2. Anne McClintock, *Imperial Leather: Race, Gender and Sexuality in the Colonial Context* (New York: Routledge, 1995), 44–45.

3. Judith Butler, *Gender Trouble: Feminism and the Subversion of Identity* (New York: Routledge, 1990), 25.

4. For an excellent analysis of this paradox, as well as a productive definition of "black nationalism," see Wahneema Lubiano, "Black Nationalism and Black Common Sense: Policing Ourselves and Others," in *The House that Race Built: Black Americans, U.S. Terrain*, ed. Lubiano, 232–52 (New York: Pantheon Books/Random House, 1997).

5. For example, some women may find it less frightful to conform to gendered expectations of "feminine" modesty and passivity (which may be rewarded with a sort of financial security through marriage as well as social affirmation) than to refuse those constraints and face such punishments as social ostracism and employment discrimination, a resulting poverty, and so forth.

6. This conceptualization of the work of middle-class ideology is discussed, for example, in Nancy Armstrong, *Desire and Domestic Fiction: A Political History of the Novel* (New York: Oxford University Press, 1987), 82.

7. Ibid.; Leonore Davidoff and Catherine Hall, *Family Fortunes: Men and Women of the English Middle Class, 1780–1850* (Chicago: University of Chicago Press, 1987), 361.

8. McClintock, *Imperial Leather*, 162.

9. Cheryl Harris's analysis of "Whiteness as Property" supports my reading of "whiteness" as having an economic value. Harris, "Whiteness as Property," in *Critical Race Theory: The Key Writings that Formed the Movement*, ed. Kimberlé Crenshaw, Neil Gotanda, Gary Peller, and Kendall Thomas (New York: New Press, 1995), 276–91.

10. Paula Giddings, *When and Where I Enter: The Impact of Black Women on Race and Sex in America*, 2nd ed. (New York: Morrow, 1984; New York: Quill/Morrow, 1996), 101; Claudia Tate, *Domestic Allegories of Political Desire: The Black Heroine's Text at the Turn of the Century* (New York: Oxford University Press, 1992), 10–11.

11. In this study, I use "African American" as a term that is to be understood as synonymous with "black," in reference to the U.S. context. That is, I use it to include, rather than exclude, Afro-Caribbean people, African immigrants (of the twentieth-century, voluntary sort), and other members of the African diaspora, along with their descendants, who live (and write) in the U.S. I recognize that this is a contested usage and stress that my aim is not to erase the specificity of different cultural identities within the African diaspora in the U.S., but to open "African American" to a more literal, inclusive definition. Note, however, that I reserve the term "black" to refer to people of African descent wherever they may reside.

12. Priscilla Wald's discussion of the "healthy carrier" informs my understanding of the dis-ease of gothic homelessness. She reports that early twentieth-century medical professionals constructed the "healthy carrier" as "a creature empirically determined to be a threat to public health" and "the healthy human vector of [contagious] disease." Under this paradigm, Wald explains, by "hovering on the border between sickness and health, the carrier turns the focus on . . . the porous and permeable borders of the body and the equally permeable borders between . . . classes, neighborhoods, municipalities, even nations." The healthy carrier, like the person suffering from gothic homelessness, need not be visibly or legibly dis(-)eased to be capable of endangering a community to which she does not belong. Wald, "Cultures and Carriers: 'Typhoid Mary' and the Science of Social Control," *Social Text*, nos. 52–53 (Autumn–Winter 1997): 185–86, 193.

13. Jamaica Kincaid, *Lucy* (New York: Plume/Penguin, 1991), 149. Further citations to this work are given in the text.

14. Diane Simmons, "Jamaica Kincaid and the Canon: In Dialogue with 'Paradise Lost' and 'Jane Eyre,'" *MELUS* 23, no. 2 (Summer 1998): 72; Lizabeth Parvisini-

Gebert, *Jamaica Kincaid: A Critical Companion* (Westport, CT: Greenwood Press, 1999), 117; Tony Tanner, introduction to *Villette*, by Charlotte Brontë (New York: Penguin, 1985), 7–8.

15. In 1903, W. E. B. Du Bois's *The Souls of Black Folk* famously set the metaphor of "double-consciousness" in motion in African American culture. He uses the term to describe the conflict felt by blacks in the United States between their racial heritage and their nationality, in a context in which "American" is understood to signify the antithesis of "Negro." Du Bois, *The Souls of Black Folk*, in *Writings*, ed. Nathan Huggins (New York: Library of America Press, 1986), 364–65.

16. Charlotte Brontë, *Villette* (London: Smith, Elder, 1853; New York: Penguin, 1985), 94. Further citations to this work are given in the text.

17. I take the phrase from the title of McDowell's book of critical essays on black women's literature, criticism, and theory, in which she states (redeploying Amiri Baraka's formulation) that "the ways things stay the same are always changing." Deborah McDowell, *"The Changing Same": Black Women's Literature, Criticism, and Theory* (Bloomington: Indiana University Press, 1995), xviii.

18. Elizabeth C. Gaskell, *The Life of Charlotte Brontë* (New York: Appleton, 1857; New York: Appleton, 1877), 220.

19. Moira Ferguson, *Jamaica Kincaid: Where the Land Meets the Body* (Charlottesville: University Press of Virginia, 1994), 1.

20. Angela Davis, *Women, Race & Class* (New York: Vintage, 1981), 95; Giddings, *When and Where*, 145, 232, 237.

21. Trudier Harris includes a compelling discussion of the indispensability of black domestic workers to white American performances of middle-class domesticity in her book *From Mammies to Militants*, noting that the low wages and high expectations that come with these jobs make it even more difficult for the women so employed to perform domesticity in their own homes. Harris, *From Mammies to Militants: Domestics in Black American Literature* (Philadelphia: Temple University Press, 1982), 10.

22. Leonore Davidoff et al., *Family Story: Blood, Contract and Intimacy, 1830–1960* (London: Longman, 1999), 162–65.

23. Deborah McDowell describes the problem by noting that, in an era in which "black sexuality [is constructed] as the deviant alternative to more culturally prescribed sexual norms," the challenge for black women "'did not consist of the right to be more sexual. It consisted of the right to be *less* sexual, the right even to be *unsexual*.'" McDowell, *"Changing Same,"* 55 (quoting Elizabeth Ammons).

The Autobiography of My Mother:
Jamaica Kincaid's Revision of *Jane Eyre* and *Wide Sargasso Sea*

JOANNE GASS

IN AN AUGUST 19, 1990 INTERVIEW, JAMAICA KINCAID SAID, "WHEN I WAS a child I liked to read. I loved 'Jane Eyre' [sic] especially and read it over and over."[1] She does not explain her fascination with *Jane Eyre*, except to say that she loved books and reading so much that she began to steal books and stash them under her house in Antigua.[2] The books she stole, however, were English books, because that was the only literature she knew or was allowed to know in that then British colony. The canon of English literature, then, and especially *Jane Eyre*, figured into Kincaid's childhood development. As a teenager attending school in England, Jean Rhys, like Jamaica Kincaid, read *Jane Eyre*; she, too, was steeped in the English literary canon. Rhys's reaction to *Jane Eyre* was one of shock and irritation; she said of it in her published Letters, "That's only one side—the English side sort of thing."[3] Rhys set out to present what she perceived to be the other side: she "renders an insider's account of the racial-harassment [sic] suffered by the Creole community and thus re-inscribes the colonial history of the West Indies from a Creole point-of-view."[4]

The genealogy of *Wide Sargasso Sea* has been examined by many critics, but no one, so far as I have been able to discover, has identified *The Autobiography of My Mother* as related to its predecessors.[5] Jean Rhys was herself a Creole, born in Roseau, Dominica; Xuela, Kincaid's "heroine," is a native of Dominica, a mulatta (her father is half African and half Scots; her mother was a Carib) who speaks both French patois and English, (Jean Rhys's languages, as well, and, the languages of Antoinette Cosway whose mother was from French Martinique (Rhys, 9)) and lives for a time in Roseau. It cannot be coincidental that Kincaid sets *The Autobiography* on the island of Dominica, Jean Rhys's birthplace, especially since her other novels are set in, or their characters' place of origin is, Antigua. Just as Rhys set *Wide Sargasso Sea* in Jamaica, to reinforce the connections between *Jane Eyre*, Bertha Rochester, and Antoinette Cosway, so does Kincaid want, I think, to forge links between Antoinette Cosway and Xuela, her "heroine" in *The Autobiography of My Mother*. Rhys shifts Antoinette and Rochester's honeymoon location from Jamaica to Dominica, specifically to Massacre, a very small town in Dominica. Kincaid makes Massacre Xuela's father's home and the place where Xuela lives with her father and stepmother. (I will come back to Massacre later.) But the coincidence of location is not the only relationship discernable amongst the three novels. All three reveal the "normative" and "natural" discourse of colonialism in general and Victorian England in particular; they focus on motherless young women victimized by colonial and/or British society and patriarchy; they explore the ways in which a woman's identity is formed by the discourses of patriarchy and imperial colonialism.[6]

Gayatri Spivak and others have explored the colonialist implications of both Brontë's and Rhys's novels. Benjamin Graves says of Spivak's analysis: "According to Spivak, Brontë's novel may well uphold its protagonist as a new feminist ideal, but it does so at the expense of Bertha, Rochester's creole bride who functions as a colonial subject or 'other' to legitimate Jane's simultaneous ascent to domestic authority. In other words, a feminist approach to theory perhaps precludes an understanding of the novel's depiction of the 'epistemic violence' (and in the case of Bertha, physical containment and pathologization) done upon imperial subjects."[7] But Rhys's novel also silences, even buries, as Spivak and others have noted, another voice or other voices. Bertha's Creole family prospered before its subjugation by the British as plantation owners who brought slaves from Africa; those freed slaves speak in the voice of Christophine, who uses her ancestral power of Obeah against Rochester and who serves as a surrogate mother to Antoinette. Christophine's voice subverts the normal role of colonizer/colonized. A number of critics, including Spivak, have noted Christophine's disappearance from the novel—her expulsion from Rochester's English home and from poor, mad Bertha's already shattered life. They have also noted the overt and covert racism in both novels. Jane Eyre's England thrives on the products of slavery; Antoinette suffers from being neither black nor English white (her husband believes that she is not purely English because of her island heritage); therefore, she is a victim without an identity.

Kincaid, through Xuela, exposes yet another level of racism—not only the racism expressed in colonial power, but the racism of the defeated survivors: "The Carib people had been defeated and then exterminated, thrown away like the weeds in a garden; the African people had been defeated but had survived. When they looked at me, they saw only the Carib people. They were wrong but I did not tell them so" (Kincaid, 15–16). Therefore, it is not only Christophine's voice that is silenced in *Wide Sargasso Sea*, it is the voice of Xuela's people, the Caribs who were the original victims of colonization and whose voices have been silenced, buried, under layers of colonization. Jamaica Kincaid, in *The Autobiography of My Mother*, unearths the buried voice of her mother and her mother's people, the Caribs, and retrieves it from the silence that both *Jane Eyre* and *Wide Sargasso Sea* consigned them to. We might even say that the books the child Jamaica stole and stashed beneath her house were, in fact, *Jane Eyre* and *Wide Sargasso Sea*, and *The Autobiography of My Mother* hybridizes them in order to subvert their colonialist repression of the voices of the originally repressed Caribs.

The resurrection of the voice of the silenced begins, then, with the mothers. Whereas Antoinette sees her mother when she looks into the mirror, Xuela tells us that her mother died when she was born and that "for [her] whole life there was nothing between herself and eternity" (Kincaid, 3). Xuela never knew her mother; she had no (M)other whose image could provide her with an identity. In this way, Xuela is like Jane. Both are orphans, or nearly so (Xuela's father sends her away, "orphaning her"). Both are sent to the homes of women who take care of them, but only in the most elementary ways. Jane suffers cruelty and abuse by her aunt and her cousins; their "home" provides only shelter; even on her deathbed, Aunt Reed refuses any kindness to Jane. Xuela likens herself to the laundry that her Ma Eunice does weekly for Xuela's father. She is something that has to be taken care of. Later, when Xuela's father brings her back to his house, Xuela's stepmother treats her cruelly, favoring the brother who will inherit her father's wealth. This, too, is reminiscent of Jane; she endures the hatred and envy of her Aunt Reed, and the heir to the house, her cousin, John Reed, torments her beyond human endurance. (Parenthetically, John Reed, the heir, parallels both Antoinette's and Xuela's brothers, in that they are the favored children. Antoinette's brother, Pierre, dies in the fire at *Coulibri*, and Xuela's brother also dies, leaving her father without the heir he desired. In all three cases, the male heir eclipses the girls.) Jane, like Xuela, has no mother to protect her. Unlike Jane and Xuela,

Antoinette has a mother, but her mother fails to protect her from the rapacious, sexual Rochester; in fact, she offers her daughter to the British colonial, a sacrifice to the conqueror. Furthermore, Antoinette's madness reflects her mother's—both become "mad" because they lose their identities. Both Antoinette and her mother are victims of the racism of the British colonials who pride themselves on their "Englishness." And yet, Annette, in her madness, rejects Antoinette, in effect, "dying" and leaving Antoinette exposed, just as Jane and Xuela are: "Early in life [Antoinette] recognizes she belongs nowhere: as a white she is hated and constantly othered in her own native Jamaican world; she is treated as an outcast by her own race. While natives contemptuously call her 'white cockroach', [sic] Europeans refer to her reproachfully as 'white nigger'.[8]

Denied a place in the dominant order and rejected by the freed slaves with whom Antoinette, at least, erroneously thought she identified, both nevertheless want a place in the dominant culture, and the way that they find it, they think, is to marry English men. Having no place in the world, Antoinette has no defenses against the constructions placed upon her by others. Jamie Thomas Dessart, in an article on mirrors and framing in *Jane Eyre* and *Wide Sargasso Sea*, points to a particular passage that is seminal in Antoinette's conception of her self. In the passage, Antoinette first looks at a painting of the Miller's Daughter, which, Dessart claims, "teaches Antoinette that she must accept the construction of others"; from the painting, Antoinette's gaze shifts toward her mother:

> So I looked away from her [the black servant, Mary] at my favourite picture, 'The Miller's Daughter', a lovely English girl with brown curls and blue eyes and a dress slipping off her shoulders. Then I looked across the white tablecloth and the vase of yellow roses at Mr. Mason, so sure of himself, so without a doubt English. And at my mother, so without a doubt not English, but no white nigger either. Not my mother. Never had been. Never could be. Yes, she would have died, I thought, if she had not met him. And for the first time I was grateful and liked him. (Rhys, 21)

In this passage, Antoinette equates happiness and tranquility with being English (or being "saved" by an Englishman). She derives her image of feminine Englishness from the painting; her image of masculine Englishness conforms to the ideal presented by Mr. Mason, who saved her mother. Mr. Mason's betrayal, his virtual selling of her to Rochester, her inability to "be" the lovely English girl in the painting, and Rochester's betrayal of her, lead to Antoinette's madness and fiery death. Rhys gives Antoinette/Bertha a voice, but, as Joya Uraizee points out, "there is no attempt to dislodge Antoinette/Bertha from her role as scapegoat, and the narrative of *Jane Eyre* is not reversed."[9]

Unlike Antoinette, Jane Eyre, initially excluded from and victimized by Victorian patriarchy, nevertheless embodies its ideals of feminine purity and English superiority, and, in the end, she triumphs *as* that ideal. Despite the fact that Jane takes control, becomes mistress of her own fortunes, and appears to be the precursor of the modern, liberated woman, she is, as Gayatri Spivak argues, the embodiment of "feminist individualism in the age of imperialism."[10] The imperialist project, Spivak asserts, "is precisely the making of human beings, the constitution and 'interpellation' of the subject not only as individual but as 'individualist.' This stake is represented on two registers: childbearing and soul making."[11] Jane's triumph, then, is the triumph of imperialist domesticity. She civilizes Rochester, tames the barbaric sexuality he claims Bertha arouses in him, remains herself pure, and, properly married, produces the male heir so necessary to the perpetuation of the ideal. Jane, the center of her house, takes her place in the order of things.

Judith Raiskin rightly points out that Jean Rhys "shows the ways in which cultural colonialism, operating through myths of home and family, is particularly implicated in the economic impoverishment and social exploitation of the colonized woman."[12] Antoinette, the exemplar of the colonized woman, sinks into madness because those myths held out to her as ideals and dramatically and graphically illustrated for her in "The Miller's Daughter" as ideals she should strive to emulate, paradoxically become barriers that bar her from achieving that status of Englishness reserved only for those women born on English soil—like Jane Eyre. How, then, does the colonized woman, interpellated into cultural colonialism, resist, much less defeat the power of those myths? How does the victim turn these myths back onto her oppressor?

By speaking out. By the time she is fourteen years old, Xuela has already learned the most important lesson—silence kills. She reflects, in the following passage, on history and silence: "to confess your bad deeds is also at once to forgive yourself, and so silence becomes the only form of self-punishment: to live forever locked up in an iron cage made of your own silence, and then, from time to time, to have this silence broken by a designated crier, someone who repeats over and over, in broken or complete sentences, a list of the violations, the bad deeds committed" (Kincaid, 59–60). Xuela, then, becomes the "designated crier" who breaks the silence. She will be the voice, which recounts, "the bad deeds committed." She begins with her mother.[13] In "Apostrophe, Animation, and Abortion," Barbara Johnson says, "The verbal development of the infant, according to Lacan, begins as a demand addressed to the mother, out of which the entire verbal universe is spun."[14] This demand occurs, according to Johnson, after the mirror stage when the child enters the symbolic order. But what if there is no mother? What if the mother, her people, and her history have been, in effect, erased? Jane Eyre has no mother, but she has the superstructure of English history and tradition and the English ideal to give her identity—she is successfully interpellated into the dominant culture. Antoinette's mother, although a victim of imperialism, nevertheless reflects the same superstructure of English imperialism that calls Jane to comfortable conformity; Antoinette becomes its tragic victim. Xuela does not have that discursive structure that would give her identity; therefore, she must "tell" her mother's story—and her history. She must fill the blank that would give her and her mother identity by providing the history for the disappeared. Xuela reflects on her vanished people: "the most bitter part was that it was through no fault of their own that they had lost, and lost in the most extreme way; they had lost not just the right to be themselves, they had lost themselves" (Kincaid, 197–98). This history, of course, is a story of annihilation. As a people, the Caribs, the last survivors, have no history other than the history of colonization. Therefore, Xuela's story (and her mother's story) will be a recitation of "violations and bad deeds." Those "violations and bad deeds" can be found in the very ideals and practices that called Jane into comfortable conformance and that drove Antoinette/Bertha mad—not because she rejected them, but because she desired to be part of them. Xuela, however, uses those practices against her oppressors.

As a child, Xuela, like Antoinette, lived with images of English power and gentility. Antoinette had the painting, "The Miller's Daughter," to remind her of what she could not have. Xuela's keeper, Ma Eunice, had a china plate that hung on her wall depicting a field of flowers and labeled in gold with the word "HEAVEN." "Of course it was not a picture of heaven at all; it was a picture of the English countryside idealized" (Kincaid, 10). Xuela broke Ma Eunice's plate. Although she did not know at the time that it depicted an idealized England, nevertheless Xuela's breaking of the plate and her recollection of it symbolize her early rejection of idealizations of anything English. That a plate depicting Heaven as an English countryside should be sold in the Caribbean illustrates the almost complete lack of recognition on the part of the colonizers that a tropical culture might view Elysium differently and emphasizes the British colonists' easy assumption that not only did civilization reside in the British Isles, but heaven did also. More importantly, the fact that Ma Eunice believed that the plate depicted heaven emphasizes the reach and influence of the discourse of the dominant culture and its ability to interpellate its subjects.

Just as the plate equates heaven with England, the educational system of Dominica identifies history, civilization, law, and geography as English history, civilization, law, and geography despite its racially mixed population, which is composed of English, French, African, and Carib peoples. The first words Xuela learns to read are printed on the wall map in her schoolroom: "THE BRITISH EMPIRE" (Kincaid, 14). That the first map she sees should name the world "THE BRITISH EMPIRE" would seem perfectly natural to her father, and it is part of the curriculum taught by the African woman (whom Xuela identifies as part of the defeated people). The schoolroom map brings the discourses of history and geography into focus for Xuela, for the history of the British Empire is depicted graphically in its conquest of geography. In that map the world *is* the British Empire—named, classified, and measured by the British. Xuela sees nothing "natural" in it; she sees in it evidence, I think, of a historical cover-up. That cover-up is exemplified in the history of Massacre—her father's hometown and the village nearest to Antoinette Cosway's estate—*Granbois*.

When Antoinette and Rochester arrive in Massacre, Rochester, upon learning the name of the place asks, "'And who was massacred here. Slaves?' 'Oh no.' She sounded shocked. 'Not slaves. Something must have happened a long time ago. Nobody remembers now'" (Rhys, 38). There are two points to make about this exchange: the first is that in Rochester's mind it goes without saying that the site of a massacre would not be a place where Englishmen were massacred, and the second is that only the name of place remains; the history has been erased. But Xuela *knows* the real story of Massacre. There Philip Warner, an Englishman, murdered his illegitimate half brother, Indian Warner, "because Philip Warner did not like having such a close relative whose mother was a Carib woman" (Kincaid, 87). Here, in a few lines, Kincaid reveals the hidden history that Xuela's story seeks to expose. Kincaid leads us to it not only through Xuela's specific invocation of the incident, but also by her invocation of the disappeared people and their absolute defeat at the hands of the English, by situating Xuela, her father, and her stepmother in Massacre, and, above all, by naming Xuela's husband—the man she will subdue, humiliate, and defeat—Philip. Philip, like Rochester, represents the patriarchal authority of the colonizer—he imposes his civilization upon those he conquers at the same time as he longs to return from the "barbaric" colonies to "civilized" England; and, paradoxically, he desires the exotic, sexually intriguing "savage" colonial woman at the same time as he hates her for her unbridled sexuality, but most of all for not being English.

Whereas Xuela's father was the successfully interpellated in-between man, the half-breed colonial victim who nevertheless victimized those below him, meted out the laws of the master, and profited from his position as go-between, her husband, like Philip Warner, sports a "pure" pedigree—he is a "legitimate" son of England and sees himself as the inheritor of the legacy of the conquerors. Xuela asks: "Could he be blamed for believing that the successful actions of his ancestors bestowed on him the right to act in an unprecedented, all-powerful way, and without consequences? He believed in a race, he believed in a nation, he believed in all this so completely that he could step outside it . . ." (Kincaid, 225). Philip lived in the past, trying to live the history his people created and believing in its truth. Xuela defines Philip's relationship to her as one of unfulfilled desire. He is easy prey to her because he represents what Robert Young identifies as "colonial desire . . . an active desire, frequently sexual, for the other."[15] The desire to conquer and colonize is also the sexual desire for the Other, most especially the female Other. At the root of this desire lurks the belief that the female Other is sexually deviant, and having declared her deviant, lascivious, and degenerate, the conqueror literally cannot keep his hands off of her. As one of the conquerors, what could Philip possibly desire? He wants *her*, entirely. He wants her to be his possession, and because she denies him that possession, he loves her. His is the desire of the conqueror.

Xuela uses her sexuality as a weapon against Philip and Monsieur LaBatte. She knows that they are easy prey. Like Rochester, who desires Antoinette/Bertha because she both repels him and enthralls him with her sexuality and racial impurity, both Philip and Monsieur LaBatte are likewise enthralled. Felicity Palmer asserts that "contamination and the association of colonized races with the worst kinds of physical, moral and mental degradations, was a convenient way to reinstate the taboos against inter-racial sexual unions."[16] In *Jane Eyre* Rochester testifies to the consequences of such an unholy union:

> "Jane, I will not trouble you with abominable details: some strong words shall express what I have to say. I lived with that woman upstairs four years, and before that time she had tried me indeed: her character ripened and developed with frightful rapidity; her vices sprang up fast and rank: they were so strong, only cruelty could check them; and I would not use cruelty. What a pigmy intellect she had—and what giant propensities! How fearful were the curses those propensities entailed on me! Bertha Mason,—the true daughter of an infamous mother,—dragged me through all the hideous and degrading agonies which must attend a man bound to a wife at once intemperate and unchaste." (Brontë, 302)

Rochester employs an extended botanical metaphor to describe Bertha's depravity; she, like a monstrous weed, destroyed the tranquility and order of his English sensibility (so often depicted in the model of the English garden). He is repulsed by her and by his own lascivious desires that she aroused in him. She poisons his garden and leads him to perdition.

Jean Rhys's Rochester, likewise, "falls" in the Caribbean. He despises himself for the lust he feels for Antoinette; to him, she is both beautiful and desirable and fearful and repulsive. Rhys most forcefully exposes his "colonial desire," however, in his reaction to Amélie, the house girl. Attracted to her, he describes her face as "lovely" and "meaningless," and, after his one-night stand with her, he says, "I had not one minute of remorse [during the encounter]." "In the morning, of course, I felt differently. Another complication. Impossible. And her skin was darker, her lips thicker than I had thought" (Rhys, 84). Rochester's morning after remorse has little to do with the sex and everything to do with her physical attributes; they repel him.

Both Rochesters depict themselves as victims of their desires, but above all, they insist that they have been victimized by women of dubious racial pedigrees and dubious intelligence. These women of mixed blood and foreign birth exhibit "rank" sexuality; their bodies appeal and appall. But it isn't just their bodies; they lack intellect as well. Rochester tells Jane that Bertha has a "pygmy intellect" (Brontë, 302), and Rhys's Rochester reflects that Antoinette is "a child . . . not a stupid child but an obstinate one" (Rhys, 56). Both depictions reinforce the racial stereotypes common to the exercise of colonial power. Both Bertha and Antoinette are defeated by this exercise of power.

Kincaid uses these racial stereotypes against the victimizers. Xuela exults in her sexuality, and she uses it as a weapon against the men who desire her. But she does not use only her body; she outsmarts them as well. Xuela achieves her ultimate, if bleak, victory by denying Philip any sort of identification with her; she speaks to him in patois, not English, even though she speaks English; she refuses to laugh or smile when he so badly wants that sort of recognition from her; she refuses to speak at all for days on end, knowing that he longs to hear her voice.[17] Xuela reduces Philip to the status of the colonized child when she refuses him these seemingly unimportant things. In fact, she turns Philip into the abandoned child she herself was when she entered her father's house for the first time and felt the vitriolic hatred and oppression emanating from her new stepmother who spoke to her only in patois when her father was absent: "I recognized this to be an attempt on her part to make an illegitimate of me, to associate me with the made-up language of people regarded as not real–the shadow people, the forever humiliated, the forever low" (Kincaid, 30–31). Just as her father moved her into his house and into the power of his new wife, so Xuela turns the tables upon Philip, the son of the conqueror, making him vulnerable to the same discourses, which his people subjected her and her people to. Just as her stepmother attempted to make Xuela an illegitimate, so does Xuela make Philip an illegitimate, countering his sense of comfortable privilege by stealing from him the power of language.

And, just as she undermines the power of language, so does she undermine his sense of ownership of the land. Xuela exacts her revenge by moving him into an alien land. She says, "After we were married we moved far away into the mountains, into the land where my mother and the people she was of were born" (Kincaid, 206). In that land, Philip stumbles; he cannot speak the language—Xuela must translate for him—, and in doing so she deliberately mistranslates; thus she deceives him, and he is lost. The land is outside history, essentially out of the reach of Philip, who, by walking its perimeters, tries to enclose it in ownership, just as he tries in other ways to own and control nature (Kincaid, 218–19). Robert Young points out that "the culture of land has always been, in fact, the primary form of colonization, the focus on the soil emphasizes the physicality of the territory that is coveted, occupied, cultivated. . . . and made unsuitable for nomadic tribes."[18]

Philip is defeated because Xuela has already reclaimed the land for herself and her defeated peoples. Recovering from the abortion of Jack LaBatte's baby, in her healing dream, Xuela walks the length and breadth of her island. In her journey, she retraces and names the history of the island, from Roseau to Massacre and beyond: "I walked through my inheritance, an island of villages and rivers and mountains and people who began and ended with murder and theft and not very much love. I claimed it in a dream. Exhausted from the agony of expelling from my body a child I could not love and so did not want, I dreamed of all the things that were mine" (Kincaid, 88–89). Xuela's near-death journey/dream bears all the earmarks of a quest: she is followed by an agouti, which she defeats by putting it to sleep; she resists the temptation to "be swallowed up whole" by the "black waters" of two channels; she rehearses the painful history of her people, and she emerges from the dream victorious, and "changed forever" (Kincaid, 93) — she claims the island for herself. She will no longer be the victim. Returned to the LaBattes by her father, Xuela understands her victory. She, Jack, and Lise stand together, forming "a little triangle, a trinity," and she knows, "at that moment someone was of the defeated, someone was of the resigned, and someone was changed forever. I was not of the defeated; I was not of the resigned" (Kincaid, 93). Xuela's reclamation of her birthright, her mapping of her land, leads directly to her conquest (if you will) of Philip and his ultimate humiliation and defeat.

When he cannot mark the land to which Xuela has moved him, when he cannot walk its perimeters without stumbling, when he cannot defeat nature, he sets out to change the natural landscape: "not gardening in the way of necessity, the growing of food, but gardening in the way of luxury, the growing of flowering plants for no other reason than the pleasure of it and making these plants do exactly what he wanted them to do; and it made great sense that he would be drawn to this activity, for it is an act of conquest, benign though it may be" (Kincaid, 143). Typical of the conqueror, Philip destroys the natural flora and fauna of "his" land and instead strips the land, growing hybrids of mangos and other exotic fruits—hybrids, which although curiosities, lack taste. They are, in fact, monstrous interventions in nature. More than that, he tries to make his garden an English garden, trying to force herbaceous borders upon a land unsuited for such things (Kincaid, 144). Sarah Brophy reports that in a gardening article entitled, "Flowers of Evil," Jamaica Kincaid asks the question, "And what is the relationship of gardening to conquest?" Brophy summarizes her answer in the following way: "gardening, especially the aesthetic cultivation of nonfood plants, provides the ruling class with the fantasy of a paradoxically natural and controlled luxury, one that allows for the retrospective minimi-

zation of the ecological devastation and agricultural exploitation that
characterized the European conquest of the Caribbean."[19] Thus, the
English garden serves as a means of forgetting; it covers up the consequences of conquest, just as forgetting the source of the name "Massacre" erases the racial incident that occurred there.

Philip also spends his time collecting specimens, exhibiting the Victorian mania for "having," for housing species in glass thereby destroying
them for the sake of science and possession. He orders nature by making list after list headed "genus" and "kingdom." But no amount of collecting, labeling, and listing can bring his property under control, and
as he watches helplessly, the ordered world, which colonial history tells
him he inherited, slips from his grasp. The land, the land of Xuela's
mother's people, which he and his forebearers believed they had conquered, defeats him. Xuela, of course, has been the willing accomplice,
but she also views this defeat as part of a larger defeat—the defeat of
"the people he came from" (Kincaid, 217). In spite of all the things that
Philip has collected and owned, he cannot own her—not her body, not
her mind, not her land. (Ironically, Xuela inherits all of her father's ac-
cumulated wealth including the land he had usurped from his victims.
That she does nothing with the land and wealth does not diminish the
irony.)

Philip's desire is a child's demand for its mother, too. But, his advantage resides in his Oedipal relationship to the Law of the Father. Although he can never *be* the father (in Lacan's model), nevertheless he
has the advantages, which accrue from the Law of the Father in that in
acquiring the language, history, and culture of the victor, he (and his
late wife) enjoyed the benefits of belonging to that discursive community—he has the power of the phallus. Nevertheless, Xuela succeeds
because she undermines Philip's authority. She, by restoring the mother's voice, in a Lacanian sense, has taken the power of the phallus from
Philip. He cannot command the land to produce; he cannot command
or even beg her to respond to him; he cannot communicate anything
except his unquenchable desire. Finally, because he cannot exercise authority over the present, he tries to recuperate the authority of the past:
"He now busied himself with the dead, arranging, disarranging, rearranging the books on his shelf, volumes of history, geography, science,
philosophy, speculations: none of it could bring him peace" (Kincaid,
224). In the end and not long before his death, he, like his ancestors,
discovers that conquest—having, possessing, owning, and collecting—
are insatiable appetites and that they never bring happiness. And "at

the moment the conqueror asks [what can bring happiness], his defeat is secure" (Kincaid, 217).

Xuela, by becoming the "designated crier," the one "who repeats over and over [the] list of the violations, the bad deeds committed," gives voice to her defeated and nearly annihilated people, the Caribs, and to her mother, for her mother's voice is her voice. Xuela's victory is, of course, a bitter one, for in order to win, she must lose. She has made herself sterile; therefore, she will not perpetuate the subjugation she and her people continue to suffer. Her victory lies in saying "No."

All three novels end with the women alone, or virtually alone, in their houses. For Jane, the house is a home, with all that that appellation entails. For the others, there is no home—only a house. *Jane Eyre* ends with Jane writing her reader ten years after her marriage. She is the model of domestic tranquility and marital happiness. Rochester's sight returns after an appropriate period in symbolic purgatory. The return of light and sight accompanies erasure and forgetfulness— Bertha, Thornfield, and Jamaica have blissfully disappeared. In a new home, Jane lives the image of the successfully interpolated English woman; she tells us, "My Edward and I, then, are happy" (Brontë, 440). *Wide Sargasso Sea*, as we know, ends with Antoinette's fiery plunge from the battlements of Thornfield Hall. Antoinette, the colonized colonial, taken from *Coulibri*, her home, and transplanted to England and Thornfield Hall, dreams of a fiery flight from her captivity, and when she awakes from the dream, her last words are: "Now, at last I know why I was brought here and what I have to do. There must have been a draught for the flame flickered and I thought it was out. But I shielded it with my hand and it burned up again to light me along the dark passage" (Rhys, 112). In her revision of *Jane Eyre*, Jean Rhys, in giving a voice to Bertha Rochester, the madwoman in the attic, has given voice to a victim, but she does not address the underlying issue of colonial racism. Antoinette herself represents the colonial oppressor; her victimization occurs because the British defeated the French. Rhys and Antoinette fail to recognize the Caribbean landowners' oppression of the slaves and obliteration of the islands' native populations.

If, as I've argued, Jamaica Kincaid, in *The Autobiography of My Mother*, set out to revise *Jane Eyre* and *Wide Sargasso Sea*, then she did it by giving voice to the lost mother, the victim of 500 years of conquest and colonial repression. In an article entitled, "To Name Is to Possess," Kincaid reflects on "the impulse to reach back and reclaim a loss" incurred at the hands of those obsessed with conquering, renaming, and possess-

ing: "This naming of things is so crucial to possession—a spiritual pad-
lock with the key thrown irretrievably away—that it is a murder, an
erasing, and it is not surprising that when people have felt themselves
prey to it (conquest), among their first acts of liberation is to change
their names. . . . That the great misery and much smaller joy of existence
remain unchanged no matter what anything is called never checks the
impulse to reach back and reclaim a loss, to try to make what happened
look as if it had not happened at all."[20] Kincaid's bleak assessment of
"acts of liberation" sheds light on the bleak ending of *The Autobiography
of My Mother*. Like Jane Eyre and Antoinette, Xuela is alone at the end
of the novel and speaking to her reader. Xuela is by now an old woman;
ever aware of her body, she feels its inevitable decline. Saying "No" and
restoring her mother's voice and her people's story have not changed
the facts of history. She reflects: "To reverse the past would bring me
complete happiness. Such an event—for it would be that, an event—
would make my world stand on its feet; it does so now and has for a
long time stood on its head" (Kincaid, 226). Resisting the power of colonial discourse and revealing the injustices of the past cannot reverse
the wrongs done; it will not make her "world stand on its feet."

NOTES

1. Leslie Garis, "Through West Indian Eyes," *New York Times*, October 7, 1990,
6:42. Garis quotes the August interview in this article.

2. Unless otherwise stated, citations are taken from the following editions: Jamaica
Kincaid, *The Autobiography of My Mother* (New York: Farrar Straus Giroux, 1996),
Charlôlte Brontë, *Jane Eyre*, ed. Beth Newman (New York: Bedford St. Martin's Press,
1996), Jean Rhys, *Wide Sargasso Sea*, ed. Judith L. Raiskin (1966; rept., New York:
Norton Critical Editions, 1999).

3. Kenny Chang, "Feminist Revision and the Recentering of a Colonial Subject:
Jean Rhys's *Wide Sargasso Sea*," *Studies in Language and Literature* 8 (December 1998):
103.

4. C. Vijayshree, "Writing Postcoloniality and Feminism: A Reading of Jean
Rhys's *Wide Sargasso Sea*," in *Women's Writing: Text and Context*, ed. Jasbir Jain, 129
(Jaipur: Rawat, 1996).

5. Two scholars have written about links between Jamaica Kincaid's work and the
Brontës. Lizabeth Paravisini-Gebert has identified a Gothic link between *Wuthering
Heights* and *The Autobiography of My Mother* in her article, "Colonial and Postcolonial
Gothic: the Caribbean," in *The Cambridge Companion to Gothic Fiction*, ed. Jerrold E.
Hogle, 229–58 (Cambridge: Cambridge University Press, 2002). Paravisini-Gebert ar-
gues that Xuela is the Heathcliff of the novel and that *The Autobiography of My Mother* is
a "narrative of symbolic renunciation [and] is rendered through the interrelated Gothic

themes of motherlessness, lovelessness, miscegenation, and the differences between the languages of the colonizer and the colonized" (251).

In a 1998 article entitled "Jamaica Kincaid and the Canon: In Dialogue with *Paradise Lost* and *Jane Eyre*," *MELUS* 23.2 (Summer 1998): 65–85, Diane Simmons traces the connections between Jamaica Kincaid and her novels *Annie John* and *Lucy*, which Simmons identifies as two volumes of a *bildungsroman*. Simmons argues that Kincaid puts to use the colonial education which, nevertheless, tried to erase her: "Like Milton, Brontë seems to have offered a way of thinking about the questions of power and powerlessness, justice and injustice that concerned Kincaid from an early age" (75). "Brontë then, like Milton, offers Kincaid the paradoxical opportunity to both identify with and to subvert the classic texts of English literature and by extension the English world view which they represent" (77).

6. Nicholas Thomas, *Colonialism's Culture: Anthropology, Travel and Government*, (Princeton, NJ: Princeton University Press, 1994). Thomas points out that colonialism is not monolithic and argues for "colonialisms." Thomas warns that failure to recognize this plurality results in the same kinds of essentializations decried by post-colonial critics. Of colonialisms, Thomas says, "that colonialism is not best understood primarily as a political or economic relationship that is legitimized or justified through ideologies of racism or progress. Rather, colonialism has always, equally importantly and deeply, been a cultural process; its discoveries and trespasses are imagined and energized through signs, metaphors and narratives; even what would seem its purest moments of profit and violence have been mediated and enframed by structures of meaning. Colonial cultures are not simply ideologies that mask, mystify or rationalize forms of oppression that are external to them; they are also expressive and constitutive of colonial relationships in themselves" (2). Thomas's advocacy of a more nuanced analysis of colonialisms is, quite frankly, obviously not endorsed by Jamaica Kincaid in her published work; however, she would, I believe, agree with Thomas that colonialism is not an event that occurred in the nineteenth century and has been "corrected" in our modern, more liberal world.

7. Benjamin Graves, "Spivak: Marxist, Feminist, Deconstructionist," <http://www.thecore.nus.edu/landow/post/poldiscourse/spivak/spivak3.html>, (1998).

8. Vijayshree, 131.

9. Joya Uraizee, " 'She Walked Away Without Looking Back': Christophine and the Enigma of History in Jean Rhys's *Wide Sargasso Sea*," *CLIO* 28, no. 3 (1999): 264.

10. Gayatri Spivak, "Three Women's Texts and a Critique of Imperialism," *Critical Inquiry* 12, no. 1 (Autumn 1985): 244.

11. Spivak, 244.

12. Judith Raiskin, "England: Dream and Nightmare," in *Snow on the Cane Fields: Women's Writings and Creole Subjectivity*," (Minneapolis: University of Minnesota Press, 1996), 144.

13. Joanne Gass, "Bitter Reconquista: Jamaica Kincaid's *The Autobiography of My Mother*," *Journal of Caribbean Studies*, (Winter 2001): 209–22. I have written on the subject of the mother in this essay.

14. Barbara Johnson, "Apostrophe, Animation, and Abortion," in *Contemporary Literary Criticism*, 3rd ed., ed. Robert Con Davis and Ronald Schleifer, 226 (New York: Longman, 1994).

15. Robert Young, *Colonial Desire: Hybridity in Theory, Culture, and Race*, (London: Routledge, 1995), 3.

16. "Sex, Hybridity and Contamination: Racial Theories of the Nineteenth Century." http://www.flea.org/thesis/html/node4.html.

17. In *Wide Sargasso Sea*, Rochester complains that Antoinette and Christophine "chatter" in patois (54). Taking Antoinette to England and expelling Christophine from his house prevents Antoinette from having the power of a language he cannot understand, just as taking away her name diminishes her as well.

18. Kenneth C. Staples, "Hong Kong culture: hybrid, bicultural, multicultural, or a continuing renewal," <http://www.asaa2000.unimelb.edu.au/papers/staples.html> (July 2000). Staples quotes Young in this article.

19. Sarah Brophy, "Angels in Antigua: The Diasporic Melancholy in Jamaica Kincaid's *My Brother*," *PMLA* 117, no. 2 (March 2002): 269.

20. Jamaica Kincaid, *My Garden (Book):*, (New York: Farrar Straus Giroux, 1996): 122.

Caribbean Impossibility:
The Lack of Jamaica Kincaid

THOMAS W. SHEEHAN

What to call the thing that happened to me and all who look like me?

Should I call it history?

If so, what should history mean to someone like me?

Should it be an idea, should it be an open wound and each breath I take in and expel healing and opening the wound again and again, over and over, and is this healing and opening a moment that began in 1492 and has yet to come to an end? Is it a collection of facts, all true and precise details, and, if so, when I come across these true and precise details, what should I do, how should I feel, where should I place myself?

Why should I be obsessed with all these questions?[1]

This account of my life has been an account of my mother's life as much as it has been an account of mine, and even so, again it is an account of the children I did not have, as it is their account of me. In me is the voice I never heard, the face I never saw, the being I came from. In me are the voices that should have come out of me, the faces I never allowed to form, the eyes I never allowed to see me. This account is an account of the person who was never allowed to be and an account of the person I did not allow myself to become.[2]

I can't say that I came from a culture that felt alienated from England or Europe. We were beyond alienation.[3]

"JAMAICA KINCAID" (THE WRITER AND SPEAKER OF THESE QUOTA-tions), who does not exist (her real name is Elaine Potter Richardson), has written a book (*The Autobiography of My Mother* (1996)) about a woman who does not exist (her name is Xuela Claudette Richardson). Kincaid has admitted that she has never "written about anyone except [herself] and [her] mother."[4] "I saw the world through her."[5] She was "an empire unto herself."[6] In *My Brother*, she remarks that "in another kind of circumstance the shape of the world might have been altered by her presence."[7] It is, however, impossible to write an autobiography of someone other than oneself. This title seems to self-destruct; it declares its own impossibility. Why? Why is there all this impossibility, this indirection, this void, this gap, this lack? There are two starting points: fiction and history. Xuela herself is something like a historical fiction, the wrong turn in the chronicle. In her historical fiction, "my mother died at the moment I was born, and so for my whole life there was nothing standing between myself and eternity; at my back was always a bleak, black wind" (*Autobiography*, 3). This black wind is really what the character of Xuela "is."

These are the first lines of the novel, of the delivery of the fiction. It opens with a deficiency, a lack. One could call it formal, but it is also historical. For one thing, Xuela's mother was a Carib Indian, an indigenous Kalinago. There are only two hundred pure Carib left on the Caribbean islands: they are mostly on the island of Dominica in a reservation,[8] and this is where the novel is set. Xuela's lack of a mother is thus also a historical lack, the felt hole of the lack of indigenous inhabitants on the islands. The Spanish conquest decimated the native population soon after Columbus arrived. Kincaid's feelings on this— and she herself is a quarter Carib: her grandmother, whom she knew, was a full-blooded Carib—are mixed in with her feelings about her African ancestry. Addressing her (white American) audience in *A Small Place* (1988), she says, "No periods of time over which my ancestors held sway, no documentation of complex civilizations, is any comfort to me. Even if I really came from people who were living like monkees in trees, it was better to be that than what happened to me, what I became after I met you."[9]

This is a blunt refusal. It is a refusal of post-Columbian history and a declaration of a constitutive lack or void for which there must be a reckoning, an account: "In a place where everything is defined by lack or absence, it is no surprise that the people ultimately mirror this place."[10] This account of absence is embodied in Xuela, in her absent mother and even her present father. Xuela's father is half Scots and half African, making her a quarter Scots and a quarter African—that is, what is living to her in her ancestry is what is living in the postslavery situation on Dominica, her father rather than her mother. All that is left is the sterile opposition of the European and the African. Xuela later marries an Englishman, "a man I did not love, but I would not have married a man I loved at all" (*Autobiography*, 205). Xuela believes that her father "came to despise all who behaved like the African people" (*Autobiography*, 187). Where does this contempt come from? Xuela explains: "an event that occurred hundreds of years before . . . continued on a course so subtle that it became a true expression of his personality, it became who he really was." This event is, of course, slavery. "Who he really was" is an exploiter and a dominator, a man who identifies with the powerful and not the powerless: "My father rejected the complications of the vanquished; he chose the ease of the victor" (*Autobiography*, 186). Xuela's father makes a choice in his life that is morally bankrupt; this is paralleled with Xuela's own choices in life, which are, in reaction, diametrically opposed, though also curiously empty.

Her father steals the supplies given to him by the British for hurricane relief and sells them. Xuela discovers this when a poor black man named Lazarus (the living dead) tries to obtain nails from her father, nails she knows to be in a barrel in his shed. She tells Lazarus this and her father denies it: "The sound of his voice was not new; it was just that I heard it for the first time" (*Autobiography*, 189). After yelling at her, her father stares out at the sea: "For my father, the sea . . . could hold no such abundance of comfort, could hold no such anything of any good; its beauty was lost to him, blank" (191). This perception of emptiness reflects a deep inner desolation.

The sea images this great emptiness or lack. Kincaid describes Antigua, the island she comes from: "it is ten by twelve miles, and it is this tiny island surrounded by two vast bodies of water. . . . At the same time we suffered constantly from drought. . . . You can't turn anywhere that you don't see this water, but you can't use it."[11] This emptiness is both torment and temptation.

This lack of water in water is also a metaphor for the situation of the African majority on Antigua or Dominica: the lack of Africa in Africans. How is such a person as Xuela's father possible? Is there more to it than Xuela's observation (or rather dismissal): "This is only to say that he proved himself commonly human" (*Autobiography*, 192)?

Antonio Benitez-Rojo quotes a Jamaican statistic that forty percent of the African slaves brought to that island died in their first three years.[12] Walter Rodney adds that "the consensus of opinion was this, take a prime African black, work him to death in five years, and you make a profit."[13] Apart from this sheer absence of human life, its active negation, Benitez-Rojo notes "a deculturating regimen that took direct action against . . . language . . . religion, and . . . customs, as African

practices were looked on with suspicion and many of them were controlled and prohibited."[14] This is an enormous amount of culture down
the memory hole, and its ceaseless rushing, its utter nonexistence, is
part of the lack that generates Xuela's father and his lack of African
culture.

This is not to say that there was no African culture left: as Benitez-
Rojo points out, Africans did certainly affect Caribbean culture before
the height of slavery and after Emancipation. In Kincaid's work and
that of other Caribbean writers, settings are saturated with the mutated
syncretic remains of African religions and cultural practices. In *Autobiography*, the main repository for this survival is Obeah, which appears
several times, always in things Kincaid's mother or Kincaid herself had
witnessed. In the context of one of these experiences—the drowning of
a boy chasing the figure of a woman (probably the goddess Erzulie or
Oshun) floating in a river—Xuela declares that "belief in that apparition of a naked woman with outstretched hands beckoning a small boy
to his death was the belief of the illegitimate, the poor, the low. I believed in that apparition then and I believe in it now." (*Autobiography*,
37–38).

Xuela takes the side of those who believe in Obeah in terms that unmistakably position it as an act of cultural resistance. It is, after all, one
of the few things that the people of African descent on these islands
have left. *At the same time*, the pure terror of this and other experiences
of Obeah, such as the death of Xuela's brother ("his entire being not
dead, not alive . . . from his body came a river of pus. Just as he died,
a large brown worm crawled out of his left leg" (*Autobiography*, 109–
11).), leads Xuela to write that "we lived in a darkness from which we
could not be redeemed. I then and now had and have no use for redemption" (*Autobiography*, 49). Obeah may be an alternative to the colonizer's culture and religion, and in the character of Xuela as Kincaid
embraces it, but for Kincaid herself its world is *also* a harsh nightmare
of emptiness that contrasts and complements the natural plenitude of
the surroundings. In her work, what she sees as the unyielding and
merciless environment of Antigua becomes intertwined with the presence of the practice of Obeah, creating a position of complete ambivalence toward Obeah and even the islands themselves. Of the many
stories she tells that illustrate this is one from her memoir of her brother
Devon, *My Brother*. The day after Devon was born, "my mother heard
her child crying, and when she awoke, she found him covered with red
ants. If he had been alone, it is believed they would have killed him"

(*My Brother*, 5–6). Kincaid also mentions being struck by the beauty of Dominica when she was living there with her mother's family, "but then I would see a light moving about in the mountains and knew that it was a jablessé[15] and would run inside to bed and pull the sheets over my head" (38). Beauty and death walk hand in hand in these islands.

Kincaid balances the two worlds she sees side by side in Antigua, its beauty and native resistance and its danger and terror, in an interview: "To be quite frank, my [Carib] grandmother's religion committed no crime against humanity"—and—"my grandmother did have friends who were souciants.[16] For a while, I lived in utter fear when I was little, of just not being sure that anything I saw was itself" (Cudjoe Interview 226). This feeling is part of Xuela's (and our) experience in *The Autobiography of My Mother*.

In *My Brother*, Kincaid sums up this last quotation epigrammatically: "Antigua is a place in which faith undermines the concrete" (35). The invisible spirit world and/or the people's beliefs in that world undermine the visible "real" world, creating voids, absences, which have a power of their own. The lack she sees in her motherland is crystallized in the fear she feels about her brother and his slow and painful death from AIDS, fears of losing herself, of falling into the void of this nonplace: "I felt I was falling into a deep hole" (*My Brother*, 20). "Every time I got on an airplane to pay him a visit, I was quite afraid that I would never come back" (*My Brother*, 92). She is terrified of becoming lost, of succumbing to the spell of the conflicted land, a spell of which Obeah is only one component. Perhaps most painful for a writer is the lack of comparison, of metaphors for what is happening to her brother, to her people (to herself). This is a lack of physical or metaphysical proportions; it is hard to even describe what happens (what happened) in the Caribbean. There is also a subtle yet pervasive fear of zombification that hovers around the edges of her narrative. As she sits by his hospital bed watching her brother for the last time, "dead really, but still breathing," she cannot find the words: "his heart beating like something, but what, but what, there was no metaphor" (*My Brother*, 107). This balancing of attraction (to overpowering beauty and fullness) and repulsion (from real danger, poverty, and lack) is part of what Giovanna Covi describes in reference to *A Small Place* as "the oxymoronic repetition of descriptions of the beauties and miseries of the land, a land that is both real and unreal and for that reason . . . is a prison of beauty."[17] Kincaid's remark to her brother that she "wanted to thank him for making [her] realize that [she] loved him" (*My Brother*, 21), perhaps also signifies her relationship to her island.

The beauty and misery of the land is a mirror image of the mother-daughter relationship at issue for Xuela and Kincaid: "This conflation of the mother and the land . . . is a 'double articulation of motherhood as both colonial and biological.'"[18] This critic is referring to Moira Ferguson's argument that the conflicted and contentious mother-daughter bond in Kincaid's work is attached to a relation to Antigua (and in Xuela's case, Dominica) as a motherland which is loved but also hated as colonially subjugated. Where is the "real" land? Are the islands Kincaid's and Xuela's real home or, given the history of slavery and transportation, the near extinction of the native population, are they false mothers, false homes? As Ferguson comments, "this relationship is always fraught with fear, alienation, and ambivalence, is always about separation."[19] Exile is always-already-prefigured here.

This separation takes another turn in Kincaid's *My Garden (Book):* (1999), where she remarks, "I do not know the names of the plants in the place I am from" (119). "What herb of any beauty grew in this place? What tree? And did the people who lived there grow them for their own sake? I do not know, I can find no record of it. I can only make a guess" (*My Garden Book*: 137). Because of the Columbian conquest, the names the natives called their plants, even in most cases the plants themselves, are simply gone. The ontology of such a situation, the nonbeing of the objects and their names, is radical; it exceeds the very European idea of ontology itself, bound up as it is with history and memory. When Derrida comments, "for us, différance remains a metaphysical name, and all the names that it receives in our language are still, as names, metaphysical," he means that there cannot actually be a term that distinguishes between being and nonbeing. That term is still "*enmeshed*, carried off, reinscribed" in the system that generates being and nonbeing.[20] Xuela is part of this system but there *is* the possibility that she is *also* part of something that is *not* part of this *Western* system. Her "nonbeing" in this sense is possibly "real" in a way unobtainable to us, to her, to you, to me. Obeah is part of this.

Kincaid and her people (and Xuela and her people) seemingly have no (access to) history or memory. It's just (merely) gone. Xuela reflects this at the end of *Autobiography*: "I long to meet the thing greater than I am, the thing to which I can submit. It is not in a book of history, it is not the work of anyone whose name can pass my own lips. Death is the only reality" (228). This refusal of history and naming is consequent upon what was taken away. But beyond even what was taken away is what was put in its place. Kincaid continues to explain her context in the piece from *My Garden (Book):* called "To Name Is To Possess," where she writes about a botanical garden on Antigua she visited as a child, which contained no plants native to the island, but many plants from around the British Empire (120).

Not only are there (for certain) no Antiguan plants but they have been replaced by nonnative plants. As Kincaid has remarked, "We were beyond alienation" (Perry Interview, 132). Beyond history, beyond memory, suffocated by colonialism and its insistent previousness. Kincaid writes of the breadfruit, which was sent to the West Indies by Joseph Banks, the English naturalist and world traveler, and the founder of Kew Gardens. It was meant to be a cheap food for feeding slaves, and Kincaid claims that it grows so readily in the Caribbean that it prevents the growing of other plants: "In a place like Antigua the breadfruit is not a food, it is a weapon" (*My Garden (Book):*, 135–37).

The breadfruit is a thus a powerful tool of dispossession. Kincaid, seeking some kind of memory of botanical resistance, observes that "the botany of Antigua exists in medicinal folklore" (137). She sees a bush in Antigua that she remembers from her childhood and asks her mother about it. Her mother says that it was used to cure bacterial infections, "but, she said, no one bothers with this anymore." Kincaid points out "not only" the ongoing erasure of memory involved here, but also the fact that it still "exists." Xuela's remark on the last page of her impossible autobiography now comes into focus: "Since I do not matter, I do not long to matter, but I matter anyway" (*Autobiography*, 228). Her existence is beyond history and beyond memory, possibly even beyond the alienation of colonialism, a human being on the far side of the West, with an existence like that of a plant, of an entire half-forgotten, half-remembered flora. And it is significant that Kincaid learns of the properties of the bush from her mother, who both remembers and transmits the memory and then dismisses it, the colonial land and the colonial mother teasing, remembering, erasing, like Derrida's différance. This is a problematic mother-daughter relation that Xuela does not have, and this lack paradoxically liberates and confines her.

One could say all this reflects Kincaid's status as an exile, as someone who left her motherland at the age of sixteen, forced into working overseas to provide money for her family. Rejecting this obligation, refusing to send money to them and refusing to even answer her mother's letters, Kincaid went her own way, eventually marrying an American and settling in Vermont.[21] Her fictionalization of this is in *Lucy* (1990), where the protagonist is likened to Milton's Satan in her independence of thought: ("There is something else from *Paradise Lost* that I seem to put in my work: 'Better to reign in hell than to serve in heaven' [Book I, line 263]. I completely believe that") (Birbalsingh Interview, 147).

Kincaid's solution to the Caribbean dilemma is escape. In this way she is a throwback to the early tradition of Caribbean women's writing, where exile is the only way of escaping the contradictions that prevent real selfhood and real consciousness. In Jean Rhys's *Wide Sargasso Sea* (1966) and Merle Hodge's *Crick Crack, Monkey* (1970), the only possible options for Caribbean women are death and exile. As Kincaid puts it in *My Brother*, "This is what my family, the people I grew up with, hate about me. I always say, Do you remember?" (19). The clear hint that memory, the basis of writing, is simply not tolerated in postcolonial Antigua is unmistakable. Kincaid cannot conceive of any writer being able to function in such circumstances. This accounts for the overwhelming emptiness of everything in Xuela's world.

The objection can easily be made that Kincaid is unfair to Antigua, Dominica, and the Caribbean because of her exilic status. Her distorted picture of her homeland(s) then results in the blighted landscape and characters of *The Autobiography of My Mother*. Certainly Kincaid is far removed from the nationalist project of someone like George Lamming. She recounts (in a 1991 interview) a confrontation she had with Lamming in Miami: "Lamming gave me a real dressing-down. . . . It was the old language of rebellion. Lamming was still fighting that battle of Independence" (Birbalsingh Interview, 142). On the other hand, she rejects a totally "diasporic" identity: "I will never become an American citizen. So I don't consider myself a diaspora writer. But we don't come from a culture that values us, and we don't know what else to do with ourselves" (143). Kincaid herself thus preserves her autonomy as a writer by refusing both Antigua and the United States of America, though she "chooses" to live in the latter.

Caribbean impossibility, for Kincaid, is thus personal. It revolves around the question "of how to respond to colonialism in any positive way."[22] It is not that death or exile is inevitable for her or others; it is her *choice*. Perhaps this is the difference between the colonial Caribbean of Rhys and Hodge and the postcolonial Caribbean of Kincaid. The way in which Kincaid seems to straddle both positions—death and exile are basic themes to her as to Rhys and Hodge, but there remains a real existence of her characters and herself in the Caribbean, a place for

them, even if defined in overwhelmingly negative terms—perhaps denotes the fact that she left Antigua in 1966, long before independence
in 1981, but the majority of her life as a writer is post-independence.

This choice is echoed in the person of the character Xuela, who
makes choices in the landscape of Dominica that, as Kincaid sees it, are
very limited choices. *But she does make them.* And these choices incarnate
lack, emptiness, and dispossession. On the one hand, there is a very
American valence to Kincaid's emphasis on choice. As she says proudly
in *My Garden (Book):*, "I returned from a visit to Antigua, the place
where I was born, to a small village in Vermont, the place where I
choose to live" (141–42). On the other hand, it is impossible to imagine
an American making the choices Xuela makes: "I refused to belong to
a race, I refused to accept a nation. . . . Am I nothing, then? I do not
believe so, but if nothing is a condemnation, I would love to be con-
demned" (*Autobiography*, 226).

This nothing that Xuela chooses to refuse to refuse is still more than
the nothingness that dispossessed her. She remains, constituted by her
refusals. The nothingness of dispossession, on the other hand, removes
everything—even the profits from slavery, the money that was its object, is drained away overseas. Xuela tells another story or parable
about her father. Showing early business acumen as a young man of
seven or eight, he sells chickens and eggs to get enough money so that
his Scots father can buy him a Sunday suit on a return trip to Britain.
On this journey, however, the ship sinks and his father, Richardson,
drowns. Xuela comments, "My father never saw his profit again, and
he may have spent the rest of his life trying to find and fit into that first
suit he had imagined himself in again and again" (*Autobiography*, 195).
There is here an economic cycle of lack that is gendered in Xuela's
father's compulsive penetration of it. Xuela then also becomes a gendered figure of this lack, a figure who can be repeatedly penetrated but
never reached or changed.

Xuela creates herself by the choice of her rejection of her father and
her embrace of the lack of her mother. The link between mother and
daughter is envisioned as far beyond the monetary and legal heir relationship of father and son. As Xuela is living in the way young people
do after leaving home for the first time—as she says, "not a man, not a
woman, not anything" (*Autobiography*, 102)—she receives a letter from
her father that refers to her relatives in terms that Xuela interprets as
signifying his outright ownership of them: "It was at that moment that
I felt I did not want to belong to anyone, that since the one person I

would have consented to own me had never lived to do so, I did not want to belong to anyone; I did not want anyone to belong to me" (*Autobiography*, 103–4). Only in lack can she be constituted.

Xuela takes the lack of her mother as an antiprinciple; her lack means she shall be a lack for everyone else. It is only in this lack that she can preserve herself, which means preserving her lack of a mother. This resolution may seem extreme until we realize how Kincaid herself feels about her own quite alive and present mother.

In 1989 she speaks of her mother as "an extraordinary person . . . the way I am is solely owing to her" (Cudjoe Interview, 219). She named her first child after her mother, Annie, and her first novel is called *Annie John*. By 1996, however, she is saying "my mother didn't like me. . . . I seemed to repel her" (Snell Interview, 28) and an interviewer characterizes her mother as "an unresponsive and often abusive mother who shipped her off to the US at 17." Kincaid gives an account of her mother's visit to her in 1990, after which she "was sick for three months. I had something near to a nervous breakdown" (*My Brother*, 28).[23] In *My Brother*, she muses about her mother: "Perhaps all love is self-serving. I do not know, I do not know. She loves and understands us when we are helpless and need her" (16–17).

In *The Autobiography of My Mother* Kincaid "explores what would have been her mother's life had [her mother] remained in Dominica and refused to have children—borrowing from her mother's life to build a narrative of emotional vacuity"[24]. Most of the external circumstances of Kincaid's real mother's life are transferred to Xuela, with the two details just mentioned inserted.

Obviously, the connection between Kincaid and her mother is psychologically quite intense. Ferguson's thesis that this relationship is metaphorical to the troubled bond between the colonizer as mother country and the colonized territory as angry child fits perfectly here. But even the willed imaginary negation of Kincaid's own self still instantiates the colonial relation, making it transindividual, an absenting that frees another voice. This voice speaks from beyond possibility, beyond most of the categories of humanity, a presentation of a (Caribbean) colonial condition. The lack Kincaid feels in the relationship with her mother is transformed into the person her mother might have been if Kincaid had never been born. The result of such an impulse might seem to be to give her mother a better life; instead we get a reoriented, colder, and more bitterly objective speaker than in Kincaid's earlier work. Xuela accepts her circumstances and lives a proud, uncompromising life; but the cost of this, maintained to (or even beyond) the full, is heavy: "That attachment, physical and spiritual, that confusion of who is who, flesh and flesh, which was absent . . . how can any child understand such a thing, so profound an abandonment? I have refused to bear any children" (*Autobiography*, 199). The painful yet needed entanglement with the mother that so transfixes Kincaid is not present for Xuela and gives her character and narrative voice a clarity that Kincaid does not have.

Such clarity I would not call "emotional vacuity." It is the acceptance of lack as an antiprinciple, a lack for Xuela that is a lack of one's mother and of one's people or nation (the Carib and the African), which she carries or bears by rejecting her stereotypically gendered roles of childbirth, love, and domesticity. This space that contains or retains Xuela must remain open for a future that does not contain Xuela herself: "I am of the vanquished, I am of the defeated. The past is a fixed point, the future is open-ended; for me the future must remain capable of casting a light on the past such that in my defeat lies the seed of my great victory, in my defeat lies the beginning of my great revenge. My impulse is to the good, my good is to serve myself. I am not a people, I am not a nation. I only wish from time to time to make my actions be the actions of a people, to make my actions be the actions of a nation" (*Autobiography*, 215–16).

In this complex mix of individuality and collectivity, the individual asserts her right to step back from people and nation (and the lack of the word "race" here is important) and to step forward into them when she chooses, a choice the outside world denies her. Her *only* individuality, her *only* choice, is to refuse, and thus hold open a space or time for an action that is not a restitution but an agency.

This space or time has something to do with gender, with gender as a lack constituted by female sexual desire, a lack that refuses to refuse, and which moves Xuela forward and through a male world, giving her a kind of agencyless agency that has no words to name itself . . . and in refusing naming, exists: "I myself had no word for it, I had never read a word for it, I had never heard someone else mention a word for it; the feeling was a sweet, hollow feeling, an empty space with a yearning to be filled"(*Autobiography*, 154).

There is an effort throughout Kincaid's dealings with sexuality and gender in her work to write out "the potential for retrieval of the colonized Caribbean body" and "the processes of female reembodiment," as Helen Tiffin puts it.[25] Kincaid admits that she herself has been sexually disembodied by her mother's insistence on protecting her from the hostile Caribbean environment: "I grew up alienated from my own sexuality and, as far as I can tell, am still, to this day, not at all comfortable with the idea of myself and sex" (*My Brother*, 68).

In the sexual encounter with the white man who eventually becomes her husband, Xuela becomes quite dominant in her submission. She takes off his belt, ties her own hands with it, and then makes him service her in several positions, each prefaced by "I made him," which is written five times. Kincaid here genders and sexualizes the history and fiction of the Caribbean in the land and waterscape of memory. The memories of slavery and the notorious mass rapes of the Caribbean natives by the Spaniards are palpable, tastable, as the Englishman "would murmur my name as if it held something, a meaning, a memory that perhaps he could not let go" (*Autobiography*, 155). Perhaps the meaning of this encounter is this: he is caught (in history, in memory) and she is not—or at least not as much, and that is a major victory. In the inherently unequal relation between them, Xuela will take her personal pleasure through her lack, the fluid lack of her desire, the lack of her love, the lack of her real engagement with him. She's not there; and yet she really is there physically, as a woman, as a (half-) native—but as a woman who will not bear (children), who will not give herself emotionally or psychologically. Her roles as (emotional and psychological) lack and (physical and spiritual) remainder cohere in her sexuality, in her choices in the practice of sex and gender. Here Xuela's name finally holds something instead of pure lack, something besides the mark of historical obliteration and its trace in colonial memory: the space created by her refusals, by her choices—perhaps the space where defeat becomes victory, the time when defeat becomes revenge, all present in the space of this room where the Englishman and the half-Carib, quarter-African, quarter-Scots woman copulate, an ongoing process that remains open.

In an essay on Kincaid's 1990 novel *Lucy*, Moira Ferguson invokes "a camera metaphor"[26] to explain the end of that novel, where Lucy, beginning a journal, "could write down only this: 'I wish I could love someone so much that I would die from it.' And then as I looked at this sentence a great wave of shame came over me and I wept and wept so much that the tears fell on the page and caused all the words to become one great big blur."[27]

Ferguson says that "the image of the blur suggests that everything is out of focus; it returns us to a camera metaphor, but one connoting a confusion coupled with determinacy."[28] Looking at the last sentence of *Autobiography*, there is a similarity only in terms of subject and theme: "Death is the only reality, for it is the only certainty, inevitable to all things" (228). Lucy wants love so badly that she wants it to sweep her off into death, and the "shame" of this immense, overwhelming need unfocuses her eyes and blurs her first attempts at writing into unintelligibility. What is this shame?

The shame is dual; Lucy is ashamed at having repressed this need in her life so brutally and impersonally and yet is also ashamed at the need itself. This necessary contradiction causes her self to disintegrate, to go out of focus. The wish for death exposes the thought and its reaction as immature and unformed, as blurred. Ferguson's exploration of the camera metaphor enables us to see how Lucy, as a character and as a voice for Kincaid, is in focus the rest of the time. When Lucy's self disintegrates, the focusing mechanism, the camera that she is for Kincaid, ceases to function and the novel ends. The character disappears as a consequence of its being a fictionalized presentation of a phase of Kincaid's life. When this phase ends, when that past self dies because of its own contradictions, everything stops.

Xuela, on the other hand, has no shame. She has contradictions, of course, but they are all part of her constitutive lack, the lack of her human and physical environments. Xuela, as a camera, as a character, always remains focused. This is inhuman, but Xuela is much more a mechanism than Lucy. The camera metaphor is different in Xuela's case. The way Xuela comes to be, the way she is focused, is through a displacement, a lack. A camera focuses on something by unfocusing other things—or alternatively, a camera frames a scene by cutting some part of the world out of that frame. Xuela as a character is Kincaid's mother if Kincaid had never been born, if her mother had not had children and had stayed on Dominica. The character is focused by what it is not, by what it leaves out as much as by what it includes. Xuela herself focuses herself within the fiction by refusing to bear children or love in a conventional manner, and by choosing to base herself on her lack of a mother. This double refusal, this choice of lack, gives her her individuality and her life, limited as it is.

This hyperfocused quality of Xuela's gives her a more mature yet more skewed view of death than Lucy; she can see (at seventy) its power and inevitability. It is the greatest lack, the annihilator, and since she has chosen to follow out her situation to its logical conclusion, almost beyond history, almost beyond memory, a mere yet pure existence, she has faced down everything else her situation has thrown at her. She understands death; she has followed its (anti) principles and its logic of absence. She faces this real, pure, absolute nonbeing head on, with appreciation. "I long to meet the thing greater than I am, the thing to which I can submit" (*Autobiography*, 228). For her, the screen will go dark, not blur; because of all the lack, because of all the death surrounding her, the focus cannot fade or waver.

Cathleen Schine, in her review of *Autobiography*, sees the novel as "pure and overwhelming, a brilliant fable of willed nihilism." She adds: "Xuela is a symbol. She sees herself as a symbol, an abstraction of an entire people's suffering and degradation, and so there is a uniformity to her cold vision and a relentless rhythmic message to her empty life that is disturbing certainly—almost unbearable—without ever feeling real."[29]

Two points should be made. Xuela is a character in a book. She is not a "real" person; she does not exist. As part of the mirrored displacement of her genesis, her nonexistence (as African, as Carib, as a woman, as poor, as a colonial subject—and also as what Kincaid's mother might have been but was not) is the basis of her existence. As she says, "I was born standing on my head . . . the world was upside down at the moment I first laid eyes on it" (*Autobiography*, 226). Her unreality is the entire point of her reality.

Xuela is also not a symbol; she is an aperture, a point of view with a recording apparatus, perhaps the "open wound" that "heal[s] and open[s], again and again, over and over" that Kincaid mentions in "In History" (*My Garden [Book]:*, 153). The metonyms and the rhythms of the penetration (insertion and withdrawal) and the breathing (inhalation and exhalation) of vagina and mouth in this formulation are instantiated in Xuela as embodied colonized (wounded) African native female. She breathes and talks, secretes and copulates, allowing us access to her, allowing her access to us. She is an incarnated camera, recording more than sight, all bodily events and their consequences. She is "confusion coupled with determinacy,"[30] consciousness coupled with flesh, a confusion (a lack [in the relationship between Kincaid and her mother]) become determinate (the *non*relationship between Xuela and her mother), a determinate and determined confusion (lack) that speaks orally to us in textual characters, an embodied machine, beyond alienation, but not beyond history or memory, not quite. Xuela exists liminally, somewhere in between a history and memory that Europe has excluded (that it could include) and something that will always remain outside these categories (that it could never include).

The lack of Jamaica Kincaid, her impossibility the impossibility of the Caribbean, inhering in both her and its name, becomes signified or indicated, deterritorialized or reterritorialized, in Xuela, who might have existed if Kincaid had not, who might have been her mother but was not, whose tale is not told by herself but by the lack of the mother she never knew and the children she never had. This lack is productive but not redemptive. It is merely a space (or wound) that is not tragic or sad or happy or healing: it is just there and here. It changes but it does not move; it moves but it does not change. It can only be addressed or recounted, and victory or revenge will not close it or heal it. It is, perhaps, a purpose.

> You can't free yourself unless you know what really happened, unless you can face what really happened. You have to tell the truth. (Birbalsingh Interview, 146)
>
> I shall never forget [my brother] because his life is the one I did not have, the life that, for reasons I hope shall never be too clear to me, I avoided or escaped.
>
> (*My Brother*, 176)
>
> Who you are is a mystery no one can answer, not even you. And why not, why not?
>
> (*The Autobiography*, 202)

NOTES

1. Jamaica Kincaid, "In History," in *My Garden (Book):* (New York: Farrar Straus Giroux, 1999), 153.

2. Jamaica Kincaid, *The Autobiography of My Mother* (New York: Plume/Penguin, 1996), 227–28.

3. Jamaica Kincaid, "Jamaica Kincaid," in *Backtalk: Women Writers Speak Out* (New Brunswick, NJ: Rutgers University Press, 1993), 132.

4. Lizabeth Paravisini-Gebert, *Jamaica Kincaid: A Critical Companion* (Westport, CT: Greenwood Press, 1999), 25.

5. Jamaica Kincaid, "Jamaica Kincaid and the Modernist Project: An Interview by Selwyn Cudjoe," in *Caribbean Women Writers: Essays from the First International Conference*, edited by Selwyn Cudjoe (Wellesley, MA: Calaloux, 1990), 227.

6. Jamaica Kincaid, "Jamaica Kincaid: From Antigua to America," in *Frontiers of Caribbean Literature in English*, edited by Frank Birbalsingh (New York: St. Martin's Press, 1996), 143.

7. Jamaica Kincaid, *My Brother* (New York: Farrar Straus Giroux, 1997), 126–27.

8. See *Encyclopedia Americana* (1973), 9:267.

9. Jamaica Kincaid, *A Small Place* (New York: Plume/Penguin, 1988), 37.

10. Simone A. James Alexander, *Mother Imagery in the Novels of Afro-Caribbean Women* (Columbia: University of Missouri Press, 2001), 83.

11. Jamaica Kincaid, "A Lot of Memory: An Interview with Jamaica Kincaid" by Moira Ferguson, *Kenyon Review* 16, no. 1 (1994): 180.

12. Antonio Benitez-Rojo, *The Repeating Island: The Caribbean and the Postmodern Perspective*, translated by James Maraniss (Durham, NC: Duke University Press, 1992), 70. See also Benitez-Rojo's chart on pp. 64–65, derived from Franklin W. Knight, *The Caribbean: The Genesis of a Fragmented Nationalism* (New York: Oxford University Press, 1978).

13. Walter Rodney, *The Groundings with My Brothers* (London: Bogle-L'Ouverture, 1969), 68.

14. Benitez-Rojo, *Repeating Island*, 70.

15. "'La diablesse' or 'bride of the dead' is a notorious creature of the night, attractively attired in fancy clothes and hat. At the end of one leg can be seen a Satanic cloven foot." See Frank Birbalsingh, *Frontiers of Caribbean Literature in English*, 136, fn. 1.

16. "A 'soucouyant' [Trinidadian spelling] is a female vampire or 'Ol' Higue . . . who can turn into a ball of fire at night, and suck the blood of her victims." See Birbalsingh, *Frontiers of Caribbean Literature in English*, 136, fn. 1.

17. Giovanna Covi, "Jamaica Kincaid's Prismatic Self and the Decolonisation of Language and Thought," in *Framing the Word: Gender and Genre in Caribbean Women's Writing*, edited by Joan Anim-Addo, 44 (London: Whiting & Birch, 1996).

18. Alexander, *Mother Imagery*, 17.

19. Moira Ferguson, *Jamaica Kincaid: Where the Land Meets the Body* (Charlottesville: University of Virginia Press, 1994), 2.

20. Jacques Derrida, "Différance," in *Margins of Philosophy*, translated by Alan Bass, 26, 27 (Chicago: University of Chicago Press, 1982).

21. Jamaica Kincaid, "Jamaica Kincaid Hates Happy Endings," interview by Marilyn Snell, *Mother Jones*, September–October 1997, 32.

22. Alison Donnell, "Writing for Resistance: Nationalism and Narratives of Liberation," in *Framing the Word: Gender and Genre in Caribbean Women's Writing*, edited by Joan Anim-Addo (London: Whiting & Birch, 1996), 34.

23. Julia Kristeva puts it succinctly: "For a heterosexual woman, the mother is the rival, which explains why the love and hatred directed at the mother are so violent. In most cases, the woman experiences a very repressed combination of love-hate, one that can be a powerful stimulus for symbolization, that can lead to the psychotic deviations of hysteria, and that can be manifested in the more mediated and productive form of sublimation and of aesthetic products." "'unes femmes': The Woman Effect" (1975), in *Julia Kristeva: Interviews*, edited by and translated by Ross Mitchell Guberman, 110 (New York: Columbia University Press, 1996).

24. Paravisini-Gebert, 38.

25. Helen Tiffin, "Cold Hearts and (Foreign) Tongues: Recitations and the Reclamation of the Female Body in the Works of Erna Brodber and Jamaica Kincaid," in *Caribbean Women Writers*, edited by Harold Bloom (Philadelphia: Chelsea House, 1997), 110.

26. Moira Ferguson, "*Lucy* and the Mark of the Colonizer," in *Caribbean Women Writers*, edited by Harold Bloom, 109 (Philadelphia: Chelsea House, 1997).

27. Jamaica Kincaid, *Lucy* (New York: Plume/Penguin, 1991), 163–64.

28. Moira Ferguson, "Lucy and the Mark of the Colonizer," in *Caribbean Women Writers*, edited by Harold Bloom, 109.

29. Cathleen Schine, "A World as Cruel as Job's," in *Caribbean Women Writers*, edited by Harold Bloom, 115–16.

30. Moira Ferguson, *"Lucy* and the Mark of the Colonizer," in *Caribbean Women Writers*, edited by Harold Bloom, 109.

My Other: Imperialism and Subjectivity in Jamaica Kincaid's *My Brother*

DERIK SMITH AND CLIFF BEUMEL

THE IMPULSE WHICH ORIGINALLY GAVE SHAPE TO THIS ESSAY RE-
sponded to generic and at times overwhelmingly positive critical evaluations of Jamaica Kincaid's work. We thought it ironic that a figure as
complex and strong willed as Kincaid could produce a body of prose
that was rarely challenged on aesthetic or political grounds—much less
taken to task. In more specific terms, it seemed as though Kincaid's
often negative appraisal of her Caribbean birthplace in salvos written
from her New England residence was more problematical than the criticism indicated. By avoiding the challenges presented by the postcolonial subject's unapologetic critique of her home while enjoying the
pleasures of exile in metropolitan space, we sensed that critics had produced lacunae ready for exploration. Our visceral response to "Kincaid
criticism" was in keeping with a general shift in postcolonial criticism
that questioned the utility of the somewhat congratulatory scholarship
that dominated journals in the 1980s and 1990s. Thus, while this piece
proceeds with the recognition that, given the historical silencing of
voices like Kincaid's, postcolonial critics have understandably champi-
oned her work in an effort to help restructure the canon in a more rep-
resentational less Eurocentric manner, it couples this awareness with a
question posed by one astute critic: "Does not the imperative to celebrate . . . generate a specter of the 'model,' acceptable postcolonial response, which both chokes critics and arrests the possibilities for
making meanings?"[1]

The need to move away from a "model" celebratory response to Kincaid's work is evidenced by her achievements as a "mainstream" writer
in the contemporary American literary landscape. Her commercial success suggests that she commands a relatively significant audience,
which appreciates her writing and is influenced by its ideas. While this
is encouraging to those of us who have welcomed the emergence of

96

postcolonial writing into the popular sphere, it also establishes an imperative for the critic. Because Kincaid is one of the few Caribbean writers to be embraced by a large American audience, her voice threatens to become representative of some monolithic Caribbean postcolonial subjectivity. The critic's duty is then, in part, to demonstrate the particularity of the author's voice by calling attention to its more problematic assertions. To shirk this task, to gloss over, or halfheartedly engage the contentious aspects of Kincaid's writing, while unreservedly praising the virtuosity of her art, is to sanction those problematic assertions and implicitly allow a single voice to wield inappropriate authority.

Not surprisingly, the tendency to extol Kincaid's work has been more pronounced in critics writing for popular rather than academic audiences. *My Brother*, Kincaid's recent memoir recounting the author's involvement with her family during her youngest sibling's AIDS-produced illness and death, and the subject of this essay, was particularly well received. Aside from an annoyed reviewer in *Time* magazine who claimed to be tired of Kincaid's obsession with "a single, anguished theme: her bitter resentment of her mother,"[2] *My Brother* enjoyed a tremendously positive critical reception, which included a nomination for a National Book Award. *The Advocate*, *Artforum*, *Booklist*, *Library Journal*, *The Nation*, the *New York Times Book Review*, and *People Weekly* all estimated the volume as worthy of an "A" grade and offered ecstatic assessments. The thread that finds its way into each of these laudatory reviews is praise for the "truth" and "honesty" of Kincaid's writing. In *Booklist*, Donna Seaman calls the memoir "unflinching" and finally characterizes it as "[h]onest, unapologetic and pure."[3] Bruce Hainley closes his review of *My Brother* in *Artforum* by declaring that Kincaid has come as "close to the truth as possible about how the world and the human beings in it live or don't live."[4] And, without mentioning Kincaid's somewhat dilettantish engagement with the discourse of homosexuality—an engagement that will receive particular attention later in this essay—the gay and lesbian newsmagazine *The Advocate* declares that "Kincaid's stark honesty makes her brother come alive in a way no reverent tribute ever could."[5]

If Kincaid's work is understood to be as "honest" and "truthful" as popular critics would suggest, we are forced to wonder how her readers then begin to assimilate unqualified assertions like: "[I]n Antigua itself nothing is made," or "[I]n Antigua people . . . never do what they say they will do."[6] It is unsettling to imagine a large audience, probably unfamiliar with the region encountered through Kincaid's prose, reading these "honest" lines in one of the only examples of Caribbean literature with which they may ever come in contact. For these readers, the Antiguan-born writer and the critics who gush at her ability to produce a textual representation of the Caribbean that is brimming with "truth" and "honesty" combine to reinforce the rhetoric of dearth and *dis*honesty that have remained attached to the colony and colonial subjects since the period of Empire. This is, of course, ironic because those critics who help to solidify Kincaid's reputation as an important writer are, on some level, engaged in a "politically correct" attempt to address the myths of inadequacy propagated by colonialism and its attendant discourse. Yet, the coupling of their brand of enthusiastic praise with Kincaid's jarring—though admittedly nuanced—critique of her home island and its people produces the figure of "honest Kincaid" who then becomes the exception that proves the rule. She is the trustworthy West Indian who exposes the mendacity of her people to a metropolitan audience ready to accept her word.

While the unchecked accolades that Kincaid has received in popular periodicals are partly a function of the hyperbole that attends the genre of reviews that these publications are expected to produce, the discernable political sensitivity that ironically helps generate these evaluations is mimicked in the scholarly treatments of Kincaid's work, which are inclined toward the laudatory. In the few academic essays that have considered *My Brother*, a similar—though more measured—refrain is also heard. For example, Louise Bernard's study of the construction of the "post-modern self" in *The Autobiography of My Mother* and *My Brother* concludes that Kincaid's "body of work actively seeks the liberatory space of 'truth-telling.'"[7] The quotation marks, which call attention to the provisional nature of any evocation of "truth," and the assertion that Kincaid's work is in a process of becoming—it "seeks," rather than achieves—are the expected signs of a scholarly approach to literature. However, there is a significant segment of Kincaid scholarship addressing her earlier work that makes less of an effort to maintain the restraint necessary for sober, discursive literary analysis. While in popular criticism Kincaid's honesty is eagerly extolled, the inclination to praise similarly manifests itself in academic writing through a proclivity to find intentionality in her writing.

Our purpose here is to question "authorial intent" and derive meaning from Kincaid's work through a skeptical critical approach that is less concerned with the imperative to celebrate than it is with gaining a

fuller understanding of the complex status of the subject in a postcolonial, globalizing world. We do not mean to suggest that scholarly evalu-
ation of Kincaid's work has been simpleminded. Just the contrary: her
work has been tagged and explored as one of the most rich and intricate
presentations of the female postcolonial subject. However, we believe
that many inquiries become self-limiting, when this richness is con-
strued as fully in the command of the author. In short, when Kincaid is
lauded as the master of her art, the very useful balance between authorial intention and interpretive possibilities opened up by poststructura-
list literary theory is lost. When critical projects not only allude to, but
are controlled by statements such as, "[T]he reader is mesmerized into
Kincaid's world, a world in which one reality constantly slides into another under cover of the ordinary rhythms of life,"[8] a chance to release
greater meaning from the text is missed. Thus, without relinquishing
the benefits derived from observing and elucidating Kincaid's intentionally constructed world—an admittedly impressive construction—we
will emphasize the equally considerable richness in meaning to be had
from observing those moments when the text appears to get beyond
Kincaid's control. We do not mean to castigate Kincaid. For what art-
work doesn't wriggle out of the artist's hands from time to time—or
even at every moment? By taking Kincaid's text to task, we are in fact
only paying it the respect it deserves as art that is insistently engaged
in the production of cultural meaning. And we are furthermore merely
answering to the demand that every text that rises to the level of serious
literature utters: one *must* take it to task. It is in the complex and contested space that opens up as Kincaid's text seems to wriggle out of control that we find its most provocative and productive material. By
admitting to Kincaid's inability to fully control her creation we are able
to discern moments in which she is made "dishonest" by her own text,
moments in which certain "truths" of subjectivity—and postcolonial
subjectivity particularly—emerge, though they seem to have been covered over.

Kincaid's recent work, *My Brother,* invites our more skeptical critical
approach that problematizes the symbolic order that most critics have
understood to be consciously and masterfully crafted by Kincaid. One
major consequence of the celebratory critical response to Kincaid has
been an overemphasis on her narratives as universally resonant tales.
Specifically, critics repeatedly, and almost exclusively, focus on Kincaid's portrayal of a female Caribbean subject as a convincing account
of the Lacanian, self-alienated subject, a version of subjectivity that has

been important to postcolonial studies. H. Adlai Murdoch reveals the link between this popular version of subjectivity and the belief that Kincaid is brilliantly and intentionally spinning it out for us: "So it is Kincaid's own Caribbean *self-reflexive* perception which provides the narrative motor for *this story for all seasons*. The maternal/filial conflict, the attempt to name and to be oneself, the struggle with difference and biculturality, and the repeated use of key tropes, generating the binary oppositions which figure the entire work, *all herald a skillful, conscious and controlled narrator*, as well as a marvelous addition to the canon of Caribbean literature [*emphasis added*]."[9] This proclivity among scholars is reminiscent of Derrida's assertion that, "Certain people, myself included, have experienced colonial cruelty from two sides, so to speak. But once again, it reveals the colonial structure of *any* culture in an exemplary way. It testifies to it in martydom, and 'vividly'"[*emphasis added*].[10] Thus, if all cultures are, at heart, colonial, then the self-alienated subject that Derrida describes is equally universal.

The point is not to disagree with these readings. Indeed, the version of identity building that critics delineate in earlier works by Kincaid (principally *Annie John, Lucy,* and *The Autobiography of My Mother*) appears to be an adequate, if also simplistic explication of Kincaid's initial portrayal of (and relationship with) her mother in *My Brother*. But while appropriating this reading we want also to point out, both in brief here and more expansively throughout this essay, that the universal, Lacanian, self-alienated subject is a rather schematic and potentially reductive version of selfhood. Indeed, that may be just the problem with these types of critique: as Derrida suggests, they may accurately describe a universal *subjectivity*, but they simultaneously cut off an exploration of a more particular *selfhood* that is constructed within this model. Elucidating this selfhood, then, will be the overarching goal of this essay, while the particular difficulties, inconsistencies, and implications involved in constructing this self will be, finally, of most interest to us. These issues, often glossed over by critics who have dealt with Kincaid's earlier fiction, become impossible to ignore in her recent memoir. As we will examine later in the essay, it is principally through the figure of her brother that the typical "Kincaidian" symbolic order is disrupted and complicated in crucial ways.

Before beginning an in-depth analysis of Devon—the "brother"—we want to briefly outline the Lacanian construction of identity that critics find in Kincaid. If one thinks again of Derrida's lines quoted above, it should be reasonable to say not only that the postcolonial subject is an exemplary model of all subjects, but that every element of that "vivid" subject's construction is also exemplary. In Kincaid's narratives, then, her mother stands in as the universal mother figure for the female subject. But much more importantly, Kincaid's mother figures also symbolically stand in for the power that alienates the self in this "exemplary" model, colonialism. Thus, remaining for the moment in this schematic mode, it is probably not an exaggeration to say that in most of Kincaid's work her mother figures represent, ironically, the colonizer. Murdoch, in her strictly Lacanian reading of *Annie John,* gestures toward this interpretation of the mother: "Annie will leave Antigua for England, replacing the mother with the colonial 'mother country'" (333). Only if the mother always latently represents the colonizer can she be replaced by yet another mother figure that is more explicitly the colonizer. Diane Simmons also recognizes this metaphorical representation: "Annie John comes of age under her mother's rule, which mirrors the attitudes of English colonial rulers."[11] Simmons asserts that by the time Kincaid writes *The Autobiography of My Mother* (the novel that Kincaid published one year prior to *My Brother*) the mother's internalization of colonial logic has become so absolute that the character becomes almost purely a representation of metropolitan power. Additionally, in her writing on Kincaid, including the book length study *Jamaica Kincaid: Where the Land Meets the Body,* Moira Ferguson identifies considerable slippage between maternal and colonial oppression in most of the author's early writing. Ferguson posits that Kincaid makes convenient use of this familial relationship (and others) in order to articulate a "sometimes veiled, often overt anticolonial discourse."[12]

Our analysis of *My Brother*—a text in which the mother-as-colonizer recognizably emerges yet again—examines what additional "discourses" show themselves when the familial relationships that Kincaid regularly uses to frame her narratives are scrutinized with uncommon circumspection. Because, however, this text does not engage issues of colonialism as explicitly as her earlier works, this mother-as-colonizer trope is ostensibly obscured even while it remains a potent and ubiquitous presence in the narrative. Kincaid constructs the memoir's somewhat hidden, yet guiding, metaphor by portraying her mother as utterly unable to relinquish parental control and mastery. Kincaid first implies, through ironic hyperbole, the darkly possessive nature of her mother's affection: "[My mother's] love for her children when they are children is spectacular, unequaled I am sure in the history of a mother's love" (17). But the dominating and ultimately stultifying nature of this love quickly becomes apparent when Kincaid explains, "It is when her children are trying to be grown-up people—adults—that her mechanism for loving them falls apart" (17). In this moment early in the text the reader can clearly discern the colonial logic which animates her "motherly" love. The mother meets her child's quest for autonomy with complete refusal; this parental "love" can be more accurately described as a desire for mastery. One cannot fail to recognize in this brief description of a mother's love the same self-delusional justification of oppressive control employed by a colonial ruler.

If Kincaid's mother is established as the consummate colonizer, then the filial relationship places Kincaid, obviously, in the role of the colonized. Throughout the memoir Kincaid portrays herself as always seeking to escape her mother's absolute control and oppression. And as anyone who is subjugated, her ultimate fantasy is to escape completely. Kincaid's self-imposed geographical and emotional separation from her mother—her establishment of an alternative "stateside" reality replete with new and self-contained family, friends, and language—represents an attempt to realize that fantastic escape. When her brother's illness draws her back within her originary sphere, dominated by her mother, Kincaid begins to appreciate her own bifurcated condition: ". . . why they invent a self that bears no resemblance to who they really are, why anyone would want to feel as if he or she belongs to nothing, comes from no one, just fell out of the sky, whole" (12–13). This wishful thinking, a dream of self-creation, in fact seems to describe Kincaid's adult life. The self-conscious critique in these lines cannot be missed. Kincaid seems aware that in her desire to escape her mother's dominion, she has been attempting to realize a myth of absolute autonomy. Simultaneously, she also admits that it is an unrealizable dream. The geographical distance Kincaid has traveled from her mother does not provide the power to absolutely sunder the psychological bonds between master and slave—nothing can. Although she has constructed an alternative and seemingly independent reality in a removed space, the moment she returns to her original "home" the repressed desires that animate her existence emerge.

It is in this textual moment that the reader learns that shame plays a significant role in Kincaid's life. It is a shame that recalls the blameless self-deprivation of the enslaved subject. The incident that provoked Kincaid to reveal the slave's fantasy of autonomy also serves to display her internalization of inordinate shame. Kincaid asks her mother of a lemon tree planted years ago by her dying brother. Her mother responds bluntly, explaining that she cut it down in order to expand her home (13). And while her mother, responsible for the obliteration of this rare symbol of her son's creative power, experiences no regret, Kincaid herself, who had nothing to do with the event, takes on the burden of shame (13). Kincaid's reaction to this event is clearly intended to differentiate herself from her mother. She experiences unwarranted shame while her imperialistic mother remains callously self-assured. Later in the text she again employs this strategy of differentiation: "And she said then, I am never wrong, I have nothing to apologize for, everything I did at the time, I did for a good reason" (27). Kincaid's mother is first the source of pain. But because of her mother's almost diabolical denial of any culpability, the shame of her actions is transferred onto Kincaid. Both the sins of the mother, and the shame of the colonial ruler are visited upon the author-protagonist. Ironically, this shouldering of unwarranted contrition seems to be one of the defining characteristics of the *successful* postcolonial subject.

Within the symbolic economy of the narrative Kincaid clearly understands herself to be the most successful postcolonial subject. Her condescendingly judgmental attitude toward the nation in which she was raised and its residents indicates that though she remains a postcolonial subject she occupies a markedly superior position than the Antiguans who have been geographically and culturally trapped within the island. It is ironic that this feeling of superiority is in great part derived from an ability to recognize the need for feelings of shame. Kincaid continually gestures toward her fellow Antiguans' (her mother chief among them) moral certainty: their inability, or unwillingness, to accept guilt. At every level Antigua is a shameless world. We must return to one of her definitive pronouncements: "[I]n Antigua people never arrive when they say they will; they never do what they say they will do" (32). Kincaid seems to prescribe an internalization of shame that is similar to her own. An unwillingness to accept shame—behavior learned from self-justifying colonial oppressors—generates a destructive cycle of repression that perpetuates the deleterious effects of colonialism.

In light of the views expressed in her important essay *A Small Place*, it is obvious that Kincaid believes these feelings of guilt and shame to have originated in the colonial oppressor. Nevertheless, as we examined in her relationship with her mother, Kincaid believes that her fellow Antiguans must cultivate recognition of this internalized shame. Kincaid's suggestion that the decolonized knowingly accept this blameless guilt in order to halt postcolonial (self-) subjugation gestures toward a

Christological redemption. It is problematical that Kincaid constructs herself as the exemplary instance of this model of post-colonial subjectivity. The rigorous demands of this ideal subjectivity prove difficult for even a person as self-examining and driven as Kincaid; her expectation that others assume this type of responsibility seems idealistic at best and reductively condescending at worst.

For Kincaid the figure that most palpably stands in opposition to her ideal subject is her AIDS-stricken brother. As the one and only example of the Christological, postcolonial subjectivity in the memoir, Kincaid is thus placed, symbolically, in diametric opposition to her brother, the figure of arch irresponsibility and naivete. Though the memoir initially presents Kincaid and her mother as antitheses, a more thorough-going analysis of the text reveals that, in fact, Kincaid and her brother represent two poles in a symbolical economy, while the mother's role in this dynamic becomes marginalized, though still important. Moreover, once this new order crystallizes, the similarities between Kincaid and her mother emerge in an increasingly important way. Thus, the vilifying characterizations of the mother that fill the opening pages of the memoir actually function as a window into the symbolic individual we refer to as "Kincaid." Before the similarities between Kincaid and her mother can be fully unpacked we must first examine the symbolic binary of Kincaid and her brother.

This sibling opposition is the product of divergent trajectories of development. Repeatedly in the memoir Kincaid and her brother are portrayed as having very similar essential beings. Though sharing a perceptible affinity and springing from the same source, they have developed along life-paths that have brought them to significantly different circumstances. On several occasions Kincaid hints toward a moment of divergence in which she was able to successfully break free from the deadening entropy of Antigua that has transformed her brother's promise into self-destructiveness. Early in the narrative Kincaid ruminates, "And when I picked up that book again, *The Education of A Gardener*, I looked at my brother, for he was a gardener also, and I wondered, if his life had taken a certain turn, might he have written a book with such a title?" (11). Though she does not explicitly contrast her brother with herself, the comparison is unmistakable. Kincaid's question seems undeniably self-referential: "I looked at my brother and wondered, if his life had taken a certain turn, might he have been the same person I have come to be?" Kincaid's love of gardening is well chronicled in the memoir and throughout her oeuvre. But she most clearly links herself to the persona that her brother might have been through authorship. A hierarchical contrast is thus drawn: she is a writer, he is not; she is productive, he is not. This contrast is more powerfully expressed later in the narrative when Kincaid passionately asserts, "He was not meant to be silent . . . locked up inside him was someone who would have found satisfaction speaking to the world in an important way, . . . but he was not even remotely aware of such a person inside him" (59–60). In this single quotation Kincaid simultaneously expresses a seminal similarity and a subsequent estrangement from her brother. By simply writing this passage in which she declares her brother's incapacity, Kincaid realizes the potential that was the common bond between them. At the same time, with this performative act Kincaid draws the contrast between her and her brother more starkly; ironically she actively (re)produces his lack of productivity.

In fact, this binary model of fecundity versus sterility characterizes Kincaid and her brother respectively. Numerous times in the narrative her brother's sterility (and the decay it eventually engenders) is emphasized as his definitive characteristic. The book insinuates that sterility and decay are his essence: "Nothing came from him; not work, not children, not love for someone else" (13). Kincaid elaborates upon and more clearly defines her brother's sterility by sketching him against his father: "He cannot make a table, his father could make a table and a chair, and a house; his father was the father of many children. [He has] [t]his compulsion to express himself through his penis, his imagination passing between his legs, not through his hands" (70). Here Devon's lack of material productivity is directly associated with a more indicting and endemic sterility. Rather than using his penis for reproductive purposes—like his father—Kincaid's brother is seen as one who has "pissed his life away." His promiscuity has yielded nothing besides destruction. This persistent sentiment that runs throughout the text is solidified when Kincaid reports her brother's self-condemnatory remark: "My brother who was lying in the hospital dying . . . [said] that he had made worthlessness of his life ('Me mek wutlessness ah me life, man')" (29). By doubling this self-indictment, and calling attention to yet another weighty distinction between her brother and herself in allowing her brother's Antiguan dialect to surface in the text after she has reported his statement in her "unproblematic" American English, Kincaid lends subtle credence to the condemnatory judgment.

Because Kincaid's portrayal of Devon bears a stark resemblance to her similarly unflattering construction of his island-home, her censorious assessments often seem refracted through Devon onto Antigua it-self. At times Antigua and Kincaid's brother cease to exist as separate entities, but serve as two halves of a bifurcated symbol. As the reader is introduced to the island, themes of decay and sterility—so typically associated with Devon—pervade Kincaid's descriptions of the island. At one point she asserts that "in Antigua itself nothing is made" (24). Like her brother, Antigua's ills are incurable; the island is caught in an irredeemable decline. Antigua's hospital, for instance, seems symboli-cally coextensive with Devon. Rather than being a site of rejuvenation and healing, the quarters in which he is confined for the greater part of the narrative, take on his qualities of decay and sterility. Kincaid's use of selective detail in her description of the hospital highlight the dual themes that epitomize her brother. She provides a catalogue of dilapida-tion summed up with, "once he spilled the pan that contained his urine and so the floor had to be mopped up and it was done with undiluted Clorox" (22). Though a seemingly minor detail, after a long list of decay and filth, the "undiluted Clorox" creates what amounts to a sensory shock in the reader. The strong, obscenely clean smell of the chemical coexists with the odor of trash. Once again, an atmosphere of decay on the one hand, and sterility—the function of the Clorox—on the other pervades the text, and serves to characterize both Devon and the island that he represents in metaphor.

The significance of Devon's lack of productivity and the sense of bar-eness that weighs in the text can only be fully understood when viewed in light of the questions of sexual orientation that are put into circula-tion by the fact that Devon has AIDS. In the opening pages of the book, Kincaid, well aware of the speculation provoked by her brother's dis-ease, invites conjecture about the possibility of homosexuality while su-perficially precluding it (7). While raising the suspicion early in the narrative, Kincaid moves away from the topic of Devon's sexual orien-tation—often stressing his heterosexual exploits, in fact—until late in the book where she reveals his homosexual life. But meantime, as we've argued, Kincaid constructs a discourse and an atmosphere of decay and sterility around her brother: indeed, she constructs him as little more than this. Thus, when Kincaid finally introduces his alternative sexual-ity, it becomes a receptacle for all the negative symbolism that revolves around him. This is a disturbingly familiar progression, for homosexual-ity and homosexual practices, as they have been constructed in the West, are already the perfect category to receive these particular char-acterizations. While it is obvious that Kincaid hopes to achieve a certain rhetorical effect by withholding her brother's homosexuality for an extended period, she, for reasons we will subsequently examine, pens a self-indictment that is instructive in spite of the fact that it is not self-reflexive. Covertly, Kincaid's text employs the derogatory and stereotypical associations of homosexuality in order to achieve a unity of identity that her strong-willed subjectivity demands. As we will soon see, that drive for unity ironically and perhaps tragically and yet also, perhaps inevitably, reveals the colonial impulse in Kincaid's own subjectivity and, quite possibly, in subjectivity wherever it appears.

Lest one doubt that Kincaid's decision to withhold her brother's homosexual practices has the effect of invoking, in a surreptitious way, the negatively charged associations around homosexuality, we need simply consider the environment in which she chooses to finally reveal her brother's hidden identity. Kincaid, remembering a mid-winter trip to Chicago recalls a barren Lake Michigan: "the lake was frozen, all the water in it tightly squeezed together, all bound up into ice, and the ice was blue, not an inviting blue" (155). Although this description may be understood as the objective-correlative for Kincaid's emotional state following Devon's death, given the accumulation of desiccated and sterile imagery in which Kincaid binds her brother, one cannot avoid associating this frozen, dead landscape with him and his just-revealed homosexuality. The narrative moment in which Kincaid reveals her brother's ambiguous sexuality serves as nodal point for discourses of sterility, decay, and death that have run throughout the text.

By withholding this revelation until the memoir's closing pages Kincaid enacts for the reader her brother's "outing." In its very nature an "outing" presupposes all the negatively coded assumptions that circulate around homosexuality; when one comes "out" he or she is prepared to confront numerous degrading stereotypes. Until this point in the narrative Kincaid has steadily constructed her brother as a figure of lack. While she responds to this "new" information concerning her brother with liberal understanding, surprisingly, she immediately continues to link barren, dehydrated images to her dead—now homosexual—brother: "And his life unfolded before me not like a map just found, or piece of old paper just found, his life unfolded and there was everything to see and there was nothing to see; in his life there had been no flowering, his life was the opposite of that, a flowering, his life was like the bud that sets but, instead of opening into a flower, turns brown and falls off at your feet" (162–63). This vegetative imagery hearkens back to one of the memoir's central images. Confined to his hospital and supremely frustrated, Devon brandishes his penis before his sister. Kincaid's strikingly vivid description of the phallus turns it into the very symbol of his nonproductivity: "[A]nd then he grabbed his penis in his hand and held it up, and his penis looked like a bruised flower that had been cut short on the stem; it was covered with sores and on the sores was a white substance, almost creamy, almost floury, a fungus" (91). By concluding her extended simile by picturing his decaying penis covered with a corrupt and poisoned semenlike substance, Kincaid collapses the images of phallus, flower, decay, and sterility into one grand metaphor for her brother. The negative energies that have been building throughout the narrative are fully unleashed when Kincaid, once again, employs symbols of her brother's physical and spiritual degradation in the midst of "outing" him. And once these forces are let loose by Kincaid, the reader is forced into a reassessment of the entire memoir. Kincaid herself invites this rereading in the passage quoted above by depicting her brother's life as a type of readable text "unfolded" before her once she discovers his homosexuality.

In an attempt to consider the full implications of Kincaid's fascinated "unfolding" of Devon's life we now turn to a piece by theorist Lee Edelman. His essay, "Homographesis," suggests that in the cultural phenomenon of "outing" we learn reading practices that can be usefully applied to our analysis of *My Brother*.

Among other things, Edelman stresses that, even someone like Kincaid, who overtly adheres to progressive attitudes towards homosexuality, can remain unwittingly confined by and in the essentialist categories that underpin heterosexist ideology. Edelman's ideas, because complex but also instructive, bear quoting at length:

> Though pursuing radically different agendas, the gay advocate and the enforcer of homophobic norms both inflect the issue of gay legibility with a sense of painful urgency. . . . Practices such as "outing" . . . arise . . . in response to the fact that homosexuality remains, for most, illegible in the persons of the gay men and lesbians they encounter at work, in their families, in their governments, on television, or in film. Just as outing works to make visible a dimension of social reality effectively occluded by the assumptions of a heterosexist ideology, so that ideology, throughout the twentieth century, has insisted on the necessity of "reading" the body as a signifier of sexual orientation.[13]

Even though Kincaid endeavors to introduce her brother's homosexual practices in a neutral, nondefining way—hoping to present the reader with "not a single sense of identity but all the complexities of who he was" (162) — her text nevertheless demonstrates a "painful urgency" to mark him as primarily and exclusively as a homosexual. As we examined above, Kincaid's "outing" of her brother consolidates in his person the negatively charged symbols of sterility and decay that continually reappear in the text. The reductive and essentialized marking of Kincaid's brother as homosexual proves so powerful at his moment of textual "outing" because, throughout the narrative, the derogatory qualities that circulate around him are qualities that are so typically tied to homosexuality in the culture at large. This type of ideological marking finally involves, as Edelman suggests, "the necessity of 'reading' the body as signifier of sexual orientation"; this function is witnessed in the mapping of negatively/homosexually charged discourse onto Kincaid's brother's body, and especially his most provocative member.

Edelman takes for granted that this drive to make legible (thus essential) the homosexual is a function of ideological heterosexual identity construction. One might well imagine that Kincaid, an obviously strong-willed, self-dependent, and self-generating individual, has unwittingly activated this ideological dynamic in this memoir in order to stabilize her own subjectivity — a subjectivity obviously and permanently fractured, not only metaphysically speaking, but more specifically because of the creolized situation in which she finds herself. Indeed, the sterility and decay that pervades *My Brother* is equaled only by Kincaid's references and allusions to her "productive" life stateside, where she gives birth to texts and children alike. At this point one might conclude the analysis, chide Kincaid for employing hegemonic strategies that replicate the policies that inform the project of colonial conquest, and further accuse her of perpetuating oppressive stereotypes exclusively for the self-serving purposes of identity building. But even a cursory reading of the memoir proves that such a simplistic and reductive choice would not do the text justice. Rather, as was indicated earlier, the unleashing of dangerously ideological energies late in the text forces one to reassess the narrative as a whole.

Edelman also suggests that the emergence of "the homosexual" in a text needn't occlude further investigation. Instead, he says, once one becomes aware that "homosexuality" proper is a negative construction erected to stabilize "and confirm the logic of identity" (22) that rests on "the binary differentiation of sameness and differance, presence and absence" (14), one can utilize this awareness. Turning ideology on its head, Edelman explains that while it is true that after the Renaissance "homosexuality becomes socially constituted in ways that not only make it available to signification," it is equally true that one finds "also ceded to it [homosexuality] the power to signify the instability of the signifying function *per se*, the arbitrary and tenuous nature of the relationship between any signifier and signified" (6). Thus, Edelman's theory also provokes a reassessment of the memoir. Because homosexuality throws all signification into flux, Kincaid's belated "outing" of her brother necessitates a rereading of the major symbolic constructions in the text. Furthermore, Edelman's theory has particularly interesting implications for a reassessed understanding of the subjectivity Kincaid constructs for herself in the text. If we follow Edelman and let "homosexuality" deconstruct categories constructed against it, then obviously the quasi-imperial, seemingly stable and unitary identity that Kincaid, knowingly or unknowingly, fashions for herself fragments at the very moment it appears to most concretize itself.

At this point we've removed ourselves yet one more stage further from the "truth" and authorial intention that serves, in this essay, as the original point of analysis. The purpose and justification for doing this is not to show how Kincaid falls short as a writer, but rather, to illuminate the extent to which she represents the dynamic, fluid, and often contradictory self-construction of the postcolonial subject. While it remains troubling that she seems to activate homophobic stereotypes in order to effect her self-construction, perhaps this essay has called ample attention to this aspect of her text. The advantage gained in the task of uncovering an ideological bias in the text was to discover the possibility that, to the extent that a subject strives toward and succeeds in gaining self-presence and unity, that subject simultaneously produces its own dissolution. The principle benefits from such a discovery seem nearly self-evident. First, an analysis like the one above calls into question the utility of striving for what we might call a unified subjectivity. Second, and equally important, the essay uncovers some of the colonial impulses that come into play when this futile project is nevertheless pursued.

When one engages in the rereading of the memoir, which the narrative itself prompts, the colonial strategies that Kincaid employs in the construction of her subjectivity become apparent. The similarities between Kincaid and her imperial mother, which upon a first reading—if even recognized at all—seem merely incidental, take on new valences. Kincaid's reemergence in her brother's life initially appears motivated by only the most selfless intentions. But how similar are Kincaid's motivations to those of her mother who loves her children only when they are "weak and helpless" (16)? Kincaid imposes an emotional and geographic separation between herself and her brother that she only bridges once aware of his abject need. This obviously recapitulates the exclusively colonial love that she accuses her mother of imprisoning her children with. Kincaid's "reunification" with her brother, which in any other context would seem innocent enough, becomes charged with the same imperial implications that are associated with her mother's interaction with her children throughout the narrative. The extent to which Kincaid adopts the colonial habits of her mother becomes fully recognizable in her ability to secure needed medicine from the metropole. In one respect this is a charitable and caring act, yet this too is refracted through the lens of her mother. Even Kincaid herself is driven to say to the reader, "I had gotten myself into debt trying to save his life" (68). Circumstances dictate that she be the sacrificing redeemer, the metropolitan agent returning to the colony at great personal expense in the attempt to "set aright" troubles that have arisen since her departure. While Kincaid's relationship to Devon is no perfect allegory for the economics of neocolonial, international politics, it is not difficult to map a "righteous foreign aid" narrative onto the portrayal of the siblings' interactions in the memoir. Like her mother who only loves her children when they are "weak and helpless," Kincaid's expression of love for her brother comes when he is most needy, when he has no choice but to take what his sister will offer. This love ensures the dominion of its projector. It is a manifestation of inequality and is its abettor; it is colonial.

Our essay has looked at a model of identity building that is deeply infused with colonial impulses. Whether or not this is the only model of subjectivity available to any individual remains unclear. At one point Kincaid hints that it is: "Perhaps all love is self-serving" (16). The possibility that all subjectivity is constructed upon this imperialistic ground only illuminates the usefulness of the analysis above. It is perhaps ironic that we find this exemplary representation of the politics of identity making in a text written from a perspective that actively seeks to resist the dialectics of colonialism. That this dialectic becomes activated even here convincingly illustrates that the drive toward mastery, at once insidious and foundational, must be constantly destabilized by its continual uncovering.

NOTES

1. Alison Donnell, "She Ties Her Tongue: The Problems of Cultural Paralysis in Postcolonial Criticism," *ARIEL* 26 (1995): 101.

2. John Skow, review of *My Brother* by Jamaica Kincaid, *Time*, November 10, 1997, 108.

3. Donna Seaman, review of *My Brother* by Jamaica Kincaid, *Booklist*, September 1, 1997, 5.

4. Bruce Hainley, review of *My Brother* by Jamaica Kincaid, *Artforum* (November 1997): 27.

5. Robert Pela, review of *My Brother* by Jamaica Kincaid, *The Advocate* (December 9, 1997): 82.

6. Jamaica Kincaid, *My Brother* (New York: Farrar Straus Giroux, 1997), 24, 32.

7. Louise Bernard, "Countermemory and Return: Reclamation of the (Postmodern) Self in Jamaica Kincaid's *The Autobiography of My Mother* and *My Brother*," *Modern Fiction Studies* 48 (2002): 134.

8. Diane Simmons, "The Rhythm of Reality in the Works of Jamaica Kincaid," *World Literature Today* 68 (1994): 466.

9. H. Adlai Murdoch, "Severing the (M)Other Connection: The Representation of Cultural Identity in Jamaica Kincaid's *Annie John*," *Callaloo* 13 (1990): 340.

10. Jacques Derrida, *Monolingualism of the Other or The Prosthesis of Origin*, translated by Patrick Mensah (Stanford, CA: Stanford University Press, 1998), 39.

11. Diane Simmons, "Coming-of-Age in the Snare of History: Jamaica Kincaid's *The Autobiography of My Mother*," in *The Girl: Constructions of the Girl in Contemporary Fiction by Women*, ed. Ruth O. Saxton, 177 (New York: St. Martin's Press, 1998).

12. Moira Ferguson, *Jamaica Kincaid: Where the Land Meets the Body* (Charlottesville: University Press of Virginia, 1994), 164.

13. Lee Edelman, "Homographesis," in *Homographesis: Essays in Gay Literary and Cultural Theory* (New York: Routledge, 1994), 4.

"Great Plant Appropriators" and Acquisitive Gardeners: Jamaica Kincaid's Ambivalent Garden (Book)

JEANNE C. EWERT

JAMAICA KINCAID'S *MY GARDEN (BOOK):*, A COLLECTION OF GARDENING essays first published in *The New Yorker* and elsewhere, is likely to surprise a reader in the American pleasure gardening tradition who expects advice on color combinations, hardy plants for cold climates, or the best way to stake delphiniums. Taken together, the essays represent a passionate gardener at work in the perennial beds, discussing catalogues and favorite tools, but also a gardener who is impassioned by the history and politics of gardening, especially as these relate to her native Caribbean. On first reading, these chapters in *My Garden (Book):* seem to present a fairly straightforward, and often enraged, indictment of the colonial practices of appropriating, renaming, and relocating plants from their native countries to other parts of the world, and imposing European gardening standards on colonial territories. A closer look at Kincaid's garden in the intermediate chapters, however, reveals the degree to which Kincaid herself engages in the very practices she criticizes. Alison Donnell makes a similar observation about *A Small Place*, arguing that while on first reading it appears to be a simple tirade "against the colonial legacy and neo-colonial tourist industry," a second, more nuanced reading reveals an "astonishingly arrogant propensity to speak for others," which suggests the adoption of colonial discourse.[1] I would argue that Kincaid's garden and Kincaid's writing enact Homi K. Bhabha's theories of hybridity, and that the goal of *My Garden (Book):* is not to argue for an ethical responsibility on the part of gardeners (or anyone) to native species in their own space, but to insist instead on the priority of an irreducible alterity—Kincaid's own and her garden's.

BOTANY, GARDENING, CONQUEST

Kincaid is both impassioned by botany and ambivalent about botanists. Botanists, she explains in *My Garden (Book):*, are like Columbus. Linnaeus and his successors emptied the newly conquered "worlds of things animal, vegetable, and mineral of their names and replaced these names with names pleasing to them," often those of conquerors of the places where the plants were found.[2] Kincaid suspects that Linnaeus deliberately based his binomial system on exotic plants whose human neighbors had been enslaved. It would not have been easy, she notes, to introduce his system by overriding the local names of beloved European plants.

The history of colonial conquest is the history of plant theft and forced resettlement. Even in Kincaid's own Antigua, the British botanical garden contained no plants native to Antigua, but only those appropriated from other people's lands somewhere else. She remembers the bamboo grove in the botanical garden where she met with lovers, and the rubber tree from Malaysia under whose shade she and her father sat each afternoon the year they were both ill. The rubber tree is such a potent symbol of colonial appropriation, transplantation, and enslavement that Kincaid deploys it as early as the stories in *At the Bottom of the River*[3] and as recently as *Mr. Potter,*[4] a span of some twenty years of writing. On a recent trip to Jamaica, Kincaid visited the Kingston botanical garden, hoping to learn about native Caribbean plants, those she remembers her mother kept in the yard, but found instead roses and lupines, plants native to the temperate zones of Europe and Asia, in a place still adhering to the English cottage garden tradition (120).[5]

When the English were a colonial presence in the Caribbean, they had grass lawns, plumbago hedges, willow topiaries, rose gardens, and chrysanthemums—all native to regions outside of the Caribbean (133). In *Autobiography of My Mother*, Kincaid's protagonist, Xuela, describes the gardening practices of her husband, Philip, who is British and part of the colonial order in Dominica, where she lives. Philip, she observes, longs to re-create the English country gardens he remembers from his childhood, but reluctantly settles for the long-dead pressed petals in one of his books. "Pressed between the pages of this book were some specimens of flowers he had known and I suppose had loved, but flowers that could not grow in this Dominican climate; he would hold them up to the light and call out to me their names: peony, delphinium, foxglove, monkshood, and in his voice was at once the triumphant chord of the victor and the discordant melody of the dispossessed; for with this roll call of the herbaceous border (he had shown me a picture of such a thing, a mere grouping of some flowering plants) he would enter an almost etherlike induced trance and would recall everyday scenes from his childhood."[6] Philip clears his land of all native species and re-creates to the best of his ability the herbaceous border he remembers. Kincaid links this activity to other colonial practices when Xuela tells us that "he had an obsessive interest in rearranging the landscape: not gardening in the way of necessity, the growing of food, but gardening in the way of luxury, the growing of flowering plants for no other reason than the pleasure of it and making these plants do exactly what he wanted them to do; and it made great sense that he would be drawn to this activity, for it is an act of conquest, benign though it may be."[7] When Philip does take an interest in tropical plant species, he does so only to hybridize them, to force them to conform to standards not part of their normal growth: "he grew fruit from the various tropical regions of the world, only he forced them to become a size they were not normally; sometimes he made them grow larger, sometimes he made them mere miniatures."[8]

Merely dumbfounded by the English who re-created their cottage gardens with plants exotic to Antigua, Kincaid is outraged by another kind of botanical colonizing: the dismissal by modern Western authors of gardening methods and aesthetics of other cultures. She cites William Warren's *The Tropical Garden*, signaling up front its lack of botanical seriousness, its status as a mere coffee table book, by pointing out that the type is "as big as a doll's teacup." She does not, she notes, even need to "read" the print; it is so large she can simply look at it (140). In *The Tropical Garden* Warren contends that people from tropical countries pay no attention to "attractive landscape design" and that "there was no such tradition of ornamental horticulture among the inhabitants of most hot weather places." To support this claim, he asserts that "a reader will search in vain" in the early accounts by travelers in the tropics for one "praising the tasteful arrangement of massed ornamental beds and contrasting lawns of well-trimmed grass around the homes of the natives."[9]

The fatuousness of supposing that all cultures must share standards for ornamental horticulture handed down from the British tradition of landed nobility (the sheep-grazed meadow/lawn), and middle to upper-class British gardening enthusiasts (the herbaceous bed/border), is obvious. *The Tropical Garden*, published in 1991, praises colonial landowners who created British-style gardens in their new empires. Kincaid counters with the narratives of Hernando Cortez in Mexico, who was astounded by "floating gardens of flowers and vegetables" and the extensive gardens of fragrant shrubs and flowers and medicinal plants. She observes angrily that after a generation or two of heavy field labor, the enslaved inhabitants of the places cited by *The Tropical Garden* might well forget how to grow plants simply for pleasure. *The Tropical Garden* itself offers ample evidence of this: it celebrates several European-established tropical botanical gardens for introducing labor-intensive crops like rubber and sugar cane that "enriched" their new host country, without mentioning that the "enrichment" went home to the colonial overlords.[10] Warren also applauds the usefulness of low-cost manual labor in colonial and former colonial gardening: a photograph of the beautiful lawns of Bombay's Gymkhana Club shows barefoot Indian men dragging heavy machinery under a blinding sun, rolling the club's grass.[11]

ON THE OTHER HAND

While the evidence for colonial abuse and enslavement of both plants and native gardeners that Kincaid marshals is incontestable, when she describes her own garden the reader is forced to question the motives behind her outrage. Kincaid's passion for plants is clearly sincere: when a visiting landscape architect recommends that she clear away all the evergreens around her house, she is outraged and goes around apologizing to them for the suggestion. Yet, Kincaid's garden in Bennington contains as many hostages as the British botanical garden in Antigua and very few plants native to Vermont. Its treasures include, we deduce over the course of the essays, a banana tree, a collection of dahlias, a buddleia, two clematis, agapanthus, and two rhododendrons, among many other plants. Kincaid does not foreground the provenance of her plants, but the reader who gardens will know that banana trees come from central America (Kincaid's variety is named after Lord Cavendish, whose family owned colonial property in Bermuda and who was a famous plant collector in his own right); dahlias are from Mexico, and are named after Sweden's Andreas Dahl, who collected and hybridized them; the buddleia is from China; the two clematis are of Himalayan origin, and their seeds were collected by a botanist Kincaid knows personally, and which she values because no one else she knows grows them; the agapanthus is from South Africa and was hybridized by Eric

Smith, another of the great botanical marauders (23); the two rhododendrons are from New Guinea (their demise will provide Kincaid with
a metaphor for her brother's death from AIDS).[12] In a nice case of stealing from the colonizers instead of the colonies, she cherishes her *Scabi-
osa ochroleuca*, from southern Europe (28). She confesses that she only
likes to grow exotic vegetables eaten by people in distant places, and
so her vegetable garden contains French *marmande* tomatoes, Turkish
cucumbers, and Russian fingerling potatoes.

Botanists, Kincaid observes with irony in her conclusion to one of *My
Garden (Book):*'s extended meditations on plant appropriation, do not
die in their own beds: David Douglas fell down a bull pit in Hawaii,
meant to entrap another kind of marauder; Reginald Ferrer died of
diphtheria in Burma.[13] After compiling the list of botanists killed in action, she notes, dryly, "I shall die in a nursery" (187). Of course, the
nurseries of Bennington, Vermont have benefited from the labors of
botanists who have gone abroad and brought back exotic specimens.
And so while Kincaid signals the ironic appropriateness of their deaths,
conquered by the very flora and fauna they had meant to kidnap, she
points also to her complicity in their actions. She is part of modern gardening's customer base, clamoring for new, different, exotic plants to
grow in their own gardens.

Kincaid has, moreover, joined the class of botanical explorers and
conquerors in a more direct way. She relates in *My Garden (Book):* stories of stealing hollyhock seeds from a public garden in the Ukraine.
"This makes sense," she says, because "the seeds of hollyhocks are very
easy to steal" (83). She does not mention that public gardens usually
collect the seeds of their own plants, especially annuals and biennials
(like hollyhocks), to save the costs of repurchasing seeds. She describes
a visit to the Chelsea flower show, where she discovers a beautiful *Verbascum* hybrid, which can't be propagated by seed but only by cuttings
(and therefore would not be easy to either steal or bring back to the
United States in her luggage). For days thereafter, Kincaid "[tramps]
around the great gardens of England plotting ways to smuggle it back"
(103). She understands perfectly the reasons for import restrictions on
agricultural products (while she is at the flower show she reads an article about an accidentally imported mite that has largely destroyed England's honeybee population), but merely wonders if the lust for a
particular plant justifies the risk. Her question implies that, had she
been able to find a way to do it, she might have justified this cost in
order to have the *Verbascum* "Helen Johnson." There is a wild verbas-

cum—with only slightly different bloom color—growing near her house in Vermont, but the appeal for her of the forbidden hybrid is its novelty, and her chance to avoid having to wait several years for nursery growers in the United States to make the plant available there. (*Verbascum* 'Helen Johnson' is widely available in the United States today.)

My Garden (Book): includes several such accounts of trips abroad in the interest of plant acquisitions. The longest of these is the story of a trip to China in the company of professional botanists.[14] Not precisely a tourist in China, and yet there not to appreciate or understand local culture, Kincaid's behavior, which she details with remarkable frankness, is very little different from that of the tourists she criticizes in *A Small Place*, her exposé of the modern exploitation of Antigua. Her journey to China is prompted by travel narratives of the great plant hunters Frank Kingdon-Ward, Ernest Wilson, and Reginald Farrer; and by nursery catalogues celebrating new plant finds from abroad (190). Moments in *A Small Place* describing the appalling assumptions of rich American tourists about the lives of the people who inhabit the Caribbean, are repeated in her own travel narrative. Ahead of her, she writes, "was an unknown landscape (unknown except for those books and people who wrote them) of mountains and valleys and meadows full of plants (in seed) that I would like to grow in my garden" (191). This formulation obviously excludes the local Chinese, to whom the mountains, valleys, and meadows full of plants are presumably well known, and from whom these much-desired seeds will be taken without consultation or consent. During her trip, Kincaid collects plants familiar to every American gardener, thanks to the efforts of colonial botanists: *Viburnum*, astilbe, roses, impatiens, dogwoods, *Clematis*, aconitum.

Enamored of a Chinese landscape she has long imagined, Kincaid frequently recoils from the Chinese people. Early in the trip she observes in a restaurant a family group who cause her to be homesick, recalling her own family back in Vermont. "I wanted to join them," she says, "but the baby of the family was having a bowel movement on the floor right then; it was all very comfortable for them, but I had come to China to collect seeds, not to be comfortable with what Chinese people did" (192). Her discomfort seems consonant with that of the hypothetical tourist she assaults in *A Small Place*: "And you look at the things they can do with a piece of ordinary cloth, the things they fashion out of cheap, vulgarly colored (to you) twine, the way they squat down over a hole they have made in the ground, the hole itself is something to marvel at, and since you are being an ugly person this ugly but joyful thought will swell inside you: their ancestors were not clever in the way yours were, for then would it not be you who would be in harmony with nature and backwards in that charming way?[15]

Kincaid's unease with Chinese sanitation practices increases until, near the end of the trip, she harangues her Chinese guide with the accusation that the hotel is the filthiest she has ever seen, not realizing that she thus embarrasses him in his own home town. Kincaid describes this behavior as "a nervous breakdown": "this is how I characterize my monumentally rude and truly insulting behavior—a temporary lapse in sanity" (200). She has never suggested that American tourists in Antigua, like her exposed to a culture and living conditions much different than their own, might also suffer from brief lapses in sanity.

Back in Vermont, Kincaid turns from botanical conquest to botanical resettlement. Her eclectic garden of flowering plants from all over the world, grouped together by color (and not, for example, provenance), has now to be protected from other marauders—the Vermont natives, the indigenous fauna that would prey on their tender shoots. Watching rabbits in her garden, she expresses a wish to be a large animal that would kill the rabbits: "The joy I would get from the snap-snap of their little necks breaking in midair would be immeasurable" (172). I suspect that some readers would echo the words of Kincaid's daughter, who, when told of this fantasy, says, "Geez, Mom, that's really mean" (172). A page later Kincaid describes a snake she sees on the stone wall of her garden and remarks, "I am afraid of snakes, and so have the impulse to kill them all immediately" (173). She refrains, remembering that snakes are useful in the garden, as they eat herbivorous animals and insects. It seems not to occur to Kincaid that, by clearing broad swathes of her property in order to plant an elaborate garden, she has driven native animals to forage among her flowers, rather than among the species that used to grow there.

She does seem to recognize a colonial impulse behind her actions when she remarks early in the book, on seeing a fox emerge from the woodland behind her house: "It is *my* woodland, for I carved it out of the chaos of wood and bramble and made it up so that it seemed like the chaos of the wood and bramble but carefully, willfully, eliminating the parts of a wood and bramble that do not please me, which is to say a part of wood and bramble that I do not yet understand" (17). But she does not delay to decide the fate of the "unpleasing" parts of the woodland until such a time as she might understand (and be pleased by) these native species.

In her repetition, from the subject position of the oppressor, of the behavior she abhorred when she was among the conquered classes, Kincaid exemplifies Paulo Freire's "adhesion" principle, in which "at a certain point in their existential experience the oppressed feel an irresistible attraction towards the oppressor and his way of life. Sharing this way of life becomes an overpowering aspiration. In their oppression, the oppressed want at any cost to resemble the oppressor, to imitate him, to follow him."[16] This occurs, according to Freire, because the oppressed have been so conditioned by the "concrete, existential situation by which they were shaped. Their ideal is to be men, but for them, to be men is to be oppressors. That is their model of humanity."[17] It does not take much of a stretch of the imagination to see in Kincaid's ruthless dominance of her yard a repetition of colonial rule in the Caribbean and elsewhere. Her activities in her garden plainly echo those of Philip in *The Autobiography of My Mother*: "He cleared the land; nothing growing on it inspired any interest in him. The inflorescence of this, he said, was not significant; and the word 'inflorescence' was said with an authority, as if he had created inflorescence itself, which made me laugh with such pleasure I lost consciousness for a moment of my own existence."[18] Kincaid mocks Philip for his domineering relationship to the garden, but like him, she is a colonial conqueror. She moves in and tries to implant an order not naturally occurring in Vermont. She imposes this on the native flora and fauna, killing some in the process and starving others. She threatens destruction to those natives who interfere with her new dominion and abides only those who may be put to useful labor there. And she willfully fails to comprehend the prior state of her newly ordered territories. This is clear in the repeated refrain of the first chapter of *My Garden (Book)*:, "What to do?" What to do when the wisteria bloom out of season or not at all? What to do when a fox appears in the garden? What to do when the woodpecker pecks at the house itself? Perhaps the wisteria are not at home in Vermont. Perhaps the fox *is* at home there. The woodpecker, at any rate, is not at home anywhere; it is poisoned by insecticide meant to kill the insects eating the house.

"What is the relationship between gardening and conquest?" Kincaid asks. "Is the conqueror a gardener and the conquered the person who works in the field?" (116). In other words, is the conqueror the one who has the luxury of owning the field and deciding what will grow in it and glorying in the tangible results and sending abroad for new and exciting crops or perhaps (great luxury indeed) going abroad to collect them herself? "I have joined the conquering class," she concedes (123). And it very likely appears that way to her readers, as well.

In defense of her own plant resettlement activities, however, Kincaid offers a somewhat problematic distinction between botanists and gardeners. On the one side are the "great plant appropriators," the scientists who dispassionately collect and label plants; on the other are the gardeners, who love, live among, and design with them. Yet her narrative straddles a difficult divide, glorying in her own plant acquisitions while confessing her botanical proclivities, suggesting her uneasiness with finding herself partially among the botanical conquerors.

Near the end of *My Garden (Book):* Kincaid relates how she saw a cotton plant in bloom in Kew Gardens under a glass house, reflecting that she'd never seen it in flower before; the flowers are similar (because related) to her favorite hollyhocks. As a child in the Caribbean she had been forced to pick cotton on her summer holidays, and so the connections between field work, conquest, plant appropriation, and her own garden are in her mind as she admires the plant's blossoms. Yet she says, "I do not mind the glasshouse. I do not mind the botanical garden. This is not so grand a gesture on my part, it is mostly an admission of defeat: to mind would be completely futile, I cannot do anything about it anyway" (151). This seems a doubtful assertion. There are many things gardeners can do about it, including planting and protecting species native to the area in which they live, learning local plant nomenclature, refusing the forced resettlement of plants from exotic locations. These practices have been carefully laid out in widely available garden literature by, for example, Sara Stein (*Noah's Garden*) and Michael Pollan (*Second Nature*). But Kincaid seems oblivious of this important strand of American garden writing. She goes on to say, "I only mind the absence of this admission, this contradiction: perhaps every good thing that stands before us comes at a great cost to someone else" (152).

In an interview with Marilyn Snell, Kincaid argues that it is best always to know at what cost your pleasures come: "The garden has a peculiar side to it, a qualifying side. For instance, most of the nations that have serious gardening cultures also have, or had, empires. You can't have this luxury of pleasure without somebody paying for it. This is nice to know. It's nice to know that when you sit down to enjoy a plate of strawberries, somebody got paid very little so that you could have your strawberries. It doesn't mean the strawberries will taste different, but it's nice to enjoy things less than we do. We enjoy things far

too much, and it leads to incredible pain and suffering."[19] Here then, is
a reason for the disarming honesty of the book, for the admission that
the plants she kills to make room for imported species are "a part of
wood and bramble that I do not yet understand." Here is also a reason
for the admission that her behavior in China is that of the ugly tourist
and the admission that she will steal seeds and smuggle plants despite
the potentially catastrophic consequences.

ALTERITY AND HYBRIDITY IN THE GARDEN

And yet, however untroubled Kincaid may be by these open contradictions, she is also sure of her right to acquire any plant she craves,
and one suspects that her project, in the garden and the book, is not to
evangelize for "nativeness" in any way. She seems, in fact, quite unaware of several decades of writings by modern native plant theorists
and students of disturbed ecosystems. The garden books she says she
reads are those of designers and travelers and nursery people. The tirade against the Kingston Botanical Garden for having no native plants
seems to be the result of her frustration at not being able to identify the
plants she grew up with because they were not available or labeled, and
from her hostility toward the imposition of a British garden aesthetic
on her childhood Antigua.

My own reading of her ambivalence is that the goal of *My Garden
(Book):* is not to argue for an ethical responsibility on the part of gardeners (or anyone) to native species, but to insist on the priority of an
irreducible, if internalized alterity—her own and her garden's. This is
suggested by the design of her Vermont gardens, always laid out in a
series of apparently random and bizarrely shaped island beds and
crowded with bright flowering plants. At some point, trying to explain
these patterns to a visiting gardener, and recognizing that her flower
beds don't conform to any recognized garden aesthetic, Kincaid realizes
that her yard reproduces the outlines of the Caribbean islands and the
surrounding sea (7). "The garden is for me an exercise in memory," she
says, and the memory is of the place where she once belonged. In *My
Garden (Book):* and in the forms of Kincaid's garden, this ambivalence
extends also to other places where she doesn't belong: China, with its
unsanitary customs; Vermont with its frigid and unwelcome winters;
England, "the old suitcase." Nor is she even "native" to the Caribbean,
where she once felt she belonged; she reiterates that her ancestors were

brought there on slave ships. Of the rubber tree in Antigua's British botanical garden she says, "it was a curiosity" at first, but that "eventually we accepted its presence in our midst, even as we accepted our own presence in our midst, for we, too, were not native to the place we were in" (145).

Kincaid's garden thus literally embodies Homi K. Bhabha's "unhomeliness" of the de-territorialized subject: ". . . the estranging sense of the relocation of the home and the world—the unhomeliness—that is the condition of extra-territorial and cross-cultural initiations."[20] Kincaid's plants are estranged from their homelands, like the rubber tree she so empathizes with as a child. It is perhaps for this reason that this little book on gardening contains a long chapter on the previous owner of Kincaid's house, the man who built it and to whom it was home. After one of this man's children calls to see if Kincaid can find a recipe, which perhaps fell behind a cupboard, Kincaid wishes wistfully that this Robert Woodworth "had given us a recipe for how to make a house a home, a home being a place in which the mystical way of maneuvering through the world in an ethical way . . . must be considered with the utmost seriousness" (48). Ordered by spatial schemes and according to aesthetic priorities bearing little relation to their origins, Kincaid's plants represent her unhomeliness to herself and to others. Her most recent book, *Among Flowers*, a travelogue of a seed-gathering trip to the Himalaya, several times reiterates this theme. The purpose for the trip and the book, she tells the reader, has its origins "in my love of the garden, my childhood love of botany and geography, my love of feeling isolated, of imagining myself all alone in the world and everything unfamiliar, or the familiar being strange."[21]

They represent her in another way, also, which Bhabha has theorized in his analysis of postcolonial subjectivity. The concept of hybridity, especially apt here as it originated in the world of horticulture, is useful for framing the conflicts Kincaid enacts in her garden. "Terms of cultural engagement, whether antagonistic or affiliative," says Bhabha, "are produced performatively. The representation of difference must not be hastily read as the reflection of pre-given ethnic or cultural traits set in the fixed tablet of tradition. The social articulation of difference, from the minority perspective, is a complex, on-going negotiation that seeks to authorize cultural hybridities that emerge in moments of historical transformation."[22] The moments of historical transformation relevant to Kincaid's garden begin with the kidnapping of her ancestors from Africa and the transplantation of cotton and sugar cane plants from their native territories to the Caribbean. They extend to the long British colonial presence in Antigua, to Kincaid's mother's rejection of her daughter and that daughter's subsequent transplantation to North America to work as a nanny. They conclude with that daughter's self-transformation into a writer, and her economic empowerment which allows for the luxury of a garden space in which to enact her alterity.

Hybridity, Bhabha points out, is "not a problem of genealogy or identity between two different cultures which can then be resolved as an issue of cultural relativism."[23] The ambivalences inscribed in Kincaid's garden cannot be resolved because she herself is both colonizer and colonized, because she exists in a liminal space, a hybrid space, in which cultural (and horticultural) difference "reverses the effects of the colonialist disavowal, so that other 'denied' knowledges enter upon the dominant discourse and estrange the basis of its authority."[24] It is this ambivalence that Barbara Edlmair, analyzing Kincaid's ambiguous relationship to Antigua after being absent since 1966 (Kincaid shifts between first and third person plural in *A Small Place*, from "we" to "they"), demonstrates in *Rewriting History*:

> While this intermediate status, combining both the insider's and the outsider's perspectives, does not disqualify her as a commentator on Antiguan history, it is nevertheless interesting that the ambiguity of her position is never problematized in the text. Indeed, Kincaid has been accused of deserting her birthplace and criticizing it from the safe distance of the affluent United States, a country with clear political and economic interests in Antigua. Thus, there is an ambivalence present in the text concerning the voice of the narrator in *A Small Place*: on the one hand, this voice seems to claim an arrogant and absolute authority, adopting the colonialist discourse and pretending to be able to judge everyone mentioned in the text; on the other hand, there is an "indeterminacy of meaning, crucially linked to the undecidability about where this voice is speaking from, and for whom."[25]

Bhabha argues in a hopeful mode for the subversive power of hybridity. "If the effect of colonial power is seen to be the production of hybridization rather than the noisy command of colonialist authority or the silent repression of native traditions," he proposes, "then an important change of perspective occurs." That change of perspective involves a fundamental ambivalence of discourses on authority, produced by the influences of hybridity, and "enables a form of subversion, founded on the undecidability that turns the discursive conditions of dominance into the grounds of intervention."[26] Kincaid's hybrid garden writing leaves perhaps less room for political optimism, offering up the anger of the colonized but acting the part of the colonizer, representing the acuity of her liminal position without proposing a solution.

Kincaid's Vermont gardens are about difference, about standing out vibrantly against the native flora and fauna (the banana tree growing in Bennington in winter is exemplary of her transplanted presence there). Her passionate acts of collection and appropriation have assembled a fantastic array of exotic flowering plants: all of them, like her, out of place, and without a means of return to the lost regions from which they came. She does not regret this act of appropriation, because their purpose in her garden is to stand in for her—to represent her alterity, to be without a place, as she is. They represent also a hybrid space—the space where the voice of the colonized inside herself speaks in the tones of the colonizer.

NOTES

I am grateful to Anne Goodwyn Jones for her perspicacious suggestions and unflagging support as I revised this essay during an NEH seminar in the summer of 2002. Linda Lang-Peralta has been a sensitive and intelligent editor and Abby Palko provided invaluable advice and a great deal of insight. As always, Terry Harpold has been both my sternest and kindest reader.

1. Alison Donnell, "She Ties Her Tongue: The Problems of Cultural Paralysis in Postcolonial Criticism," in *Jamaica Kincaid: Modern Critical Views*, ed. Harold Bloom, 42–43. (Philadelphia: Chelsea House, 1998).

2. Jamaica Kincaid, *My Garden (Book):* (New York: Farrar Straus Giroux, 2001), 160. All subsequent references will be to this edition.

3. Jamaica Kincaid, *At the Bottom of the River* (New York: Farrar Straus Giroux, 1983), 10.

4. Jamaica Kincaid, *Mr. Potter* (New York: Farrar Straus Giroux, 2002), 156.

5. For a thorough and useful overview of colonial gardening and plantation practices in the Caribbean, see Helen Tiffin's "Replanted in this Arboreal Place," in *English Literatures in International Contexts*, ed. Heinz Antor and Klaus Stierstorfer (Heidelberg: C. Winter, 2000).

6. Jamaica Kincaid, *The Autobiography of My Mother* (New York: Plume/Penguin, 1997), 144.

7. Ibid., 143.

8. Ibid., 209.

9. William Warren, *The Tropical Garden* (London: Thames and Hudson, 1991), 14.

10. Ibid., 37.

11. Ibid., 62. See also Tiffin, 149.

12. Jamaica Kincaid, *My Brother* (New York: Farrar Straus Giroux, 1997), 177. The metaphor of the unproductive plant ("in his life there had been no flowering, his life

was the opposite of that, a flowering, his life was like the bud that sets but, instead of opening into a flower, turns brown and falls off at your feet") is deployed to contrast Kincaid's own fruitful, productive life to her brother's (162–63; see also 167). When Kincaid first learns of her brother's illness, and as she sits with him in the hospital, she is reading Russell Page's *The Education of a Gardener* (London: William Collins, 1962), a sort of bildungsroman of the landscape architect. Her brother's life, as told by Kincaid, is an antibildungsroman: there is no flowering, no productivity, and an early death.

13. Kincaid actually says Douglas died in a bear pit, but it was a trap for wild cattle (he was, in fact, gored by a bull who fell into the pit after him). Yet another victim of the animal trap was Robert Fortune, who narrowly survived a fall into a boar pit in China and who mentioned in his journal that he thought the whole time of Douglas. On the list of botanical marauders who perished in action she might also have mentioned Philibert Commerson who died of dysentery in Mauritius; Francis Masson who froze to death in Canada; and Joseph Dombey who died in a British prison on Montserrat, accused of being a French spy.

14. Sarah Casteel suggests that Kincaid's description of this trip to China constitutes a parody of the classic botanical conquest narrative. This interesting possibility would be predicated on Kincaid's seeing her own gardening activities ironically, and there is some evidence that she does, but, as Casteel also notes, *My Garden (Book):* is ambivalently, incompletely ironic. Kincaid frequently takes her plant conquests very, very seriously. Sarah Phillips Casteel,"Rethinking Roots in Jamaica Kincaid's Garden Writing" (lecture, American Comparative Literature Association Convention, San Juan, Puerto Rico, 2002).

15. Jamaica Kincaid, *A Small Place* (New York: Farrar Straus Giroux, 1988), 16–17.

16. Paulo Freire, *Pedagogy of the Oppressed* (New York: Continuum, 1989), 49.

17. Ibid., 30.

18. Kincaid, *The Autobiography*, 222.

19. Marilyn Snell, "Jamaica Kincaid Hates Happy Endings: Interview with Jamaica Kincaid," *Mother Jones* (September/October 1997), <http://www.motherjones.com/mother_jones/SO97/snell.html>

20. Jamaica Kincaid, *Among Flowers* (Washington, DC: National Geographic, 2005), 7.

21. Homi K. Bhabha, *The Location of Culture*. (London: Routledge, 1994), 9.

22. Ibid., 2.

23. Ibid., 114.

24. Ibid.

25. Barbara Edlmair, *Rewriting History: Alternative Versions of the Caribbean Past in Michelle Cliff, Rosario Ferré, Jamaica Kincaid and Daniel Maximin* (Vienna: Braumüller 1999), 79–80. Edlmair is quoting Donnell, 42–43. See also Antonia MacDonald-Smythe, *Making Homes in the West/Indies: Constructions of Subjectivity in the Writings of Michelle Cliff and Jamaica Kincaid* (New York: Garland, 2001), 145–56 for a valuable discussion of Kincaid's position as both native and tourist in *A Small Place*.

26. Bhabha, 112.

"Another line was born . . .":
Genesis, Genealogy, and Genre in
Jamaica Kincaid's *Mr. Potter*

JANA EVANS BRAZIEL

> *In the beginning, God created the heavens and the earth, and the earth was formless and void, and darkness was over the surface of the deep, and the spirit of God was moving over the surface of the waters. Then God said, Let there be light and there was light and God saw that the light was good. And God separated the light from the darkness. And God called the light day and the darkness he called night.*
>
> —Genesis 1:1–5[1]

> *. . . and this [her absence] was followed by a large blank space of darkness and light, sometimes separated, the darkness and light, sometimes mingling, the darkness and the light, and this single blank space of only darkness and light—separated or commingled—was where Elfrida Robinson, his mother, stayed.*
>
> —*Mr. Potter*[2]

JAMAICA KINCAID'S *MR. POTTER* IS THE AUTHOR'S MOST RECENT FORAY into the complex and challenging terrain of autofiction (a hybrid genre intermingling fiction and autobiography); or more precisely, *alterbiography*, a textual rending of autobiography through the inscriptions of alterity and difference. The novel is subtle, nuanced, lyrical, passionate, and literary. For those who know Kincaid's work well and are committed to the ardor that reading her texts demands, it is not only an immensely rewarding read, but a new and unexpected episode in a literary drama that continues to unfold with breathtaking poetry and philosophical brilliance. *Mr. Potter* recounts the simple, sparse life of a chauffeur (who first works for an exiled Lebanese merchant and later for himself) on the island of Antigua, the place of Kincaid's own birth. The story reveals the daily events of Mr. Potter's life: his affairs and the numerous daughters (who all share his nose) that he fathered, but for whom he

127

never provided and certainly never loved; his illiteracy; and his humble attempts to make a life for himself, if not for his children. The novel is not just a biography of this man (who could not read or write), but also the autobiographical reflections of his daughter (the one who could read and write): Elaine Cynthia Potter. In the novel, Kincaid movingly tells of Mr. Potter's abandonment and rejection of the young girl (born on May 25, 1949), after her own mother, Annie Victoria Richardson (then Drew), seven months pregnant at the time, left with his money that had been saved and hidden under the mattress and with which he intended to buy a car. Through his story, we discover that he too has suffered loss and abandonment: his father, Nathaniel Potter, refused to acknowledge paternity of the boy Roderick, and his mother, Elfrida Robinson, walked into the sea one day when he was just a small child, never to return. The book is a painful account of loss and desire, and it memorializes the pain itself as much as the man who suffered it, the man who in his own turn passed this line of disinheritance to his daughters, the legatees of his illegitimacy, anonymity, and illiteracy, save one: the author of his life.

Mr. Potter is a postcolonial, postmodernist creation myth — postmodern in its sensibilities (language constructs transitory truths), yet modern in its historical crises (the past haunts not only the fleeting moments of the present but also of the future). In the novel, Kincaid engages her paternal genealogy, breathing life into anonymous ancestors and in-name-only fathers, without eclipsing maternal obsessions, which always recur in Kincaid's writing of worlds. Genealogy, in the novel *Mr. Potter*, becomes the foundation for genre, as it does in Kincaid's *The Autobiography of My Mother*; genealogy inflects genre and the writing of genre; in this sense, genealogy is inseparable from genre. The inflections of genre imbue other historical and mythological relations — those of genesis and genocide, creation and annihilation. Kincaid weaves and knots the entangled threads of genre, genealogy, genesis, and genocide. For Kincaid, this knot is woven and unwoven, tangled and untangled in the genres of biography and autobiography — a Gordian knot not exclusively of mother, father, me; but more vastly, of lineage, language, history, and subjectivity. Throughout the text, a preoccupation and engagement with Genesis informs the narrative subtext, forms the backdrop for this humble narrative about a simple, if not always honorable Antiguan man; yet genesis is also absolutely crucial to Kincaid's philosophical framing of the novel.

This paper proposes an inquiry into a phenomenon that I define as

"*Caribbean Genesis*,"[3] reading Glissant's theoretical writings in *Caribbean Discourse*[4] alongside Kincaid's engagements with genesis in *Mr. Potter*. In this paper, I have several interrelated objectives: First, I situate Kincaid's preoccupation with genesis as myth and as a response to history. I outline what Glissant identifies as a Caribbean "quarrel with history," discussing how Kincaid's engagements with genesis are intimately related to this "quarrel."[5] Then, I examine genre and the writing of genre in relation to genesis—particularly as it relates to biography and autobiography, and more specifically in relation to the writing of biography *as* autobiography. Probing Kincaid's aesthetic and philosophical play on genesis (and genocide) in the novel, I ask how these forces shape her writing of auto/biography. And finally, I analyze the presence and import of Kincaid's biographical autograph in the novel *Mr. Potter*.

GENESIS, "IN THE BEGINNING WAS THE WORD . . ."
(AS LIGHT TO DARKNESS)

"In the beginning . . ."

—Genesis 1:1

"In the beginning was the Word . . ."

—John 1:10[6]

"And to start again *at the beginning*"

—*Mr. Potter*[7]

"In the beginning"—so begins the book of Genesis and so begins a world. The words reverberate across centuries and new myths of creation, history, and time, echoed *anno Domini* in the Gospel of John, "In the beginning was the Word." The creation of worlds in words for a new age. For Jamaica Kincaid, writing in the twenty-first century of the third post-Christian millennium, words and worlds remain imbued with creative power, if only transitorily, and the author as creator takes up her pen to write new lives and new worlds into being. In *Mr. Potter*, a novel that swirls around creations, Kincaid reiterates these biblical beginnings, but forces creation and creativity to her will, wielding her pen to confront history and so-called divine orders (the fatal European belief in the "Great Chain of Being"). "And to start again *at the beginning*" (188) telling and writing (and *creating*) Mr. Potter and his story, if not history (or, *History with a capital H*), Kincaid laments, and yet embraces the fact that "Mr. Potter was *not an original man, he was not made from words*, his father was Nathaniel and his mother was Elfrida and neither of them could read or write; his beginning was just the way of everyone, as would be his end. He began in a long day and a long night and after nine months he was born . . ." (55–56). Kincaid's portrait of Roderick Nathaniel Potter renders him an ordinary man, not original; a real flesh-and-blood—or as she later states it, "tissue, bones, and blood" (62)—man. Kincaid makes the man, her father, in words, and yet she claims here, *"he was not made from words"* (56; emphasis added). Working within, but also against *Logos* (both the principle of order in Greek thought, as well as divine word and its incarnation in biblical terms), Kincaid creates a portrait of her father. Here Kincaid's tracing of genealogy evokes the begotten sons of biblical fathers; in Kincaid's cosmogony, they are begotten and forgotten sons, or more accurately, disinherited daughters. The passage is ambivalent; its movement twofold; its effect double—as Kincaid first renders her father humble and material, and then, second, creates his image *in language* even as she renounces the idea of transcendent ideas. Does Kincaid's portrait of Mr. Potter evoke divine creation even as she renounces that possibility? Does Kincaid's novel *Mr. Potter* mark a return to or a *revenant* of mythic beginnings? or contrarily, a creative writing away of all possibilities for divine creation, for definitive origins? In Kincaid's engagements with genesis, she joins a Caribbean "quarrel with history" that is above all a preoccupation with genesis (origins, creation, filiation), even through its disavowal or a Caribbean turning away from the possibility of creative beginnings. In this sense, Kincaid joins other Caribbean writers such as Derek Walcott and Édouard Glissant in their poetic revisions of genesis, creation, and myth.[8] Glissant returns again and again to notions of genesis in his pioneering work on Caribbean aesthetics, *Caribbean Discourse*, not to locate an origin and point of beginning, but as a way of recreating past in present and future, even without origins. So with Kincaid and her engagements with genesis.

Genesis: as narrator, writer, daughter, Kincaid writes worlds into being and fills her worlds with mythic characters. A Potter descended from a long line of potters—she is the demiurge creating and destroying worlds at will: in the text, she is divine and diabolic, godlike and fallen, moving across spheres celestial, earthly, and infernal that she has created in words. Traversing genres, Kincaid's *mythos* is at once epic and tragic, narrating the trajectories of modern diasporas (African, Lebanese, Czechoslovakian, Dominican, and finally, Antiguan) through the biographical and textual lives of Nathaniel Potter, Elfrida Robinson, Mr. Shoul, Dr. Samuel "Zoltan" Weizenger, his nurse and wife Mae Weizenger, Roderick Nathaniel Potter, Annie Victoria Richardson, and their biological daughter Elaine Cynthia Potter (Richardson). It narrates the epic movements of modernity and the cultural clashes that created a "New World"—so-called discovery, conquest, colonialism, indigenous subjugation, forced migration in the Middle Passage and then forced labor on the British Caribbean's sugar cane plantations, the Second Middle Passage and Asian indenture. The stories are both intimate and abstract: Roderick Nathaniel Potter is both "Caribbean Everyman," whose history began and ended, as Kincaid states, 500 years ago in 1492, and the five-year-old orphaned boy (nicknamed Drickie) whose father Nathaniel Potter never acknowledged him and whose mother Elfrida Robinson walked into the sea one day to deliberately drown herself.[9]

As in Genesis, Kincaid begins (and I thus begin) with a meditation on light and darkness, "sometimes separated . . . sometimes mingling" (83). From the very first page of *Mr. Potter*, Kincaid establishes a play on light and darkness that is both metaphoric and metaphysical, that is biblical, creating the contrasting boundaries that demarcate day from night, and human being from human being in the novel. In the opening chapter, a contrast—as dark to light, and night to day—is painted between the character Mr. Potter, the Antiguan chauffeur of African descent, and Dr. Weizenger, the exiled Czechoslovakian doctor who has newly arrived and who will be driven to his new home by Mr. Potter. Unaccustomed to the brilliant light of the Caribbean sun, Dr. Weizenger embraces the sun's rays, while fearing the darkness (or absence of light): "And Dr. Weizenger was thinking how beautiful light of any kind was, light that did not come from a furnace, a real furnace fed by the fuel of coal or human bodies; light, real light, with its opposite being darkness, real darkness, not a metaphor for the darkness from which Mr. Potter and his ancestors had come" (16). As a man escaping the Jewish Holocaust and fleeing European anti-Semitism, Dr. Weizenger remains plagued and haunted by images of annihilation: "And his own extinction had almost succeeded and how surprised he was by this, and how he would remain for the rest of his life" (23). Despite this near-death brush with genocide, Dr. Weizenger also remains unaware of other earlier historical genocides, oblivious to the same fatality suffered by others in the world; he experienced his confrontation with death and annihilation "as if such a thing had never happened before, as if groups of people, one day intact and building civilization and dominating heaven and earth, had not the next found themselves erased and not even been remembered in a prayer or in a joke by the rest of humanity; as if groups of people had not been erased from the beginning of life and human memory" (23).

For Dr. Weizenger, his own exile in Antigua is like a "descent" into darkness, a darkness that borders on the metaphysical, yet also remains too palpably physical or material: too visible, too epidermal. In his worldview, Dr. Weizenger racializes the terrains of light and darkness, even as he maintains the distinction between metaphysical darkness and material darkness. He thus disallows the African Antiguans around him even the space of a negative ontology, an ontological negation: for him, they remain too earthbound, too physical even to ascend (or descend) to metaphysical absence (of light). Dr. Weizenger overwhelmingly feels that he has "vanished into darkness, yes darkness!" (33). Is Dr. Weizenger's absorption into darkness annihilatory or lifesustaining? This darkness is mental as well as corporeal, and his experience of it is as if "a vast darkness had descended over many things he had known" (33). He finds this darkness indistinct, unknowable; he cannot quite describe it. It is "not a darkness like the night, and not a darkness that was the opposite of the light in which he was now standing, not a darkness that was the opposite of the light into which Mr. Potter had temporarily disappeared"; for Weizenger, it is a racialized darkness. It is "more like the darkness from which Mr. Potter and all he came from had originated" (33). Dr. Weizenger's racism is made manifest again later in the novel when he insists that his young medical assistant, Annie Victoria Richardson, scrub the black children, his patients, before he will treat them. Ironically, although Dr. Weizenger feels himself absorbed into darkness and thus destroyed, his escape to Antigua, to the island's "darkness" as he conceives it, saves him from an otherwise certain death at the hands of "white" German fascists who erroneously and homicidally proclaimed their own so-called "enlightened" worldview.

The passage remains marked by a fundamental ambivalence: black absorbs white, darkness light. Does the passage reveal light returning to darkness? Darkness from whence it came? In the passage, Dr. Weizenger both (negatively) racializes darkness and strips it of potential metaphysical valence; yet, this darkness persists as an a priori cosmic force, as if prior to creation (a divine force in and of itself). In the biblical account of Genesis, there are three fundamental divine separations—light from darkness; sky from water; land from sea. The proclaimed separation of created light (*Let there be light* . . . , Genesis 1:3) from darkness is primary; the separation of heavens from waters secondary; and the division of land from sea tertiary. Kincaid reminds her readers that these divisions are acts of (divine and human and ideological and mythic and historical) power; however, even within myth, there is an indivisible a priori. In Genesis, darkness is the a priori. Darkness precedes light; darkness exists prior to created light; it is a priori, before. Within biblical accounts of creation, the a priori darkness casts a fundamentally ambivalent shadow over divine creation: if it exists a priori, before creation, then it exists outside of the reach of God's creative hand. Kincaid draws on this fundamental ambivalence—the a priori nature of darkness within the created universe—to establish darkness as a field outside of divine or human intervention, a source of energy, power, and unbound nature that precedes the created world. As such, it remains beyond creation, even as it is separated or divided from creation (*And God separated the light from the darkness*, Genesis 1:4).

Contrasting with a priori darkness, light is substanceless, yet translucent, imbuing all objects on which it falls with "substance" although light itself is without substance. The light has no spatially defining characteristics of its own; like water, it takes on the attributes of the object into which it streams or flows. Compare the line from *Mr. Potter* in which the biological grandfather Nathaniel likens light and water: "And there was the world of sky above and light forcefully illuminating and forcefully streaming through the sky and the awe of great bodies of water flowing into each other even as they remained separate" (37). In another passage, we see through Mr. (Roderick) Potter's eyes, rather than those of Dr. Weizenger. Arriving at Dr. Weizenger's new house in St. Johns, Mr. Potter opens the doors and then the windows. Struck by the light, Mr. Potter gazes through the window at the world outside the house (in this passage as in many others in Kincaid's oeuvre, the house itself is a world contained). When Mr. Potter sees the light, he observes its translucence: "it was the light as he had always known it, so bright that it eventually made everything that came in contact with it transparent and then translucent, the light was spread before Mr. Potter as if it were a sea of water, it covered and yet revealed all that it encompassed; the light gave substance to everything else: the trees became the trees but only more so, and the ground in which they anchored themselves remained the ground but only more so, and the sky above revealed more and more of the sky and into the heavens, into eternity, and then returned to the earth. (19–20). Mr. Potter destabilizes the cultural privileging of light (over dark), without negating light's beauty, its power, its translucence. Mr. Potter can sustain a world of light and dark intermingled, mixed, creating shadows, unlike Dr. Weizenger for whom the light and the darkness remain fundamentally separated (as if by divine decree; compare Genesis 1:4), or else one threatens to destroy and erase the other (thus, Dr. Weizenger's fear and feeling that he has vanished into darkness!). For Dr. Weizenger, even though he inhabits the shadows (like Mr. Potter and Mr. Shoul who live in the diasporic shadows of new worlds), he remains part of the singular world (and worldview) that cannot admit or "speak of the shadows" (114). Kincaid blurs the boundaries of created light and a priori darkness in the passage in which the young boy Roderick Nathaniel Potter (nicknamed Drickie) grieves for his dead mother (Elfrida Robinson) who committed suicide by drowning, a death by water, and abruptly left her son, from that moment on an orphan, to the world alone. The five-year-old boy naively awaits his mother's hoped-for, but never-fulfilled return, craving a glimpse of her face, but "all this [expectation and desire] was followed by a large blank space of darkness and light, sometimes separated, the darkness and the light, sometimes mingling, the darkness and the light, and this single blank space of only darkness and light—separated or commingled—was where Elfrida Robinson, his mother, stayed" (83–84).

Kincaid also writes genesis into the novel in other ways—first, in creating a life for Mr. Potter; second, in creating a life for herself through Mr. Potter's story; and finally, through evoking biblical language throughout the novel in the creation of her own chaosmos, a world with constellations and infernal fires and geologic subterranean shifting plates. By writing genesis into the novel, Kincaid powerfully revisits Glissant's idea that "Genesis legitimates genealogy."[10] I turn now to the Caribbean "quarrel with History" and Kincaid's role in this quarrel.

THE CARIBBEAN "QUARREL WITH HISTORY"

Édouard Glissant's *Le discours antillais* (*Caribbean Discourse*) was a groundbreaking work for theorizing Caribbean identity, history, and literature in ways that resisted dominant colonialist paradigms. One of the most provocative ideas in Glissant's text is the idea that History and Literature in the West have functioned as totalizing systems that consolidate grandiose ideals about Western civilization; for Glissant, "History (whether we see it as expression or lived reality) and Literature form part of the same problematics."[11] As Glissant further theorizes, "History (like Literature) is capable of quarrying deep within us, as a consciousness or the emergence of a consciousness, as a neurosis (symptom of loss) and a contraction of the self."[12] Critiquing the transcendence of History and Literature in the West, Glissant remarks on an Antillean "quarrel with History" in *Caribbean Discourse*, wherein he refigures the relations of history and literature and notes the colonialist imbrications of myth making and history defining.[13] History and Literature, which Glissant argues "first come together in the realm of myth," have operated in the West through an ideology of "dominant sameness" that relegates diversity and difference to the peripheries of documentation or representation: according to Glissant, this dynamic is deeply embedded within the notion of Genesis.[14] Caribbean writers' contestations of history also mark their engagements with genesis. And Genesis (*capital G*), according to Glissant, is the foundational narrative for History (*capital H*) and Literature (*capital L*): "Genesis, which is the fundamental explanation, and ordering, which is the ritualized narrative, anticipate what the West would ascribe to Literature (that is almost divine creation: the Word made Flesh)—the notion of Genesis—and what would be the realm of historical consciousness (a selective evolution)—that of Ordering."[15] And "the encounter between genesis and ordering" in myth separates, opposes, and structures the relations between the realms of nature and culture.[16] Within Western myths of genesis, Glissant argues that nature is almost always subdued to the ordering principles of culture and that "the control of nature, and of one's nature, by culture was the ideal of the Western mind."[17] In genesis myths of the West, Glissant contends, "it is a matter of learning the natural Genesis, the primordial slime, the Eternal Garden, and embarking—even at the risk of condemnation (like the myth of Adam and Eve . . .)—on a journey to an ordering-knowledge."[18] This dynamic, according to Glissant, operates both within History and within Literature, manifest in History's notions of evolution and progress and in Literature's, particularly realism's, privileging of the linear, chronologically ordered narrative: "the linear nature of narrative and the linear form of chronology take shape in this context."[19] Herein lies the idea that "Genesis legitimates genealogy": for Glissant, time, history, lineage all affirm myth's quest for origins, legitimacy, and filiation. In contrast, the modern American hero, Glissant argues, "will have to return to the demands of the 'here and now' (which is, not the known, but the done), so renouncing, the beginning of history. . . ."[20]

Does Jamaica Kincaid also so renounce the "beginning of history"? Or does she pose the aporia of history and historical beginnings as *her* fundamental question? After all, as Glissant intimates, "the important thing is not the reply but the question."[21] Indeed, Kincaid's *Mr. Potter* continually evokes the idea of "beginnings": in the novel, she meditates on "my beginnings" (54); to tell Mr. Potter's story, his history, she says that she must "start again at the beginning" (188); of the diasporic individuals (Mr. Potter, Mr. Shoul, Dr. Weizenger) living in Antigua, Kincaid notes, "they had to begin again, re-create their own selves, make something new" (194). In Kincaid's tangled narrative, though, beginnings border on and merge with endings. Kincaid thus also paradoxically meditates on beginnings that end in *Mr. Potter*: writing about her biological grandfather, Nathaniel Potter, and his place on earth, Kincaid explains that "he was part of its mysterious and endless beginnings" (40); commenting on Mr. Potter's death, Kincaid laments his end, but more hopefully articulates that "his end has a beginning" (178); she also grieves, though, that life with "its glorious *beginnings end* and the end is always an occasion for sadness" (184, emphasis added). Even endings are not final, and in the novel, endings almost always spill over into new points of becoming, into new beginnings: in a passage recounting Dr. Weizenger's flight from Prague through Budapest, Vienna, Berlin, and Shanghai to St. Johns, Antigua, the exile recalls conversations about the "end of the world" with "days of the world ending *again and again*, and within the very days were *ends*, as if the day did not constitute and define a limitation" (32, 32–33; emphasis added).

Kincaid thus stages her own "quarrel with History." She also enters this Antillean "quarrel" in her numerous meditations on "history" in the West Indies in published interviews. In a 1990 interview with Selwyn Cudjoe, Kincaid noted how a childhood fascination with history remained an adult preoccupation, if not obsession, for her: "I read *A History of England*. . . . I read about the history of the West Indies, all different books, because I keep thinking that someone will say it happened differently. I can never believe that the history of the West Indies happened the way it did[:] . . . the wreck and the ruin and the greed."[22] Kincaid told Donna Perry in 1993, "When I was little I had this great mind for history. And I never really understood it until I realized that the reason I like history is because I also reduce the past to domestic activity. History was what people did. It was organized along the lines of who said what and who did what, not really unlike how the society in which I grew up was organized. The idea that things are impersonal occurrences is very alien to me. I personalize everything.[23] In the interview with Perry, Kincaid also commented that she "personalize[s] everything"—even, or perhaps especially, her history and her heritage, and these elements are, of course, entangled with notions of genealogy, genesis, genre, and ultimately, even genocide. In a 1993 interview with Allan Vorda, Kincaid defines her history and heritage in a way that mirrors Xuela's, the protagonist of *The Autobiography of My Mother*: "I'm part African, part Carib Indian, and part—which is a very small part by now—Scot. All of them came to Antigua by boats. This is how my history begins"[24] . . . *how my history begins*. This engagement, or quarrel, with history, then, is very much an autobiographical venture; Kincaid explains how one "struggle[s] to make sense of the external from the things that have made you what you are and the things that you have been told are you: *my history of colonialism, my history of slavery*, and imagining if that hadn't happened what I would have been."[25] Kincaid's words reveal how one's autobiography must necessarily be written within and against the parameters of history and those historical forces (such as colonialism, slavery, and genocide) that have shaped the Caribbean "New World." To Perry, Kincaid attests this relationship of self to history, stating, "my history is so much about dominion; in fact we were called 'the dominion,' and all the colonies were 'the dominions.'"[26] The relationship of self to history, although intimately personalized in these quotations, is also abstracted and collectivized: it is the collective histories of colonialism, slavery, and genocide in the Caribbean that must be confronted within the autobiographical. For Kincaid, history is autobiography, and autobiography history. One cannot be disentangled from the other. It is in this sense that Kincaid writes history's autobiography and deconstructs autobiography's history.

Fictionally, Kincaid meditates once again on history and its profound (indeed devastating) effects on lives lived under its spell in the novel *Mr. Potter*. The year 1492, as a simultaneous point of historical beginning and ending, is reiterated in *Mr. Potter*, and in the novel, it is associated with genealogy, descent, and a search for origins. In the novel, Kincaid writes, "the sound of Mr. Potter's voice, [was] so full of all that had gone wrong in the world for almost five hundred years that it could break the heart of an ordinary stone" (23). Mr. Potter's voice rings with tragic "discoveries," and his birth from a "motherless" mother named Elfrida Robinson descends from a long line or sentence of "motherless mothers." Kincaid directs her readers in the imperative, "See her as a small girl motherless, and see her mother before her motherless and that mother, too, motherless, and on and on reaching back not so much into eternity as into a sentence that would begin with the year fourteen hundred and nine-two; for eternity is the unimaginable awfulness that makes up the past and the unimaginable peace and pleasure that is to come" (72). History and genealogy are intertwined here, even if in broken lines; Roderick Nathaniel is born to Elfrida Robinson, a motherless mother who is herself the daughter of a motherless mother who is herself this motherless daughter. For the boy Drickie and his mother Elfrida, this historical and genealogical disinheritance is a "sentence," a damnation, a condemnation to ancestral anonymity; it is also a tragic consequence of European colonial history and its abominable enslavement of people of African descent.

The year 1492 ("fourteen hundred and ninety-two") thus marks a broken line of historical descent for people of African origins in the "New World." Time, and the movement of time, is marked differently for those who are the victors and those who are the vanquished. In the novel, the Anglican cathedral, which stands on the spot at which Market Street ends on Newgate Street, is the temporal and spatial landmark of both victory and defeat: it has been built for the Anglican believers by the African slaves "from whom Mr. Potter could trace his ancestors"; the tower clock on the cathedral ("with four faces looking north, south, east, and west, making the cathedral seem as if it simultaneously captured and released time") marks time for the victors, but for Mr. Potter (as for all who looked like him), "he was all by himself: a definition of time captured and released, released and captured" (177). The tower clock, Kincaid notes, was built "hundreds of years before," by Mr. Potter's ancestors, "And Mr. Potter's lifetime began in the year fourteen hundred and ninety-two but he was born on the seventh day of January, nineteen hundred and twenty-two, . . . And all through this small narrative of this small life was the loud and harsh ringing of the church's bell, and this loudness and this harshness was such a surprise to the people who had ordered the cathedral and its clock and bell that these two peoples agreed to call the harsh loudness a chime and the chiming of the church bells marking off time eventually became a part of the great and everlasting silence" (177–78).[27] Time ultimately is measured *not* through the chiming of the church's bell, but rather in the "great and everlasting silence" of history and defeat and death. Mr. Potter's death, his end (*as if* in a narrative; *as if* written by his daughter

Elaine Cynthia Potter), is associated with this "great and everlasting silence" that is both temporal and eternal; however, "his end has a beginning," a textual return: "And Mr. Potter did not move with great hurry or inexorably toward his inevitable end, it was only that the end is so inevitable, his end was beyond avoidance, and yet like the hours trapped in a clock—let it be the clock on the top of the cathedral with its four faces, each facing a corner of the earth—the end of each hour is the beginning of the next, his end has a beginning . . ." (178). Mr. Potter's movement toward death is monumental: a temporal entrapment ("hours trapped in a clock"), yet as each hour ends, it begins again in the new hour to which it gives birth. Mr. Potter's end, his beginning: a narrative cycle of return and creative force: he creates the child—Elaine Cynthia Potter—whom he abandons and who creates his life (*Mr. Potter*) in narrative for eternal recurrence, removing Mr. Potter from the eternal and vast silence that is death and that is history. Kincaid shrouds her dead father in mythic layers, making him an artifact not only of history and literature, but also of myth. Here, I want to return to a discussion of genesis in order to illustrate how the Caribbean "quarrel with History" is intimately bound to ideas about myth.

"CARIBBEAN GENESIS": WRITING NEW WORLDS

In *Mr. Potter* Kincaid sets a world spinning on its axis, creates a chaosmos of creative beginnings and tragic endings wrought through the forces of creation and annihilation, of genesis and genocide. Kincaid's Antiguan chaosmos is one in which "the sun, a planetary body [is] indifferent to the significance of individuals" and the world "in all its parts, was complicated, with plates beneath its surface shifting and colliding, with vast subterranean cauldrons of steam and gases mixing and then exploding violently through the earth's crust" (140, 125). This chaosmos is not only planetary and geologic; it is also psychic and metaphysic, haunted and driven by the question to her father, "What am I to call you? [which] seemed to arrange not only a singular world but a whole system of planetary revolutions" (169). This world is volatile and changing, not static. Kincaid writes, "The world as we know it will from time to time do that, collapse, engulfed by a fire" (104). Unsurprisingly, Annie Victoria Richardson is a force (both divine and diabolic) in this world: she is sulfuric and volcanic, "flames in her own fire and . . . very beautiful" (135); she is an unstable archipelago, "herself already a series of beautifully poisonous eruptions, a boiling cauldron of strange fluids, a whirlwind of sex and passion" (141). Later, evoking the same language of infernal destruction, Kincaid takes on the fiery force of her mother, and the author sees her life "in a tunnel, ablaze with torrents of fire, . . . and at that time I glowed not like an ember surging toward ashes but like a stout log enveloped in flames" (165). To maternal fire, Kincaid contrasts paternal, oceanic flow: in the writer's elemental engagements, father is likened to sea and sky, with "the end of his life itself rushing like a predictable wave in a known ocean" (194); his death deeply affects Kincaid (though she writes that her existence did not seem to alter him at all), and she mourns "that a source from which [she] flowed had been stanched" (185). On the day of his burial "the sun was blotted out, blotted out by an eternal basin of rain" (182). If mother is godlike, father is a lowly man, like his own father Nathaniel Potter, "and their worlds, the one in which they lived and the one in which they existed, ceased, and the small irregular stumble that their existence had made in the vast smoothness that was the turning of the earth on its axis was no more" (55). Mother is to father as God is to man; as fire is to water.

In Kincaid's created world, readers bear witness to plagues and curses and prayers and betrayals and destructions that rival those of the Torah or the Old Testament. Kincaid's paternal grandfather Nathaniel, in this Caribbean chaosmos, is accursed, cast out, among the banished: he becomes an Antiguan Job, a fisherman whose catch dwindles daily, finally to nothing, rather than increasing ten fold, and who curses God; he then is smote by the God he cursed, stricken with deadly, festering boils, "and when he died, his body was blackened, as if he had been trapped in the harshest of fires, a fire that from time to time would subside to a dull glow only to burn again fiercely, and each time the fierce burning lasted for an eternity" (47). Nathaniel suffers infernal destruction (hellfire and brimstone?), as one cast out, as if by God, to the margins of history and culture. Kincaid shocks our emotions, pulling us toward this "New World" Job and his dreadful reversal of fortune. One sympathizes with Nathaniel, not the God who dared to strike him down; feels pity for the man, not adoration for the God.

Mr. (Roderick) Potter, like his own father Nathaniel who abandoned him, is not only a mortal inhabitant of this created world; his body is the world itself. Mr. Potter's heart is not only corporeal, but also a human geography, a bodily map of Kincaid's Antigua. Kincaid charts a cartographic journey across "the many interstices of Mr. Potter's heart: valleys of regret and hope and disappointment; mountains of regret and hope and disappointment; seas of longing; plains barren of vegetation and plains full of dust; shallow gutters of joy; deep crevices of sorrow; a sharp ledge of awe" (152). Mr. Potter's heart is the world that his lovers and daughters inhabit, although "all of this was a secret to him" (152): it "resembled the surface of some familiar but not yet found planet"—his heart inhabited by the lovers (and mothers), girls (and daughters) that he abandons (153). The sorrow he creates for his abandoned lovers and disinherited daughters also creates new geographical *alterrains* (or alternative terrains): once deserted, each woman "was recomposed, not made new, only recomposed into an ordinary mother with her girl child, and their tears could make a river and their sighs of sorrow and regret could make mountains, and the pangs of hunger in their stomachs could make a verdant valley" (152). If for Glissant, the quintessential unconquered territory is the forest, for Kincaid it is the body of Mr. Potter and the worlds spawned in the sorrow he creates for those who love and lose him, for the girls he fathers and then forgets.[28]

So what do Jamaica Kincaid's worlds create in their creation? Why does she engage genesis to write new worlds? Does she attempt in *Mr. Potter* to write new worlds destroyed by the myth of the "New World"? If European colonial history constructed a worldview that subsumed all other worlds into its own, eclipsing alternative terrains (other histories, other peoples, the planets spawned in their imaginations) through a "dominant sameness,"[29] then Kincaid rends this singular and cyclopean world with textual worlds that were or might have been. Her creation is less a past remembering of worlds lost (is paradise lost ever regained?) than a future remembrance—creating for posterity what might have been, what will be (or the yet to become) in worlds of words—in honor of histories erased, if not in their stead. If European myths of creation (or genesis) obliterated and destroyed other worlds— those of the Africans forcibly deracinated from homeland and enslaved in new lands; of the Americans (the Taino, the Aruac, and Carib Indians) decimated under early Spanish colonial rule; and of the Asians exiled and indentured throughout the Caribbean, primarily by British colonialists—then Kincaid's revisions recast the relations of encounter, contact, and power, re-envisioning those other worlds; she does so on a scale that is both cosmic and human, celestial and mundane. The so-called New World brought together—by force, if not by choice— peoples from across the globe; yet it established and echoed the hierarchical relations of the Old World. Rewriting genesis, and creating worlds (new and old, discovered or lost), Kincaid settles the scores of history: she evokes history's wounds, its legacies of disinheritance for those who live in "the shadows": for "the world would not allow them to . . . speak of the shadows in which they lived, the world would first shudder and then shatter into a million pieces of something else before it would allow them to do so" (114). In the final section, I examine how Kincaid's engagements with genesis also manifest a concern with transmuting genres, particularly those of autobiography and biography.

TRANSMUTATIONS OF GENRE: KINCAID'S BIOGRAPHICAL AUTOGRAPH IN *MR. POTTER*

"And I, writing all this now, came into being just at that moment and I, who am writing all this now, came into being a very long time before that" (142) — So writes Jamaica Kincaid, the narrative figuration in the present of the past child Elaine Cynthia Potter in her fictional biography, *Mr. Potter*, of her biological father, Mr. Potter. Kincaid's self-creation in language, in words, both parallels and subverts divine creation (an extension of deity into language and flesh: *In the beginning was the Word*). In this section, I address the question of biography as *alterbiography*[30] in Kincaid's novel *Mr. Potter*, an *alterbiographic* text that decenters and deterritorializes the matrix of self-other-text. The novel displaces the autobiographical "I" and its referentiality into the biographical Mr. Potter, a fictional portrait of the author's biological father, and yet, a historical figuration of an African descendant of slaves in the Caribbean island of Antigua. In the novel, Kincaid confounds the referentiality of biographical texts, and thus, transmutes or alters our understanding of auto/biography; she writes *alter biographically*. I plumb here Kincaid's writing of autobiography *as* biography in *Mr. Potter*, focusing on the novel's preoccupation with genealogy, genesis, and even genocide as frames for rethinking the boundaries of genre. Father and daughter are related not exclusively through genealogy, but also through genealogical abandonment: each is marked at birth by "an empty space with a line drawn through it" where the father's name should have been inscribed on their birth certificates (100). I will trace, then, "the line" that Kincaid believes is "drawn through [her] which [she] inherited from him, and this line drawn through [her] binds [her] to him even as it was very much meant to show that [she] did not belong to him" (161). I read this "line" as Kincaid's biographical autograph. This autobiographical extension—the inscription of her biographical autograph in the text—is intensely linked (through genesis and genealogy) to her transmutations of genre in the novel *Mr. Potter*.

"I began to realize," Kincaid noted in a 1993 interview, "how my writing and my use of images are based on my understanding of the word as good and evil as influenced by two books in the Bible, Genesis and Revelation"; in the interview, she also intimates that "the beginning and the end are the real thing."[31] These biblical resonances—Genesis, Revelation—sweep through Kincaid's texts as the forces of creation and destruction, of genesis and genocide, and these forces enter into Kincaid's writing of genealogy and genre, specifically those of "life" writing—or, of autobiography and biography. Kincaid philosophically tests the generic frames of autobiography and biography in literary texts such as the short story "Biography of a Dress," the novel *The Autobiography of My Mother*, the memoir *My Brother*, and most recently, in the novel *Mr. Potter*.[32] For Kincaid, the genres of biography and autobiography are intricately woven into the parameters of memory and history, but also more indelibly, they are marked with the fractures of genesis, genealogy, and genocide in the Caribbean. In this section, I theorize the relations of *genre* to genealogy, focusing specifically on Kincaid's transmutations of autobiography and biography.

Biography is, of course, by definition necessarily situated within the frame of autobiography. Having emerged alongside the genre of autobiography in the eighteenth century, biography stands between the literary expectations of autobiography and the documentary demands of reflective historiography. Feminist and literary scholars such as Liz Stanley and Laura Marcus, and more recently (and in my mind, more sophisticatedly) Alison Donnell and Leigh Gilmore have explored the imbrications of biography and autobiography.[33] According to Gilmore in *The Limits of Autobiography: Trauma and Testimony*, "Kincaid maximizes the nonmimetic capacities of autobiography through her emphasis on autobiographical extension, a self-representational practice allied with and knowable through metonymy"; in her reading of Kincaid's literary texts as serial autobiography, Gilmore explains that "insofar as autobiography represents the real, it does so through metonymy, that is, through the claims of contiguity, wherein the person who writes extends the self in the writing, and puts her in another place."[34] I argue here that the places where Kincaid situates the autobiographical self or selves are in other lives, or even objects—a dress in "Biography of a Dress," and the lives of Xuela Claudette Richardson in *The Autobiogra-*

phy of My Mother, Devon Drew in *My Brother*, or Roderick Potter in *Mr. Potter*. In the most recent novel, Kincaid writes, "I see now that all change is its same self and all different selves are the same" (139). These biographical and metonymic displacements push autobiography to its generic limits, but they also allow Kincaid to create lives—her own and others—from memory and imagination, and to refuse the destruction of those lives through anonymity and historical erasure.

Autobiography, then, almost always exceeds the individual who writes it, exceeds the life and the subjective experiences of the writing subject; autobiography will also be about the others who surround the writing subject and whose experiences are enmeshed with those of the writer. Autobiography is inherently entangled with biography, the writing of other people's lives. These biographical others may or may not include one's family—one's mother and father, siblings, spouse or partner, and child(ren)—and they are certainly not limited to genealogy and filiation; however, even when absent, genealogy is still silent and invisibly present in the autobiographical text. In Kincaid's *alterbiographic* texts, she challenges the presumed insularity and discreteness of the autobiographical form, opening it to representations of alterity: through *alterbiography*, Kincaid powerfully writes other into self, biography into autobiography, annihilation into creation, and death into life. She thus forces us to rethink the presumed boundaries of these terrains; she does so through her transmutations of genealogy and genre.

What, then, is the relation between genealogy and genre, particularly in autobiographical and biographical forms? Genealogy, as autobiography and as biography, are also embedded within history *writ large*: New World "Discoveries"; British maritime history and its legacies of piracy, pillaging, and ceremonious parading of one's loot or booty (human, mineral, and botanical); the Atlantic Slave Trade; chattel slavery in the Antilles, the enslaved Africans beginning a life of drudgery in this "New World"; and lost to posterity, the Caribs and other indigenous peoples of the West Indies who suffered the worst and most irrevocable form of historical "progress" (always to the gain of one group of people, but to the insurmountable and incalculable loss of another): genocide. Kincaid's alterbiographical texts are not just about the imbrications of autobiography (or the autobiographical form) and biography (or the biographical form); nor are they just about the interweaving of autobiography with genealogy or filiation; but they are also about the inherent entanglement of autobiography with history.

Here, an etymological turn is instructive in understanding Kincaid's constructions and deconstructions of genres — autobiography and biography. Both genre and genealogy (like genesis and genocide and many other modern English words) have their root in the Greek term *genos*, which (like many Greek nouns) has a somewhat broad denotation. Its most common (or pervasively documented) meaning is "sort or kind" — from which we derive words like *generic, general, generally*, and even *gender*, but also clearly, *genre*. The word *genos* also denotes a family; hence, modern equivalents in English, such as *genealogy, genealogical*, and even more scientifically, *genes, genomes, genetic*, and *genetics*. This last meaning is also closely parallel to a third meaning denoted by *genos*: a race, tribe, or other group of people. This third meaning (or usage) for *genos* is similar to another Greek term, *ethnos*, which also means a race, tribe, or group of people and from which modern English words such as *ethnic* and *ethnicity* are derived.[35] From these etymological insights, we must examine how language itself is part of the matrix — if not *the* matrix — from which ideas about genre, race, literature, and nationality emerge. (This etymological relation or affiliation — between genre and genealogy and genocide, from the root *genos* — also raises the question of the racialization of genres, which is regrettably beyond the scope of the current paper.) Kincaid's weaving and unraveling of genres (autobiography, biography) opens one space for doing so, and her transmutations of genre are informed by genealogy (both familial and racial, as the root *genos* supports); Kincaid's transmutations of genre also perspicaciously expose racial violence at the heart of history, of colonialism, of slavery, of genocide, and even of the modern nation-state (which emerged from these historical parameters).

The philosophical and textual transmutations of genealogy and genre inform the novel *Mr. Potter*, a text in which Kincaid indelibly inscribes her biographical autograph. In the novel, Kincaid unequivocally links not only the story of Mr. Potter's life to her own, through genealogy, but more intimately, through its biographical telling: "he could not read and he could not write and he could not render the story of life, his own in particular, with coherency and I can read and I can write and I am his daughter" (130). The genesis of Mr. Potter's story through language (wherein text is likened to "a bolt of cloth" and writing is figured as both weaving and dyeing) also borders on its unraveling or unfolding. Kincaid writes, "in this way I make Mr. Potter and in this way I unmake Mr. Potter and apart from the fact that he is now dead, he is unable to affect the portrait of him I am rendering here, the scenes on the bolt of cloth as he appears in them: the central figure" (158). In her telling and untelling, or making and unmaking, of Mr. Potter's biography, genealogical and chronological order are reversed, as daughter gives birth to father. The writer speaks and names and creates two lives—her father's and her own: "And I now say, 'Mr. Potter,' but as I say his name, I am reading it also, and so to say his name and to imagine his life at the same time makes him whole and complete, not singular and fragmented, and this is because he is dead and beyond reading and writing and beyond contesting my authority to render him in my own image" (193). This image—though seemingly based on self-sameness and similitude—is not metaphoric, but rather metonymic: it displaces self (daughter) into other (father), while inverting time, paternity, and knowledge ("reading and writing"), as well as gendered and biblical myths of genesis. Daughter divinely creates father in *her* own image, but this image is shifting; it is imagined, as all images ultimately are; and it is written. Kincaid reveals how "Mr. Potter's life advanced and exploded on the page" that narrates his genesis.[36]

Reflecting on the novel (then in-process) in an essay printed in *The New York Times*, Kincaid describes Mr. Potter's home as "on the page, the white page, the clean white page,"[37] an image evoking Xuela Claudette Richardson's description of her own birth in the novel *The Autobiography of My Mother*: "I was new, the pages of my life had no writing on them, they were unsmudged, so clean, so smooth, so new."[38] The "page," though, is not a metaphor for the autobiographical self; rather, it is the textual site of auto/biographical extension, of creative possibilities for genesis, of future and past becomings; it is the metonymic starting point for new autobiographical beginnings. Writing lives into being, Kincaid metonymically writes and rewrites her own lives. Writing biography, Kincaid enters autobiography.

Throughout the novel *Mr. Potter*, Kincaid incessantly comments on Mr. Potter's illiteracy and her own ability to read and write; this difference between her and her father is profound. Because she can read and because she can write, she can also write Mr. Potter's story, his biography, and thereby save him from eternal loss. This difference is a difference of power—she can read, he could not; yet, Kincaid desires to save her father, despite his paternal abandonment of her as an infant, from an unknown and unrecorded life. (One poignant memory vividly, if ironically, recalls the self-absorbed man waving a young Elaine away as she comes to him for money to buy a writing tablet.) Kincaid's power, though, is surrendered in her generosity toward this man who, in part, gave her life. She writes, "because I am his daughter, for I have his nose, and because I learned how to read and how to write, only so is Mr. Potter's life known, his smallness becomes large, his anonymity is stripped away, his silence broken. Mr. Potter himself says nothing, nothing at all" (189). Kincaid, the abandoned and renamed (self-named) daughter, "creates" a story for the illiterate Mr. Potter and so saves him from eternal oblivion and everlasting anonymity.

Kincaid's life is thus intimately connected to her father's, even if she did not know him well during his lifetime: they share a line of "illegitimacy"—a line that joins father and daughter in name and in disinheritance, in life as in death. Kincaid writes, "he died and will never be heard from again, except through me, for I can read and I can write my own name, which includes his name also, Elaine Cynthia Potter, and like him and his own father before him, I have a line drawn through me, a line has been drawn through me" (191–92). Elaine Cynthia Potter, the disinherited daughter—later self-defined as Jamaica Kincaid—"creates" a story for Mr. Potter and in so doing "creates" her own narrative and rewrites herself: here the writing of biography becomes the writing of autobiography; the writing of other (father) becomes a reclamation of self (daughter). She thus breaks the "line" (of illegitimacy, of illiteracy, of disinheritance) in her auto/biographical reclamation. And Kincaid sadly notes that Mr. Potter "lived his life deliberately ignorant of [her] existence, as if [she] were in a secret chamber separated from the rest of the world and the world would never know of [her], or suspect that [she] was in the world" (193). This secret chamber is a sepulcher of sorts, condemning daughter to genealogical death; yet the author bestows narrative life on Mr. Potter, freeing herself both from her father's death and from the internal death that his indifference toward her created within the girl that she was. In writing Mr. Potter's story, Kincaid is excavating the effigy of the child Elaine Cynthia Potter, "laid to rest in the pose of the newborn which is also the pose of the dead" (147). Life, death; daughter, father—both are entangled together in "this borning and dying" that becomes the auto/biographical writing of worlds. Herein lies Kincaid's biographical autograph (101).

Kincaid's engagements with genesis are deeply imbricated with her profound "quarrel with History" and her radical critiques of historical consequence (material and political and cultural). Returning to broken points in severed genealogical lines, Kincaid rewrites the stories—indeed the histories—of her own genesis and that of her biological father (and her biographical protagonist), Mr. Potter. Kincaid's *alterbiographic* engagements with genesis and genealogy in *Mr. Potter* also offer powerful literary transmutations of genre (or categories of division and difference): she textually and aesthetically erodes the boundaries dividing biography and autobiography, autobiography and history; just as she philosophically blurs the boundaries between self and other, life and death, light and darkness. Kincaid thus writes alternative histories (to contest the dominant forms of European colonial history in the "New World"): these created (and past-driven, yet future-oriented) histories are marked by different times, different points of geneses—creating new worlds for those who have suffered the erasures of historical time *writ large* in the Caribbean (slavery and genocide and colonialism). In closing, then, I return full circle, or to quote Kincaid:

> And to start again *at the beginning*: Mr. Potter's appearance in the world was a combination of sadness, joy, and a chasm of silent horror for his mother (Elfrida Robinson) and indifference to his father (Nathaniel Potter), who had so many children that none of them could matter at all; and to the world he was of no consequence at all, for the world is filled with many people and each of them is like a second in a minute and a minute is in an hour and an hour is in a day and a day is in a week and a week is in a month and a month is in a year and a year is in a century and a century is in a millennium and a millennium is in the world and the world eventually becomes a picture trapped in a four-sided frame. (188)

NOTES

The quotation in the paper's title, taken from *Mr. Potter* (New York: Farrar Straus Giroux, 2002) 148, reveals the importance of auto/biographical writing to the author's creation of self and to the process of autogenesis.

1. Genesis (Septuagint, Bible) All subsequent references will be to this version.

2. Kincaid, *Mr. Potter*, 83–84. With the exception of epigraphic quotations, all further citations to *Mr. Potter* are provided parenthetically within the text.

3. I am currently completing a book manuscript entitled *"Caribbean Genesis"—Jamaica Kincaid and the Writing of New Worlds*.

4. Édouard Glissant, *Le discours antillais* (Paris: Seuil, 1981); *Caribbean Discourse*, translated by J. Michael Dash (Charlottesville: University Press of Virginia, 1989, 1999).

5. See Édouard Glissant, "The Quarrel with History," in *Caribbean Discourse*, 61–95.

6. Gospel of John (Greek New Testament, Bible).

7. Kincaid, *Mr. Potter*, 188.

8. Walcott's theoretical writings, especially "The Muse of History," has borrowed from Christian mythological symbols: naming, creating, Adam in his "New World". D'Aguiar has written eloquently about Walcott as Adamic creator, and Dance titled his

collection of interviews with West Indian writers *New World Adams*. See the following: Derek Walcott, "The Muse of History," in *What the Twilight Says: Essays* (New York: Farrar Straus Giroux, 1998), 36–64; Fred D'Aguiar, "Adam's Other Garden: Derek Walcott's Exploration of the Creative Imagination," *Caribana* 3 (1992–93): 67–77; and Daryl Cumber Dance, ed., *New World Adams: Conversations with Contemporary West Indian Writers* (Leeds, UK: Peepal Books, 1992).

9. See Donna Seaman's "*Mr. Potter* (Book Review)," *Booklist* 98.13 (March 1, 2002): 1052 (1).

10. Glissant, *Caribbean Discourse*, 140.

11. Ibid., 69.

12. Ibid., 70.

13. Ibid., 61.

14. Ibid., 71, 70.

15. Ibid., 72.

16. Ibid., 73.

17. Ibid.

18. Ibid., 73.

19. Ibid.

20. Ibid., 82, 140.

21. Ibid., 81.

22. Selwyn R. Cudjoe, "Jamaica Kincaid and the Modernist Project: An Interview," in *Caribbean Women Writers*, edited by Cudjoe (Wellesley, MA: Calaloux, 1990), 215–31. Quotation from 223–24.

23. See Donna Perry, "Jamaica Kincaid (Interview)," in *Backtalk: Women Writers Speak Out. Interviews by Donna Perry* (New Brunswick, NJ: Rutgers University Press, 1993), 127–41. Quotation from Perry 137.

24. See Allan Vorda, "I Come from a Place That's Very Unreal: An Interview with Jamaica Kincaid," in *Face to Face: Interviews with Contemporary Novelists* (Houston, TX: Rice University Press, 1993), 79–95. Quotation from Vorda 81.

25. Ibid., 83; emphasis added.

26. Perry, 134–35.

27. Compare the critique of history as silenced in Michel-Rolph Trouillot, *Silencing the Past: Power and the Production of History* (Boston: Beacon Press, 1995).

28. Conquering space and territory within the Americas—quintessentially for Glissant, the forest—is also the quest of the American hero; however, "this is not the Eternal Garden, it is energy fixed in time and space, but which conceals its site and its chronology. The forest is the last vestige of myth in its present literary manifestation. In its impenetrable nature history feeds our desire" (*Caribbean Discourse*, 82–83). Compare Kincaid's meditations on Eden and the Garden in Eden in *My Garden (Book):* (New York: Farrar Straus Giroux, 1999).

29. Glissant, *Caribbean Discourse*, 70.

30. *Alterbiography*, and its generic contours, are further conceptualized in an article addressing Kincaid's short story "Biography of a Dress" and *The Autobiography of My Mother*. See the following: Jana Evans Braziel, "*Alterbiographic* Transmutations of Genre in Jamaica Kincaid's 'Biography of a Dress' and *The Autobiography of My Mother*," *A/B: Auto/Biography Studies* 18 no. 1 (Summer 2003): 85–104.

31. Vorda 93, 94.

32. Kincaid "Biography of a Dress," *Grand Street* 11 no. 3 (1992): 93–100; *The Autobiography of My Mother* (New York: Farrar Straus Giroux, 1996); and *My Brother* (New York: Farrar Straus Giroux, 1997).

33. See the following contributions: Liz Stanley, *The Auto/biographical I* (Manchester: University of Manchester Press, 1992); Laura Marcus, *Auto/biographical Discourses: Theory, Criticism, Practice* (Manchester: University of Manchester Press, 1994); Leigh Gilmore, *The Limits of Autobiography: Trauma and Testimony* (Ithaca, NY: Cornell University Press, 2001); Alison Donnell, "When Writing the Other Is Being True to the Self: Jamaica Kincaid's *The Autobiography of My Mother*," in *Women's Lives into Print: The Theory, Practice and Writing of Feminist Auto/Biography*, edited by Pauline Polkey, 123–36 (New York: St. Martin's Press, 1999).

34. Gilmore, 101.

35. These ideas are explored more fully in book manuscript *"Caribbean Genesis"—Jamaica Kincaid and the Writing of New Worlds*.

36. Kincaid, "Those Words that Echo . . . Echo . . . Echo Through Life," *New York Times*, June 7, 1999 http://www.nytimes.com/ (accessed May 15, 2002). Quotation from page 3.

37. Ibid., 3.

38. Kincaid, *The Autobiography of My Mother*, 214–15.

Bibliography

WORKS BY JAMAICA KINCAID

1976. "The Fourth." *New Yorker* (19 July): 23.

1977. "Jamaica Kincaid's New York." *Rolling Stone* (6 October): 71–73.

1977–83. "The Talk of the Town." *New Yorker* (17 October): 37; (3 January): 23.

1978. "Antigua Crossing." *Rolling Stone* (29 June): 48–50.

1978. "Girl." *New Yorker* (26 June): 29.

1978. "In the Night." *New Yorker* (24 July): 22–23.

1979. "Wingless." *New Yorker* (29 January): 26–27.

1981. "The Apprentice." *New Yorker* (17 August): 25.

1981. "The Letter from Home." *New Yorker* (20 April): 33.

1981. "What I Have Been Doing Lately." *Paris Review* 23:129–32.

1981–82. "Annie John." In *First Person Feminine*, ed. C. H. Bruner and D. K. Bruner, Second Series, 12:20. Audiocassette. Iowa State University WOI-FM. Ames, IA.

1982. "At the Bottom of the River." *New Yorker* (3 May): 46.

1983. *At the Bottom of the River*. New York: Farrar Straus Giroux.

1983. "The Circling Hand." *New Yorker* (21 November): 50–57.

1983. "Columbus in Chains." *New Yorker* (10 October): 48–52.

1983. "Figures in the Distance." *New Yorker* (9 May): 40–42.

1983. "The Red Girl." *New Yorker* (8 August): 32–38.

1984. "Gwen." *New Yorker* (16 April): 46–52.

1984. "The Long Rain." *New Yorker* (30 July): 28–36.

1984. "Somewhere in Belgium." *New Yorker* (14 May): 42–51.

1984. "A Walk to the Jetty." *New Yorker* (5 November): 45–51.

1985. *Annie John*. New York: Farrar Straus Giroux.

1986. *Annie, Gwen, Lilly, Pam, and Tulip*. New York: Library Fellows of the Whitney Museum of Modern Art.

1988. *A Small Place*. New York: Farrar Straus Giroux.

1988. "The Ugly Tourist." *Harper's* (September): 32–34.

1989. "Mariah." *New Yorker* (26 June): 32–38.

1989. "Ovando." *Conjunctions* 14:75–83.

1989. "Poor Visitor." *New Yorker* (27 February): 34–46.

1989. "The Tongue." *New Yorker* (9 October): 44–54.

1990. "Athol Fugard: Interview with South African Playwright." *Interview* 20 (August): 64.

1990. "Cold Heart." *New Yorker* (25 June): 28–40.

1990. "The Finishing Line." *New York Times Book Review* (2 December): 18.

1990. *Lucy*. New York: Farrar Straus Giroux.

1990. "Lucy." *New Yorker* (24 September): 44–53.

1991. *Lucy*. New York: Plume/Penguin.

1990. "My Mother." In *Caribbean New Wave: Contemporary Short Stories*, ed. Stewart Brown, 111–15. London: Heinemann.

1991. Foreword to *Babouk*, by Guy Endore. Voices of Resistance. New York: Monthly Review Press.

1991. "On Seeing England for the First Time." *Transition* 51 (1991): 32–40.

1991. "Out of Kenya." With Ellen Pall. *New York Times* (16 September): A-15 +.

1992. "Biography of a Dress." *Grand Street* 11 (3): 93–100.

1992. "Flowers of Evil." *New Yorker* (5 October): 154–59.

1993. "Alien Soil." *New Yorker* (21 June): 47–51.

1993. "Dear John: Five Ways to Leave a Lover." *Mademoiselle*, March 1993, 202–3.

1993. "A Fire by Ice." *New Yorker* (22 February): 64–67.

1993. "Just Reading." *New Yorker* (29 March): 47–51.

1993. "Song of Roland." *New Yorker* (12 April): 94–98.

1993. "This Other Eden." *New Yorker* (20 and 23 August): 69–73.

1994. "Christmas Pictures from a Warm Climate." *Vogue* December 1994, 314–15.

1994. "Early Delights." *New Yorker* (12 December): 63–71.

1994. "A Small Place." In *Writing Women's Lives: An Anthology of Autobiographic Narratives by Twentieth-Century American Women Writers*, Edited by Susan Neunzig Cahill, 415–22. New York: HarperPerennial.

1994. "The Season Past." *New Yorker* (7 March): 57–61.

1994. "Xuela." *New Yorker* (9 May): 82–92.

1995. *Best American Essays*. Edited by Jamaica Kincaid and Robert Atwan. Boston: Houghton Mifflin.

1995. "Homemaking." *New Yorker* (16 October): 54–59.

1995. "In Roseau." *New Yorker* (17 April): 92–99.

1995. "Plant Parenthood." *New Yorker* (19 June): 43–46.

1995. "Putting Myself Together." *New Yorker* (20 February): 93–101.

1996. *The Autobiography of My Mother*. New York: Farrar Straus Giroux.

1996. *The Autobiography of my Mother*. New York: Plume/Penguin.

1996. "The Flowers of Empire." *Harper's* (April): 28–31.

1996. "From Antigua to America." In *Frontiers of Caribbean Literature in English*, ed. Frank Birbalsingh, 138–151. New York: St. Martin's Press.

1997. "In History." *Callaloo* 20:1–8.

1997. *My Brother*. New York: Farrar Straus Giroux.

1988. Intro. to *Generations of Women: In Their Own Words*, ed Mariana Ruth Cook, 9–11. San Francisco: Chronicle Books.

Ed. 1998. *My Favorite Plant: Writers and Gardeners on the Plants They Love*. New York: Farrar Straus.

1998. *Poetics of Place*. With Lynn Geesaman. New York: Umbrage.

1999. *My Garden* (Book): New York: Farrar Straus Giroux.

1999. "Those Words that Echo . . . Echo . . . Echo Through Life." *New York Times*, June 7, 1999. http://www.nytimes.com/ (accessed May 15, 2002).

2001. *Talk Stories*. New York: Farrar Straus Giroux.

2002. *Mr. Potter*. New York: Farrar Straus Giroux.

2003. "The Circling Hand." In *Mending the World: Stories of Family by Contemporary Black Writers*, ed. Rosemarie Robotham, 20–34. New York: BasicCivitas Books.

2003. "From Lucy." In *Crossing into America: The New Literature of Immigration*, ed. Louis Gerard Mendoza and Subramanian Shankar, 89–96. New York: New Press.

2003. "Girl." In *The Next American Essay*, ed. John D'Agata, 43–44. Saint Paul, MN: Graywolf.

2003. Preface to *In the Land of the Blue Poppies: The Collected Plant-Hunting Writings of Frank Kingdon Ward*. Ed. Tom Christopher. New York: Modern Library.

Written and narrated. *Life and Debt*. DVD. Produced and directed by Stephanie Black. Tuff Gong Pictures. New York: New Yorker, Video, 2003.

2003. "A Small Place." In *Women Writing Resistance: Essays on Latin America and the Caribbean*, ed. Jennifer Browdy de Hernandez, 147–56. Cambridge, MS: South End Press.

2003. "Winter as a Time of Sorrow and Barrenness. A Fire by Ice." In *Winter: A Spiritual Biography of the Season*, ed. Gary Schmidt and Susan M. Felch, 8–16. Woodstock, VT: SkyLight Paths.

Literatures of Latin America from Antiquity to the Present, edited by Willis Barnstone. Princeton, NJ: Recording for the Blind & Dyslexic, 2003. Compact disc.

2004. From "The Autobiography of My Mother." In *Black Satin: Contemporary Erotic Fiction by Writers of African Origin*, ed. by J. H. Blair, 93–96. New York: Berkley Books.

2004. "Desert Blooms: New Cactus Plantings Bring Prickly Beauty to Santa Barbara's Lotusland." *Architectural Digest* 61, no. 4: 58–120.

2004. "Girl." In *40 Short Stories: A Portable Anthology*, ed. by Beverly Lawn. Boston: Bedford/St. Martin's.

2004. "'Girl' (read by Jamaica Kincaid)." In *Speaking of Literature, Writers Read and Discuss Their Stories, Poems, and Plays: An Audio Companion to Literature and Its Writers*, edited by Ann Charters and Samuel Charters. Boston: Bedford/St. Martin's. Compact disc.

2004. From "My Brother." In *How I Learned to Cook: And Other Writings on Complex Mother-Daughter Relationships*, ed. by Margo Perin, 130–35. New York: Jeremy P. Tarcher/Penguin.

2004. "Song of Roland." In *More Stories We Tell: The Best Contemporary Short Stories by North American Women*, ed. by Wendy Martin, 146–55. New York: Pantheon.

2004. *Speaking of Literature, Writers Read and Discuss Their Stories, Poems, and Plays: An Audio Companion to Literature and Its Writers* Charters, ed. by Ann Charters, Samuel Charters, John Gielgud, Basil Rathbone, Julie Harris, and Richard Burton. Boston: Bedford/St. Martin's, Compact disc.

2005. *Among Flowers: A Walk in the Himalaya.* National Geographic Directions. Washington, DC: National Geographic.

2005. *My Favorite Tool.* New York: Farrar Straus Giroux.

INTERVIEWS WITH JAMAICA KINCAID

Balutansky, Kathleen M. "On Gardening: An Interview with Jamaica Kincaid." *Callaloo* 25 (2002): 790–800.

Birbalsingh, Frank. "Jamaica Kincaid: From Antigua to America." In *Frontiers of Caribbean Literature in English*, edited by Frank Birbalsingh, 138–51. New York: St. Martin's Press, 1996.

Bonetti, Kay. "An Interview with Jamaica Kincaid." In *Conversations with American Novelists: The Best Interviews from The Missouri Review and the American Audio Prose Library*, edited by Kay Bonetti et al, 26–38. Columbia: University of Missouri Press, 1997.

———. "Interview with Jamaica Kincaid." In *Speaking of Literature: Writers Read and Discuss Their Stories, Poems, and Plays: An Audio Companion to Literature and Its Writers*, edited by Ann Charters. Boston: Bedford/St. Martin's, 2004. Compact disc.

Cudjoe, Selwyn. "Jamaica Kincaid and the Modernist Project: An Interview." In *Caribbean Women Writers: Essays from the First International Conference*, edited by Selwyn Cudjoe, 215–32. Wellesley, MA: Calaloux, 1990.

Dance, Daryl Cumber, ed. In *New World Adams: Conversations with Contemporary West Indian Writers*. Leeds, UK: Peepal Books, 1992.

Dilger, Gerhard. "Jamaica Kincaid with Gerhard Dilger (1992)." In *Writing across Worlds: Contemporary Writers Talk*, edited by Susheila Nasta, 80–92. New York: Routledge, 2004.

Ferguson, Moira. "A Lot of Memory: An Interview with Jamaica Kincaid." *Kenyon Review* 16 (1994): 163–88.

Garner, Dwight. "Jamaica Kincaid." *Salon Magazine* (January 13, 1996), http://www.salon.com/05/features/kincaid.html (accessed February 16, 2005).

Muirhead, Pamela Buchanan. "An Interview with Jamaica Kincaid." *Clockwatch Review* 9 (1994–95): 39–48.

Perry, Donna. "Jamaica Kincaid (Interview)." In *Backtalk: Women Writers Speak Out*, edited by Donna Perry, 127–41. New Brunswick, NJ: Rutgers University Press, 1993.

Snell, Marilyn. "Jamaica Kincaid Hates Happy Endings: Interview with Jamaica Kincaid." *Mother Jones* 22, no. 5. (September–October 1997): 28–32. http://www.motherjones.com/mother_jones/SO97/snell.html.

Vorda, Allan. "I Come from a Place That's Very Unreal: An Interview with Jamaica Kincaid." In *Face to Face: Interviews with Contemporary Novelists*, edited by Allan Vorda, 79–95. Houston, TX: Rice University Press, 1993.

————. "An Interview with Jamaica Kincaid." *Mississippi Review* 20 (1991): 7–26.

Wachtel, Eleanor. "Eleanor Wachtel with Jamaica Kincaid." *Malahat Review* 116 (1996): 55–71.

SECONDARY SOURCES

Alberghene, Janice M., and Beverly Lyon Clark, eds. *"Little Women" and the Feminist Imagination: Criticism, Controversy, Personal Essays*. New York: Garland, 1999.

Alcott, Louisa May. *Little Women*. Introduction by Susan Cheever. 1868. New York: Modern Library, 2000.

Alexander, Simone A. James. *Mother Imagery in the Novels of Afro-Caribbean Women*. Columbia, MO: University of Missouri Press, 2001.

Armstrong, Nancy. *Desire and Domestic Fiction: A Political History of the Novel*. New York: Oxford University Press, 1987.

Ashcroft, Bill, Gareth Griffiths, and Helen Tiffin. "Ambivalence." In *Key Concepts in Post-Colonial Studies*. New York: Routledge, 1998.

Ashcroft, Bill, Gareth Griffiths, and Helen Tiffin, eds. *The Post-Colonial Studies Reader*. London: Routledge, 1995.

Ben Beya, Abdennebi. "Mimicry, Ambivalence and Hybridity." http://www.emory.edu/ENGLISH/Bahri/1WEBPAGE.HTML

Benedict, Helen. "Tone Deaf: Learning to Listen to the Music in Prose." *Poets & Writers Magazine* 29 (6): 4–18.

Benitez-Rojo, Antonio. *The Repeating Island: The Caribbean and the Postmodern Perspective*. Translated by James Maraniss. Durham, NC: Duke University Press, 1992.

Bernard, Louise. "Countermemory and Return: Reclamation of the (Postmodern) Self in Jamaica Kincaid's *The Autobiography of My Mother* and *My Brother*." *Modern Fiction Studies* 48 (1) (2002): 113–39.

Berrian, Brenda. "Snapshots of Childhood Life in Jamaica Kincaid's Fiction." In *Arms Akimbo: Africana Women in Contemporary Literature*, edited by Janice Liddell and Yakini Belinda Kemp, 103–16. Gainesville: University Press of Florida, 1999.

Bhabha, Homi K. *The Location of Culture*. London: Routledge, 1994.

Blaisdell, Robert. "Short Take on Writing: Teaching Jamaica Kincaid's 'Putting Myself Together.'" *College Teaching* 46 (4) (1998): 134–35.

Bloom, Harold, ed. *Caribbean Women Writers*. Philadelphia: Chelsea House, 1997.

————. ed. *Jamaica Kincaid: Modern Critical Views*. Philadelphia: Chelsea House, 1998.

Bouson, J. Brooks. *Jamaica Kincaid: Writing Memory, Writing Back to the Mother*. Albany: State University of New York Press, 2005.

Brontë, Charlotte. *Jane Eyre*. Edited by Beth Newman. New York: Bedford St. Martin's Press, 1996.

————. *Villette*. London: Smith Elder. 1853. Introduction by Tony Tanner and notes by Mark Lilly. New York: Penguin, 1985.

Brophy, Sarah. *Witnessing AIDS: Writing, Testimony and the Work of Mourning*. Toronto: University of Toronto Press, 2004.

———. "Angels in Antigua: The Diasporic of Melancholy in Jamaica Kincaid's *My Brother*." *PMLA* 117 (2) (2002): 265–78.

Burrows, Victoria. *Whiteness and Trauma: The Mother-Daughter Knot in the Fiction of Jean Rhys, Jamaica Kincaid, and Toni Morrison*. New York: Palgrave Macmillan, 2004.

Butler, Judith. *Gender Trouble: Feminism and the Subversion of Identity*. New York: Routledge, 1990.

Byerman, Keith E. "Anger in *A Small Place*: Jamaica Kincaid's Cultural Critique of Antigua." *College Literature* 22 (1) (1995): 91–102.

Byrne, K. B. Conal. "Under English, Obeah English: Jamaica Kincaid's New Language." *CLA Journal* 43 (3) (2000): 276–98.

Casteel, Sarah Phillips. "New World Pastoral: Landscape and Emplacement in Contemporary Writing of the Americas." PhD diss., Columbia University, 2003.

———. "Rethinking Roots in Jamaica Kincaid's Garden Writing." Lecture given at the American Comparative Literature Association Convention, San Juan, Puerto Rico, 2002.

Caton, Louis Freitas. "Romantic Struggles: The Bildungsroman and Mother-Daughter Bonding in Jamaica Kincaid's *Annie John*." *MELUS* 21 (3) (1996): 125–42.

———. "'. . . Such Was the Paradise That I Lived' Multiculturalism, Romantic Theory, and the Contemporary American Novel." PhD diss., University of Oregon, 1995.

Chanda, Swati. "Narratives of Nation in the Age of Diaspora (Salman Rusdie, Jamaica Kincaid, Gurinder Chadha, Linton Kwesi Johnson)." PhD diss., Purdue University, 1996.

Chang, Kenny. "Feminist Revision and the Recentering of a Colonial Subject: Jean Rhys's *Wide Sargasso Sea*." *Studies in Language and Literature* 8 (December 1998): 103–18.

Chick, Nancy. "The Broken Clock: Time, Identity, and Autobiography in Jamaica Kincaid's *Lucy*." *College Language Association Journal* 40 (1) (1996): 90–103.

Clore, Melanie. "A Following Sea: Charting Sea Imagery and Identity in Jamaica Kincaid's *Annie John* and Paule Marshall's *Praisesong for the Widow*." Master's thesis, University of Richmond, 2003.

Cobham, Rhonda, ed. "Jamaica Kincaid: A Special Section." *Callaloo* 25 (2002):773–989.

Comfort, Susan Marguerite. "Memory, Identity, and Exile in Postcolonial Caribbean Fiction." PhD diss., University of Texas at Austin, 1994.

Cousineau, Diane. "Women and Autobiography: Is There Life Beyond the Looking Glass?" *Caliban* 31 (1994):97–105.

Covi, Giovanna. "Jamaica Kincaid and the Resistance to Canons." In *Out of the Kumbla: Caribbean Women and Literature*, edited by Carole Boyce Davies and Elaine Savory Fido, 345–54. Trenton, NJ: Africa World Press, 1990.

———. "Jamaica Kincaid's Political Place: A Review Essay." *Caribana* 1 (1990):93–103.

———. "Jamaica Kincaid's Prismatic Self and the Decolonialisation of Language and Thought." In *Framing the Word: Gender and Genre in Caribbean Women's Writing*, edited by Joan Anim-Addo, 37–68. London: Whiting and Birch, 1996.

———. *Jamaica Kincaid's Prismatic Subjects: Making Sense of Being in the World*. London: Mango, 2003.

———. "Jamaica Kincaid's Voyage of Recovery: The Cliffs of Dover Are Not White." In *Deferring a Dream: Literary Sub-Versions of the American Columbiad*, edited by Gert Buelens, 76–84. Boston: Birkhauser Basel, 1994.

Cudjoe, Selwyn R., ed., *Caribbean Women Writers: Essays from the First International Conference*. Wellesley, MA: Calaloux, 1990.

Curry, Renee R. "'I Ain't No Friggin' Little Wimp': The Girl 'I' Narrator in Contemporary Fiction." In *The Girl: Construction of the Girl in Contemporary Fiction by Women*, edited by Ruth Saxton, 95–106. New York: St. Martin's Press, 1998.

D'Aguiar, Fred. "Adam's Other Garden: Derek Walcott's Exploration of the Creative Imagination." *Caribana* 3 (1992–93): 67–77.

D'Amore, Alice M. "A Fourth Garden of Self-Awareness in the Works of Jamaica Kincaid." Master's Thesis, Kutztown University of Pennsylvania, 2003.

Dance, Daryl Cumber, ed. *Fifty Caribbean Writers*. Westport, CT: Greenwood, 1986.

Davidoff, Leonore. et al. *Family Story: Blood, Contract, and Intimacy, 1830–1960*. London: Longman, 1999.

Davidoff, Leonore, and Catherine Hall. *Family Fortunes: Men and Women of the English Middle Class, 1780–1850*. Chicago: University of Chicago Press, 1987.

Davies, Carole Boyce. "Writing Home: Gender and Heritage in the Works of Afro-Caribbean/American Women Writers." In *Out of the Kumbla: Caribbean Women and Literature*, edited by Carole Boyce Davies and Elaine Savory Fido, 59–73. Trenton, NJ: Africa World Press, 1990.

Davis, Angela. *Women, Race & Class*. New York: Vintage, 1981.

De Abruna, Laura Niesen. "Jamaica Kincaid's Writing and the Maternal-Colonial Matrix." In *Caribbean Women Writers: Fiction in English*, edited by Mary Conde and Thorunn Lonsdale, 172–83. New York: St. Martin's Press, 1999.

Deloughrey, E. "Island Ecologies and Caribbean Literatures." *Tijdschrift voor Economische en Sociale Geografie* 95 (3) (2004): 298–310.

Derrida, Jacques. "Differance." In *Margins of philosophy*. Translated by Alan Bass, 1–28. Chicago: University of Chicago Press, 1982.

———. *Monolingualism of the Other or The Prosthesis of Origin*. Translated by Patrick Mensah. Stanford, CA: Stanford University Press, 1998.

Dessart, Jamie Thomas. "'Surrounded by a Gilt Frame': Mirrors and Reflection of Self in *Jane Eyre*, *Mill on the Floss*, and *Wide Sargasso Sea*." *Jean Rhys Review* 8 (1–2) (1997): 16–24.

Dilger, Gerhard. "'I Use a Cut and Slash Policy of Writing': Jamaica Kincaid." *Wasafiri: Journal of Caribbean, African, Asian and Associated Literatures and Film* 16 (1992): 21–25.

DiMarco, Danette. "Taking Their Word: Twentieth-Century Women Reinvent the Victorian." PhD diss., Duquesne University, 1996.

Dolby, Nadine. "A Small Place: Jamaica Kincaid and a Methodology of Connection." *Qualitative Inquiry* 98 (1) (2003): 57–74.

Donaldson, Laura E. "The Miranda Complex: Colonialism and the Question of Feminist Reading." *Diacritics* 18 (3): (1988): 65–77.

Donnell, Alison. "Dreaming of Daffodils: Cultural Resistance in the Narratives of Theory." *Kunapipi* 14 (1992): 45–52.

———. "She Ties Her Tongue: The Problems of Cultural Paralysis in Postcolonial Criticism."*ARIEL* 26, no. 1 (1995): 101–16. Reprinted in *Jamaica Kincaid: Modern Critical Views*, edited by Harold Bloom, 37–49. Philadelphia: Chelsea House, 1998.

———. "When Daughters Defy: Jamaica Kincaid's Fiction." *Women: A Cultural Review* 4 (1993): 18–26.

———. "When Writing the Other Is Being True to the Self: Jamaica Kincaid's *The Autobiography of My Mother.*" In *Women's Lives into Print: The Theory, Practice and Writing of Feminist Auto/Biography*. Edited by Pauline Polkey, 123–36. New York: St. Martin's Press, 1999.

———. "Writing for Resistance: Nationalism and Narratives of Liberation." In *Framing the Word: Gender and Genre in Caribbean Women's Writing*. Edited by Joan Anim-Addo. London: Whiting & Birch, 1996.

Doyle, Jacqueline. "Developing Negatives: Jamaica Kincaid's *Lucy.*" In *The Immigrant Experience in North American Literature: Carving Out a Niche*, edited by Katherine B. Payant and Toby Rose, 59–72. Westport, CT: Greenwood, 1999.

Du Bois, W. E. B. *The Souls of Black Folk*. 1903. In *Writings*, edited by Nathan Huggins, 357–574. New York: Library of America, 1986.

Dutton, Wendy. "Merge and Separate: Jamaica Kincaid's Fiction." *World Literature Today* 63 (3) (1989): 406–10.

Edelman, Lee. "Homographesis." *Homographesis: Essays in Gay Literary and Cultural Theory*, edited by Lee Edelman, 3–23. New York: Routledge, 1994.

Edlmair, Barbara. *Rewriting History: Alternative Versions of the Caribbean Past in Michelle Cliff, Rosario Ferré, Jamaica Kincaid and Daniel Maximin*. Vienna: Braumüller, 1999.

Edmondson, Belinda. *Making Men: Gender, Literary Authority, and Women's Writing in Caribbean Narrative*. Durham, NC: Duke University Press, 1999.

Edwards, Brent Hayes. "Selvedge Salvage." *Cultural Studies* 17 (1) (2003): 27–42.

Ellison, Elizabeth. ""'. . . Leaving You With Neither Here Nor There,' The power of hybridity in Jean Rhys' *Wide Sargasso Sea.*" In *Proceedings of The Ninth Annual Acacia Conference*, 36–41. Fullerton: California State University, Fullerton, 2001.

Emery, Mary Lou. "Refiguring the Postcolonial Imagination: Tropes of Visuality in Writing by Rhys, Kincaid, and Cliff." *Tulsa Studies in Women's Literature* 16 (2) (1997): 259–81.

Estes, Angela M., and Kathleen M. Lant. "Dismembering the Text: The Horror of Louisa May Alcott's *Little Women.*" *Children's Literature* 17 (1989): 98–123.

Ferguson, Moira. *Colonialism and Gender Relations from Mary Wollstonecraft to Jamaica Kincaid: East Caribbean Connections*. New York: Columbia University Press, 1993.

———. *Jamaica Kincaid: Where the Land Meets the Body*. Charlottesville, VA: University Press of Virginia, 1994.

———. "*Lucy* and the Mark of the Colonizer."*Modern Fiction Studies* 39 (2) (1993): 237–59. Reprinted in Bloom, ed. *Jamaica Kincaid.*

Flockemann, Miki. "'If I Were Her'—Fictions of Development from Cape Town, Canada and the Caribbean: A Relational Reading." *Journal of Literary Studies* 15 (1999):176–94.

Flower, Dean. "Three Novels and Fifty-three Short Stories." *Hudson Review* 49 (3) (1996): 483–91.

Forbes, Curdella. "Writing the Autobiography of My Father." *Small Axe: A Caribbean Journal of Criticism* 13 (2003): 172–81.

Frederick, Rhonda D. "What if You're an 'Incredibly Unattractive, Fat, Pastrylike-Fleshed Man'?: Teaching Jamaica Kincaid's *A Small Place*." *College Literature* 33 (3) (2003): 1–18.

Freire, Paulo. *Pedagogy of the Oppressed.* New York: Continuum, 1989.

Garis, Leslie. "Through West Indian Eyes." *New York Times,* October 7, 1990, sec. 6.

Gaskell, Elizabeth C. *The Life of Charlotte Brontë.* 1857. Reprint, New York: Appleton, 1877.

Gass, Joanne. "Bitter Reconquista: Jamaica Kincaid's *The Autobiography of My Mother*." *Journal of Caribbean Studies* (Winter 2001): 209–22.

George, Rosemary Marangoly. "Home-Countries and the Politics of Location: Home, Nationalism, Feminist Subjecthood." PhD diss., Brown University, 1992.

Giddings, Paula. *When and Where I Enter: The Impact of Black Women on Race and Sex in America.* 2nd ed. New York: Quill/Morrow, 1996.

Gilkes, Michael. "The Madonna Pool: Woman as 'Muse of Identity.'" *Journal of West Indian Literature* 1 (June 1987): 1–19.

Gilmore, Leigh. "There Will Always Be a Mother: Jamaica Kincaid's Serial Autobiography." In *The Limits of Autobiography: Trauma and Testimony,* edited by Leigh Gilmore, 96–119. Ithaca, NY: Cornell University Press, 2001

Glissant, Édouard. *Caribbean Discourse.* [1989] Translated by J. Michael Dash. Charlottesville: University Press of Virginia, 1999.

———. *Le discours antillais.* Paris: Seuil, 1981.

Graves, Benjamin. "Spivak: Marxist, Feminist, Deconstructionist." http://www.thecore.nus.edu/landow/post/poldiscourse/spivak/spivak3.html.

Hainley, Bruce. Review of *My Brother* by Jamaica Kincaid. *Artforum International* 36 (3) (1997): S27.

Harkins, Patricia. "Family Magic: Invisibility in Jamaica Kincaid's *Lucy*." *Journal of the Fantastic in the Arts* 4 (1991): 53–68.

Harris, Cheryl I. "Whiteness as Property." In *Critical Race Theory: The Key Writings that Formed the Movement,* edited by Kimberlé Crenshaw, Neil Gotanda, Gary Peller, and Kendall Thomas, 276–91. New York: New Press, 1995.

Harris, Trudier. *From Mammies to Militants: Domestics in Black American Literature.* Philadelphia: Temple University Press, 1982.

Hegel, G. W. *The Philosophy of History* [1892]. Reprint, New York: Dover Publications, 1956.

Henry, Paget. *Caliban's Reason: Introducing Afro-Caribbean Philosophy.* New York: Routledge, 2000.

Herndon, Crystal Gerise. "Gendered Fictions of Self and Community: Autobiography and Autoethnography in Caribbean Women's Writing." PhD diss., University of Texas at Austin. 1993.

———. "Returns to Native Lands, Reclaiming the Other's Language: Kincaid and Danticat." *Journal of International Women's Studies* 3 (2001): 1–10.

Hirsch, Marianne. "Resisting Images: Rereading Adolescence." In *Provoking Agents: Gender and Agency in Theory and Practice*, edited by Judith Degan Gardiner, 249–79. Urbana: University of Illinois Press, 1995.

Hodge, Merle. *Crick Crack, Monkey.* London: Andre Deutsch, 1970.

———. "Caribbean Writers and Caribbean Language: A Study of Jamaica Kincaid's *Annie John.*" In *Winds of Change: The Transforming Voices of Caribbean Women Writers and Scholars*, edited by Adele Newson and Linda Strong-Leek, 47–53. New York: Lang, 1998.

Hogan, Patrick Colm. *Colonialism and Cultural Identity.* Albany: SUNY Press, 2000.

Holcomb, Gary E. "Travels of a Transnational Slut: Sexual Migration in Kincaid's *Lucy.*" *Critique* 44 (3) (2003): 295–313.

Hoving, Isabel. "Remaining Where You Are: Kincaid and Glissant on Space and Knowledge." *Thamyris/Intersecting: Place, Sex & Race* 9, no. 1 (2003): 125–41.

Insanally, Annette. "Contemporary Female Writing in the Caribbean." In *The Caribbean Novel in Comparison: Proceedings of the Ninth Conference of Hispanists*, edited by Ena V. Thomas, 115–41. St. Augustine, Trinidad: University of the West Indies, Department of French and Spanish Literatures, 1986.

———. "Sexual Politics in Contemporary Female Writing in the Caribbean." In *West Indian Literature and Its Political Context*, edited by Lowell Fiet, 79–91. Rio Piedras: University of Puerto Rico, 1988.

Ippolito, Emilia. "Room as a Catalyst of Differences: In Search of Autonomous Subjectivity in the Caribbean (Con)Text of Jamaica Kincaid." In *Borderlands: Negotiating Boundaries in Post-Colonial Writing*, edited by Monika Reif-Hulser. Amsterdam: Rodopi, 1999.

Irline, Francois. "The Daffodil Gap: Jamaica Kincaid's *Lucy.*" *MaComere* 4 (2001): 84–100.

Ismond, Patricia. "Jamaica Kincaid: 'First they must be children.'" *World Literature Written in English* 28 (1988): 336–41.

Jacobus, M. "Jane Austen in the Ghetto." *Women: A Cultural Review* 14 (1) (2003): 63–85.

Jain, Veena. "Jean Rhys's *Wide Sargasso Sea*: A Re-writing of History." *Women's Writing: Text and Context*, edited by Jasbir Jain, 114–23. Jaipur: Rawat, 1996.

"Jamaica Kincaid Reinvente Son Pere." *Jeune Afrique L'intelligent* 46 (January 9, 2005): 92–93.

James, Louis. "Reflections, and the Bottom of the River: The Transformation of Caribbean Experience in the Fiction of Jamaica Kincaid." *Journal of Caribbean, African, Asian and Associated Literatures and Film* 9 (1988–89): 15–17.

Jayasundera, Ymitri. "Jamaica Kincaid (1949–)." In *Contemporary African American*

Novelists: A Bio-Bibliographical Critical Sourcebook, edited by Emmanuel Nelson and Deborah G. Plant, 260–66. Westport, CT: Greenwood, 1999.

Johnson, Barbara. "Apostrophe, Animation, and Abortion." In *Contemporary Literary Criticism*. 3rd ed., edited by Robert Con Davis and Ronald Schleifer, 215–31. New York: Longman, 1994.

Johnson, Freya. "The Male Gaze and the Struggle Against Patriarchy in *Jane Eyre* and *Wide Sargasso Sea*." *Jean Rhys Review* 5 (1–2) (1992): 22–30.

Kanhai, Rosanne. "Sensing Designs in History's Muddles: Global Feminism and the Postcolonial Novel."*Modern Language Studies* 26 (1996): 119–30.

Kaplan, Caren. "Reconfigurations of Geography and Historical Narrative: A Review Essay." *Public Culture* 3 (1990): 25–32.

Karafilis, Maria. "Crossing the Borders of Genre: Revisions of the Bildungsroman in Sandra Cisneros's *The House on Mango Street* and Jamaica Kincaid's *Annie John*." *Journal of the Midwest Modern Language Association* 31 (1998): 63–78.

Karim, Persis Maryam. "Fissured Nations and Exilic States: Displacement, Exile, and Diaspora in Twentieth-Century Writing by Women." PhD diss., University of Texas at Austin, 1998.

Kendall, Elaine. Review of *Lucy* by Jamaica Kincaid. *Los Angeles Times*, October 21, 1990, Book Review section.

Kenney, Susan. *New York Times*, April 7, 1985, Book Review section.

King, Jane. "A Small Place Writes Back." *Callaloo* 25 (2002): 885–909.

Kristeva, Julia. "'unes femmes': The Woman Effect." In *Julia Kristeva: Interviews*. Interview by Elaine Boucquey, edited and translated by Ross Mitchell Guberman, 103–12. New York: Columbia University Press, 1996.

Lanser, Susan Sniader. "Compared to What? Global Feminism, Comparatism, and the Master's Tools." In *Borderwork: Feminist Engagements with Comparative Literature*, edited by Margaret Higonnet, 280–300. Ithaca, NY: Cornell University Press, 1994.

Ledent, Benedicte. "Voyages into Otherness: *Cambridge* and *Lucy*." *Kunapipi* 14 (1992): 53–63.

Lee, Judith. "Lucifer: A Fantastic Figure." *Journal of the Fantastic in the Arts* 8 (1997): 218–34.

Lenk, Cynthia Ruth. "Race, Gender, and Personal Power in Selected Contemporary Caribbean Works of Fiction." PhD diss., University of Arkansas, 1990.

Lenz, Brooke. "Postcolonial Fiction and the Outsider Within: Toward a Literary Practice of Feminist Standpoint Theory." *NWSA Journal* 16 (2) (2004): 98–111.

Levin, Amy K. *Africanism and Authenticity in African-American Women's Novels*. Gainesville: University Press of Florida, 2003.

Loe, Thomas. "Jamaica Kincaid's *Lucy* as a Short Story Sequence." *Notes on Contemporary Literature* 26 (1996): 2–3.

Loichot, Valérie. "Fort-de-France: Pratiques Textuelles et Corporelles D'une Ville Coloniale." *French Cultural Studies* 15 (1) (2004): 48–60.

Lubiano, Wahneema. "Black Nationalism and Black Common Sense: Policing Ourselves and Others." In *The House that Race Built: Black Americans, U.S. Terrain*, edited by Wahneema Lubiano, 232–52. New York: Pantheon Books/Random House, 1997.

MacDonald-Smythe, Antonia. "Authorizing the Slut in Jamaica Kincaid's *At the Bottom of the River*." *Macomere* 2 (1999): 96–113.

———. "Making Herself at Home in the West/Indies: The Gendered Construction of Identity in the Writings of Michelle Cliff and Jamaica Kincaid." PhD diss., Ohio State University, 1996.

———. *Making Homes in the West/Indies: Constructions of Subjectivity in the Writings of Michelle Cliff and Jamaica Kincaid.* New York: Garland, 2001.

Mahlis, Kristen. "Gender and Exile: Jamaica Kincaid's *Lucy*." *Modern Fiction Studies* 44 (1) (1998): 164–84.

Mangum, Bryant. "Jamaica Kincaid." In *Fifty Caribbean Writers*, edited by Daryl Cumber Dance, 255–63. Westport, CT: Greenwood Press, 1986.

Marcus, Laura. *Auto/biographical Discourses: Theory, Criticism, Practice.* Manchester: University of Manchester Press, 1994.

Martin, Janette May. "The Dynamics of Expatriatism in the Writing of Jean Rhys and Jamaica Kincaid." PhD diss., Bowling Green State University, 1994.

McClintock, Anne. *Imperial Leather: Race, Gender and Sexuality in the Colonial Contest.* New York: Routledge, 1995.

McDowell, Deborah. *"The Changing Same": Black Women's Literature, Criticism, and Theory.* Bloomington: Indiana University Press, 1995.

Mendelsohn, Jane. "Leaving Home: Jamaica's Voyage Round Her Mother." *Village Voice Literary Supplement* 89 (1990): 21.

Mistron, Deborah E. *Understanding Jamaica Kincaid's "Annie John": A Student Casebook to Issues, Sources, and Historical Documents.* Westport, CT: Greenwood Press, 1999.

Morris, Ann R. and Margaret M. Dunn. "'The Bloodstream of Our Inheritance': Female Identity and the Caribbean Mothers'-Land." In *Motherlands: Black Women's Writing from Africa, the Caribbean and South Asia*, edited by Susheila Nasta, 219–37. London: Women's Press, 1991.

Murdoch, H. Adlai. "The Novels of Jamaica Kincaid: Figures of Exile, Narratives of Dreams." *Clockwatch* 9 (1994–95): 141–54.

———. "Severing the (M)other Connection: the Representation of Cultural Identity in Jamaica Kincaid's *Annie John*." *Callaloo* 13 (1990): 325–40.

Nagel, James. "Desperate Hopes, Desperate Lives: Depression and Self-Realization in Jamaica Kincaid's *Annie John* and *Lucy*." In *Traditions, Voices, and Dreams: The American Novel Since the 1960s*, edited by Melvin Friedman and Ben Siegel, 237–53. Newark: University of Delaware Press, 1995.

Nasta, Susheila. "Motherlands, Mothercultures, Mothertongues: Women's Writing in the Caribbean." In *Shades of Empire in Colonial and Post-Colonial Literatures*, edited by C. C. Barfoot. Amsterdam: Rodopi, 1993.

———. *Writing Across Worlds: Contemporary Writers Talk.* New York: Routledge, 2004.

Natov, Roni. "Mothers and Daughters: Jamaica Kincaid's Pre-Oedipal Narrative." *Children's Literature: Annual of The Modern Language Association Division on Children's Literature* 18 (1) (1990): 1–16.

Niesen de Abruna, Laura. "Family Connections: Mother and Mother Country in the Fiction of Jean Rhys and Jamaica Kincaid." In *Motherlands: Black Women's Writing from Africa, the Caribbean and South Asia*, edited by Susheila Nasta, 257–89. London: Women's Press, 1991.

Nixon, Nicola. '*Wide Sargasso Sea*' and Jean Rhys's interrogation of the "nature wholly alien" in '*Jane Eyre.*' *Essays in Literature* 21 (2) (1994): 267–82.

O'Brien, Susie. "The Garden and the World: Jamaica Kincaid and the Cultural Borders of Ecocriticism." *Mosaic* 35, no. 2 (2002): 167–85.

———. "New Postnational Narratives, Old American Dreams; Or, the Problem with Coming-of-Age Stories." In *Postcolonial America*, edited by C. Richard King, 65–80. Urbana: University of Illinois Press, 2000.

Oczkowicz, Edyta. "Jamaica Kincaid's *Lucy*: Cultural 'Translation' as a Case of Creative Exploration of the Past." *MELUS* 21, no. 3 (1996): 143–57. Reprinted in *Jamaica Kincaid*, edited by Harold Bloom, 117–30. Philadelphia: Chelsea House, 1998.

———. "The Metaphor of 'Translation' in Multicultural Writing by Contemporary American Women Writers." PhD diss., Lehigh University, 1994.

Page, Russell. *The Education of a Gardener*. London: William Collins, 1962.

Palmer, Felicity. "Sex, Hybridity and Contamination: Racial Theories of the Nineteenth Century." http://www.flea.org/thesis/html/node4.html.

Paravisini-Gebert, Lizabeth. "Colonial and Postcolonial Gothic: The Caribbean." In *The Cambridge Companion to Gothic Fiction*, edited by Jerrold E. Hogle, 229–58. Cambridge: Cambridge University Press, 2002.

———. *Jamaica Kincaid: A Critical Companion*. Westport, CT: Greenwood Press, 1999.

Payette, Patricia Ruth. "Jane Eyre and the Postcolonial Bildungsroman." Master's thesis, University of Louisville, 1995.

Pela, Robert. Review of *My Brother* by Jamaica Kincaid. *The Advocate* 748 (1997):82.

Perlman, Karen Beth. "Memory Speaks: The Revision of History and the Subject in Contemporary Women's Fiction." PhD diss., University of Michigan, 1994.

Perry, Donna. "Initiation in Jamaica Kincaid's *Annie John*." In *Contemporary American Women Writers: Gender, Class, Ethnicity*, edited by Lois Parkinson Zamora, 128–37. London: Longman, 1998.

Pigeon, Elaine. "Jamaica Kincaid's *Annie John*: The Trauma of Colonial Education." In *Literature of Region and Nation: Proceedings of the 6th International Literature of Region and Nation Conference*, edited by Winnifred M. Bogaards. Saint John, NB: Social Sciences and Humanities Research Council of Canada, 1998.

Poon, Angelia. "Re-Writing the Male Text: Mapping Cultural Spaces in Edwidge Danticat's Krik? Krak! and Jamaica Kincaid's *A Small Place*." *Jouvert* 4 (2000): 30.

Prentice, Christine. "Out of the Pre-Texts of Imperialism into 'A Future They Must Learn': Decolonizing the Allegorical Subject." *ARIEL* 31 (1–2) (2000): 203–29.

Rafi, Iris Fawzia. "'You of Age to See about Youself Now! So Pull Up You Socks!': Themes of Bildung in Select Novels by West Indian Women Writers." PhD diss., Emory University, 1995.

Raiskin, Judith. "England: Dream and Nightmare." In *Snow on the Cane Fields: Women's Writings and Creole Subjectivity*. Minneapolis: University of Minnesota Press, 1996.

Ramchand, Kenneth. "West Indian Literary History: Literariness, Orality and Periodization." *Callaloo* 11 (1988): 95–110.

Rejouis, Rose-Myriam. "Caribbean Writers and Language: The Autobiographical Po-
    etics of Jamaica Kincaid and Patrick Chamoiseau." *Massachusetts Review* 44 (1–2)
    (2003): 213–33.

Renk, Kathleen J. "The Shadow Catchers: Creole/Womanist Writers in the Anglo-
    phone Caribbean." PhD diss., University of Iowa, 1995.

Rhys, Jean. *Wide Sargasso Sea*. 1966. Edited by Judith L. Raiskin. New York: Norton
    Critical Editions, 1999.

Rice, Anne P. "Burning Connections: Maternal Betrayal in Jamaica Kincaid's *My
    Brother*. *A/B: Auto/Biography Studies* 14 (1999): 23–37.

Robbins, Bruce. "Soul Making: Gayatrt Spivak on Upward Mobility." *Cultural Studies*
    17 (1) (2003): 16–27.

Rodney, Walter. *The Groundings with My Brothers*. London: Bogle-L'Ouverture Publica-
    tions, 1969.

Schine, Cathleen. "A World as Cruel as Job's." In *Caribbean Women Writers*. Edited by
    Harold Bloom. Philadelphia: Chelsea House Publishers, 1997.

———. Review of Kincaid's *Autobiography of My Mother*, by Jamaica Kincaid. *New York
    Times Book Review* (February 4): 1996, 5.

Schlosser, Donna. "Recurring Vocabularies: Narrating Voices in *Annie John*, *Jasmine*,
    and *Middle Passage*." PhD diss., Florida Atlantic University, 1997.

Schultheis, Alexandra W. *Regenerative Fictions: Postcolonialism, Psychoanalysis, and the Na-
    tion as Family*. New York: Palgrave Macmillan, 2004.

Seaman, Donna. Review of *My Brother*, by Jamaica Kincaid. *Booklist* 94 (September 1,
    1997): 5.

———. Review of *Mr. Potter*, by Jamaica Kincaid. *Booklist* 98 (March 1, 2002): 1052.

Sherrard, Cherene. "The 'Colonizing' Mother Figure in Paule Marshall's *Brown Girl,
    Brownstones* and Jamaica Kincaid's *The Autobiography of My Mother*." *MaComere* 2
    (1999): 125–33.

Showalter, Elaine. *Sister's Choice: Tradition and Change in American Women's Writing*. Ox-
    ford: Clarendon, 1991.

Simmons, Diane. "Coming-of-Age in the Snare of History: Jamaica Kincaid's *The Auto-
    biography of My Mother*." In *The Girl: Constructions of the Girl in Contemporary Fiction by
    Women*, edited by Ruth O. Saxton, 107–18. New York: St. Martin's Press, 1998.

———. *Jamaica Kincaid*. New York: Twayne, 1994.

———. "Jamaica Kincaid: A Critical Study." PhD diss., City University of New York,
    1995.

———. "Jamaica Kincaid and the Canon: In Dialogue With 'Paradise Lost' and 'Jane
    Eyre.'" *MELUS* 23, no. 2 (Summer 1998): 65–85.

———. "The Mother Mirror in Jamaica Kincaid's *Annie John* and Gertrude Stein's *The
    Good Anna*." In *The Anna Book: Searching for Anna in Literary History*, edited by Mickey
    Pearlman, 107–18. Westport, CT: Greenwood, 1992.

———. "The Rhythm of Reality in the Works of Jamaica Kincaid." *World Literature
    Today* 68 (3) (1994): 466–72.

Skow, John. Review of *My Brother*, by Jamaica Kincaid. *Time*, November 10, 1997,
    108.

Smyth, Heather. "Psychoanalytic Feminism and Caribbean Women's Relationships in the Works of Jamaica Kincaid and Paule Marshall." Master's thesis, University of Guelph (Canada), 1994.

Spivak, Gayatri. "Three Women's Texts and a Critique of Imperialism." *Critical Inquiry* 12 (1985): 243–61.

Stanley, Liz. *The Auto/biographical I.* Manchester: University of Manchester Press, 1992.

Stanton, Katherine Ann. "Worldwise Global Change and Ethical Demands in the Cosmopolitan Fictions of Kazuo Ishiguro, Jamaica Kincaid, J. M. Coetzee, and Michael Ondaatje." PhD diss., Rutgers University, 2003.

———. *Cosmopolitan Fictions: Ethics, Politics, and Global Change in the Works of Kazuo Ishiguro, Michael Ondaatje, Jamaica Kincaid, and J. M. Coetzee.* New York: Routledge, 2005.

Staples, Kenneth C. "Hong Kong culture: hybrid, bicultural, multicultural, or a continuing renewal." http://www.asaa2000.unimelb.edu.au/papers/staples.htlm (July 2000).

Steavenson, Wendell. "Mercurial Maternalism." *San Francisco Review* 21 (1996): 36–37.

Stewart, Karen. "'A' Is for Annie: A Post It Note on Autobiographies and Postcoloniality in Jamaica Kincaid's *Annie John.*" PhD diss., University of Vermont, 1996.

Sugg, Katherine. "'I would rather be dead': Nostalgia and Narrative in Jamaica Kincaid's *Lucy.*" *Narrative* 10 (2) (2002): 156–74.

Tanner, Tony. Introduction. *Villette*, by Charlotte Bronte 7–51. New York: Penguin, 1985.

Tapping, Craig. "Children and History in the Caribbean Novel: George Lamming's *In the Castle of my Skin* and Jamaica Kincaid's *Annie John.*" *Kunapipi* 11 (1989): 51–59.

Tate, Claudia. *Domestic Allegories of Political Desire: The Black Heroine's Text at the Turn of the Century.* New York: Oxford University Press, 1992.

Thomas, Greg. Review of *"Jamaica Kincaid: A Critical Companion," Research in African Literatures* 33 (3) (2002): 225–28.

Thomas, Nicholas. *Colonialism's Culture: Anthropology, Travel and Government.* Princeton, NJ: Princeton University Press, 1994.

Thum, Angela M. "*Wide Sargasso Sea*: A Rereading of Colonialism." *Michigan Academician* 30 (3) (1998): 147–62.

Tiffin, Helen. "Cold Hearts and (Foreign) Tongues: Recitation and the Reclamation of the Female Body in the Works of Erna Brodber and Jamaica Kincaid." *Callaloo* 16, no. 4 (1993): 909–21. Reprinted in *Jamaica Kincaid*, edited by Harold Bloom, 141–56. Philadelphia: Chelsea House, 1998.

———. "Decolonization and Audience: Drna Brodber's *Myal* and Jamaica Kincaid's *A Small Place. SPAN* 30 (1990): 27–38.

———. "'Flowers of Evil,' Flowers of Empire: Roses and Daffodils in the Work of Jamaica Kincaid, Olive Senior and Lorna Goodison." *SPAN* 46 (1998): 58–71.

———. "'Replanted in this Arboreal Place': Gardens and Flowers in Contemporary Caribbean Writing." In *English Literatures in International Contexts*, edited by Heinz Antor and Klaus Stierssstorfer. Anglistische Forschungen, Bd. 283. Heidelberg: C. Winter, 2000.

Timothy, Helen Pyne. "Adolescent Rebellion and Gender Relations in *At the Bottom of the River* and *Annie John.*" In *Caribbean Women Writers: Essays From the First International Conference*, edited by Selwyn R. Cudjoe, 233–42. Wellesley, CT: Calaloux, 1990.

Tolchin, Karen Rebecca. "Part Ketchup: Coming of Age in America with J. D. Salinger, Philip Roth, John Irving, Edith Wharton and Jamaica Kincaid." PhD diss., Brandeis University, 2000.

Trotman, Althea Veronica. "African-Caribbean Perspectives of Worldview: C. L. R. James Explores the Authentic Voice." PhD diss., York University, 1993.

Trouillot, Michel-Rolph. *Silencing the Past: Power and the Production of History*. Boston: Beacon Press, 1995.

Ty, Eleanor. "Struggling with the Powerful (M)Other: Identity and Sexuality in Kogawa's Obasan and Kincaid's *Lucy*." *International Fiction Review* 20 (1993): 120–26.

Uraizee, Joya. "'She Walked Away Without Looking Back': Christophine and the Enigma of History in Jean Rhys's *Wide Sargasso Sea*." *CLIO* 28 (3) (1999): 261–77.

Valens, Keja. "Obvious and Ordinary." *Frontiers: A Journal of Women's Studies* 25 (2) (2004): 123–50.

Vijayshree, C. "Writing Postcoloniality and Feminism: A Reading of Jean Rhys's *Wide Sargasso Sea*." In *Women's Writing: Text and Context*, edited by Jasbir Jain, 124–33. Jaipur: Rawat, 1996.

Vilches Norat, Vanessa. *De(s)madres o el rastro materno en las escrituras del yo: a prop[226]osito de Jacques Derrida, Jamaica Kincaid, Esmeralda Santiago y Carmen Boullosa*. Santiago, Chile: Editorial Cuarto Propio, 2003.

Walcott, Derek. *What the Twilight Says: Essays*. New York: Farrar Straus Giroux, 1998.

Wald, Priscilla. "Cultures and Carriers: 'Typhoid Mary' and the Science of Social Control." *Social Text*, nos. 52–53 (Autumn–Winter 1997): 181–214.

Wallace, Jo-Ann. "De-scribing The Water Babies: 'The Child' in Post-Colonial Theory." In *De-Scribing Empire: Post-Colonialism and Textuality*, edited by Chris Tiffin and Alan Lawson, 171–84. New York: Routledge, 1994.

Warren, William. *The Tropical Garden*. London: Thames and Hudson, 1991.

Weber, Jean. "From 'Bad' to 'Worse': Pragmatic Scales and the (De)construction of Cultural Models." *Language and Literature* 14 (1) (2005): 45–63.

Welsh, Sarah Lawson. "The West Indies." *The Journal of Commonwealth Literature* 32 (3) (1997): 187–200.

Wilt, Judith. *Ghosts of the Gothic: Austen, Eliot, & Lawrence*. Princeton: Princeton University Press. 1980.

Yang, Ming-tsang. "Vision and Revision in Jamaica Kincaid's 'On Seeing England for the First Time.'" *Studies in Language and Literature* 6 (1994): 143–52.

Yeoh, Gilbert. "From Caliban to Sycorax: Revisions of *The Tempest* in Jamaica Kincaid's *Annie John*." *World Literature Written in English*, 33–34 (1993–94): 103–16.

Young, Robert. *Colonial Desire: Hybridity in Theory, Culture, and Race*. London: Routledge, 1995.

Contributors

Jana Evans Braziel is an Assistant Professor in the Department of English and Comparative Literature at the University of Cincinnati, where she teaches African, African diasporic, and Caribbean literatures. With Anita Mannur, Braziel recently co-edited *Theorizing Diaspora* (2003). She has also published *Bodies Out of Bounds: Fatness and Transgression* (2001), co-edited with Kathleen LeBesco.

Jeanne Ewert holds a PhD in Comparative Literature from the University of Pennsylvania, and is an independent scholar living and working in Gainesville, FL. Her current project is a monograph exploring the treatment of ethical issues in American garden writing of the nineteenth and twentieth century.

Joanne Gass is Professor of English and Comparative Literature at California State University, Fullerton. She has a PhD in Comparative Literature from the University of California, Irvine, with a specialization in the contemporary novel, and she has published articles on the novels of Angela Carter, Jamaica Kincaid, Virginia Woolf, Helena Parente Cunha, Manuel Puig, Don DeLillo, and Carlos Fuentes.

Linda Lang-Peralta is Associate Professor of English at The Metropolitan State College of Denver. She earned a PhD in Comparative Literature at the University of California, Irvine. She has contributed to *Women's Life-Writing: Finding Voice, Building Community* (1997) and *Modern Kenya: Social Issues and Perspectives* (1999). She also is editor of *Women, Revolution, and the Novels of the 1790s* (2001).

Maria Soledad Rodriguez holds a PhD from Princeton University and is Professor of English at the University of Puerto Rico at Rio Piedras. She teaches Caribbean, U.S., and women's literature, and critical approaches to Caribbean children's and young adult literature. She is currently working on a book about the sources of folk figures in comparative Caribgean literature.

Tom Sheehan is currently an Assistant Professor of English at Florida Atlantic University. He has articles under review on Jean Rhys, Jamaica Kincaid, and James Joyce. He is working on a manuscript on space, time, and framing in European and Caribbean modernist literature, and film.

Derik Smith and Cliff Beumel: Derik Smith is an Assistant Professor of English at Zayed University in the United Arab Emirates. He is currently at work on a book project engaging politics and aesthetics in the poetry of Robert Hayden. He lives with his wife and two sons in Dubai. Cliff Beumel is an independent scholar with interests in eco-criticism and nineteenth century American literature. He received his MA in English from Northwestern University in 2000.

Evie Shockley: Evie Shockley holds a PhD from Duke University and is Assistant Professor of English at Rutgers University. Her current research projects include a manuscript tentatively titled "Gothic Homelessness: Domestic Ideology, Identity, and Social Terror in African American Literature" and an investigation of the relationship of race and innovation in African American poetry.

Index